LEADING THE
WORKFORCE
OF THE FUTURE

INSPIRING A MINDSET OF
PASSION, INNOVATION AND **GROWTH**

By

Brigette Tasha Hyacinth

OTHER BOOKS BY

Brigette Tasha Hyacinth:

- **The Future of Leadership:**
  Rise of Automation, Robotics and Artificial Intelligence.

- **Purpose Driven Leadership:**
  Building and Fostering Effective Teams.

- **The Ultimate Leader:**
  Learning, Leading and Leaving a Legacy of Hope.

- **The Edge of Leadership:**
  A Leader's Handbook for Success.

Dedication

First and foremost, I have to thank God for His mercies, grace, and loving kindness towards me, and for blessing me with wisdom to complete this book.

This book is dedicated to my family. I love you all so much.

My heartfelt thanks goes to my dear mother, Marguerite Joseph, who has made huge sacrifices for me to be where I am today.

A big thank you to Frank Hyacinth, my father, and to my brothers and sisters—Troy Hyacinth, Onica Hyacinth, Gavery Enrico Hyacinth—and to Alicia Hyacinth (my sister-in-law), Che Nigel Hyacinth (deceased), Cheron Hyacinth, and Brent John for the huge support they provided.

Thank you to my nieces and nephew, Nicholas Hyacinth, Celeste Hyacinth, Tinique Hyacinth and Sarah Davis. I am so proud of you all. May you continue to grow in the grace and knowledge of our Lord and Saviour, Jesus Christ.

In remembrance of my cousin, Roger Marshall, and my dear friends, Anthony (Tony) Ramlogan, Gregory Hospedales, Jome Lalmansingh, Winston Marcano and Elizabeth Edwards who all passed away from illnesses, before I completed this book. I am thankful for their support.

Preface

Leading the workforce of the future mandates' new levels of self-awareness. As the workplace evolves in the direction of innovation, digitalization, and rapid change, leaders must follow suit in order to remain relevant and engaging to this multigenerational workforce.

This book provides concrete advice and best practices on how to engage and retain top talent. It addresses several areas to focus on to future proof yourself and your business.

In this book you will discover strategies to:

- Become the leader your team needs you to be.
- Accelerate talent development.
- Reshape your culture.
- Reskill your workforce.
- Create an innovation mindset.
- Succeed with purpose.

The future is no longer some far-off destination; it is already here. Don't be caught off guard!

Table Of Contents

SECTION ONE:

YOUR LEADERSHIP IDENTITY

CHAPTER ONE

DO YOU LEAD WITH PURPOSE: WHAT'S YOUR WHY?

Everybody is driven by something. We search for meaning, for a purpose, for direction — and sometimes we search in some strange ways, too. To have purpose is to give meaning to the goals we are striving to achieve. This is the reason for your journey. A life without purpose is like a ship drifting aimlessly without a sail, a compass, or a port to call home.

Your leadership purpose is the essence of who you are. The difference between average and successful leaders is their purpose. Your purpose and focus become your driver.

Purpose is increasingly being called the key to navigating this multifaceted, unpredictable, and uncertain world we live in today. The best leaders create an environment that allows people to succeed. They do this by having a deep awareness of their purpose. Purpose must tap into people's hearts and help them give their best when the odds are against them. You cannot achieve the goals that you have until you can establish your "WHY" factor. It's your reason for doing what you are doing. "Why do I want to lead?" "What's the purpose of my leadership?" Research shows us that fewer than 20% of leaders have a strong sense of their individual purpose. If you haven't clearly articulated your "why," your influence will be shaky. Igniting passion starts with defining your purpose. Leaders must activate people's emotions. This requires a strong sense of self and an authentic vision.

The greatest tragedy in life is not death but a life without purpose.
~Dr Myles Munroe

The "5 Whys" technique can be very helpful in getting to the root of what you truly desire.

Make a chain of "Why?" questions. You start by asking yourself why you want to achieve a particular goal. For example, "Why do I want this position?" You might answer, "Because I want to advance in my career." Then ask again. "Why do I want to advance in my career?" Continue with "Why?" on each answer at least five times. Eventually, you will end up with your real motives and the deeper value behind your wishes. We can never know for sure the motives of others. We can only work on ourselves and model the right way for others, leading by example.

"My leadership purpose is _____." It's your personal mission statement. Develop a vision and a mission statement to go with it. Ask yourself what's really important to you, what you are good at, and what you would like to have achieved when, at the end of your life, you look back.

Reflection is paramount. It can help you reconnect with your dreams. Set aside time daily to pause and reflect. To enhance your self-awareness, you must be willing to look within yourself through regular self-reflection. It's impossible to see the big picture, and where you are in that picture, if you keep going nonstop. The practice of visualizing can be very useful. One exercise I do every morning is to visualize the goals I am working towards coming to life and bearing fruit. And don't forget to visualize the impact you'll have on others as a result of living your purpose.

Your leadership purpose is made up of who you are and what you're here to accomplish. There is some area of life where you are meant to make a positive impact and complete that assignment. When you find your purpose, it will be easy to pursue it even in the face of obstacles because it is naturally embedded within you. It will bring you great fulfilment. Your gifts are not to be used primarily for selfish gain, but to connect with, even edify, others.

A team depends on its leader to tell them where they are going, why they are taking that particular course, and how they're going to reach the destination. People are more motivated when a leader articulates his or her vision for the organization, along with the steps and goals needed to achieve it.

One cold winter in South Wales, a mother was travelling cross-country with her baby and was caught in a terrible snowstorm. The next day, upon learning she never reached her destination, a search group went looking for her. They soon spotted a large bank of snow on the road. They quickly swept it away only to find the frozen body of the barely clothed woman. In her arms was her baby—alive and wrapped in a bundle of clothing. In the brunt of the snowstorm, the mother had removed most of her clothing and wrapped it around her baby to keep him alive. She knew that she would die, but that there was a chance the baby might survive. This baby boy grew up to become a successful businessman in the UK. One of the reasons he achieved such great success is that he never forgot about his mother's sacrifice.

Purpose often arises from experiences in your own life. What obstacles have you encountered? What qualities helped you to overcome them? How did your strengths help make life better for others?

WHAT IS YOUR PASSION?

To find your purpose, you need to figure out your passions and skills. For some of us, our purpose in life is clear. Our natural talents ended up being clear indicators of what we were ultimately passionate about. For others, though, it's not that easy. Your purpose is already there. You just have to uncover it in order to make an impact and to live the life you are supposed to.

Many times, I hear individuals that I am coaching say, "**I don't have a purpose.**" "**I can't find my passion.**" **Everyone has a purpose on this earth.** Sometimes we can be our greatest enemies. "But the worst enemy you can meet will always be yourself." — Friedrich Nietzsche. That voice we hear in our head recites some false narratives so often and so frequently, that we really start believing them after a while. The thing is, they only distort reality which keeps us trapped. Fear is a powerful tool, but it can also cripple you from taking positive actions or seeing the truth.

There is something you can do better than most people. What are you passionate about? What comes easy to you? What do you love to do? It could be the simple things you love doing and you are good at. Think about the times you've experienced the greatest joy in your life. If your life were perfect right now, what would it look like? What kind of job would you have? Where would you be right now? What qualities do you enjoy expressing the most in the world? Mine are hope and love.

You can also listen to what other people appreciate about you. When I was working in the corporate world, most people would often tell me, "Brigette you are in the wrong profession. You need to be a psychologist or a motivational speaker. You are really good at counselling and inspiring us." My employees would literally line up to speak to me about their issues or problems. Sometimes even after I left the office, they would be waiting for me in the carpark just to get a word of encouragement.

Fill in the blank. **My life is ideal when I'm_____**. For me, my life is ideal when I'm being of service to others, when I am inspiring others and helping them to be their best. Once you are clear about what you want — keep your mind constantly focused on it. The things that bring you the innermost joy are in alignment with your purpose.

> *"The best and most beautiful things in the world cannot be seen or even touched - they must be felt with the heart."*
> — Helen Keller

Of course, it takes work to develop your talents. Even the most gifted individuals such as musicians, artists, athletes, etc., still have to practice. But it should feel natural to you. It shouldn't be a continuous struggle. I love speaking, writing, coaching and training leaders. These things come easy for me, but I am always looking for ways to improve my craft.

While reflecting, you may discover something altogether different than what you do. That's okay. **It's never too late to change direction.** Once you are alive and there is breath in your body. You can start working on a plan and take small steps, to get to where you need to be. Even the slightest contribution in any form to make this world a better place to live, can be seen as fulfilling your purpose.

Our world doesn't need more numbers-centered leaders but purpose-driven leaders. The key to accelerating growth and strengthening your impact in both your professional and personal life is purpose. The process of finding your purpose, and finding the courage to live it, is the single most important progressive task you can embark on as a leader.

CHAPTER TWO

YOUR LEADERSHIP IDENTITY—YOU CANNOT LEAD OTHERS UNTIL YOU LEAD YOURSELF FIRST!

WHO ARE YOU?

Who Are You? I have been asked this question so often. I don't usually share much about my private life, but today I want you give you a snippet of why I am so passionate about leadership and HR, and it starts with...Who am I? I always ask people to speak from the heart, so today I am going to be an open book. I believe this is what it's going to take to really succeed as a leader and build influence in this new world. It's about being human and vulnerable.

MY STORY

My leadership journey started quite early in my childhood. As long ago as I can remember, I had that desire to take the initiative, to lead change and inspire and help others. Today people tell me that I am so successful, but little do they know my story began at the bottom, rock bottom. Some people climb their way up the ladder to their dreams, but I had to do a lot extra – I needed ropes of strength, a ladder of commitment, and a harness of faith. I grew up in Trinidad and Tobago, the island of the hummingbird and steelpan. My early childhood was riddled with hardships, but I knew early on I wanted to make a difference in the world.

From the time I was little, all the elderly villagers (who have long passed) would tell my mother, "This child is different." I was always focused and driven. I was not born with a golden spoon, a silver spoon, or any other spoon for that matter.

I was raised by my mother, a single parent, together with my five other siblings. Things were incredibly difficult. We had nothing. Our stove was made of clay. We didn't even have beds. We slept on mattresses and makeshift bedding made from worn out clothes in our meager abode. I went to school with holes in my shoes; the other kids would laugh at me, but my mother could not do any better.

She herself had had a very rough life. My mother grew up in Soufriere, St Lucia. Her paternal grandmother took her from her mother when she was around the age of three because she was severely malnourished. When her grandmother went to the police station to state her intention to keep my mother, she told the officers that if my mother lasted more than three days, she would keep her. If not, her mother would have to bury her. My mother recites that she was so skinny, and her belly was so swollen, the officers thought she wouldn't make it. At 13, my mother's father brought her to Trinidad. She never got the chance to acquire an education since my grandfather kept her at home to attend to the animals. A couple of years later when my mother had us, she did odd jobs, such as washing, ironing, babysitting, and taking care of the elderly. She even worked as a janitor to take care of us.

I remember two moments from my early childhood quite vividly. The first was having a conversation with my mother when I was around five, telling her I wanted to go to school. But at that time, she could not afford to send me. The second was playing marbles when I was around seven or eight with a neighbor and hearing his mother whisper to him, "Why are you playing with Brigette? She is so serious." I guess I have always been very focused and driven.

The road was quite bumpy. It was a constant struggle. At the age of 12, on the day I was writing my common entrance exam. I didn't have a pencil. My mother took me to the shop to buy a pencil, but we came up $0.05 short. The shop keeper refused to overlook that in spite of how much my mother pleaded with her. As I write this, I can feel the sickening feeling I felt on that day. My mother then remembered my sister's friend Miss Anne lived in an adjacent street.

Miss Anne was so disturbed that she gave me pencils, breakfast, and money so I could be comfortable taking my exam.

As we were leaving, I told my mother, "Don't worry, one day you will not have to beg anyone for anything, I will be able to provide for you." (Thank God for making this happen.) It's still amazing to me to go from begging for a pencil to authoring five books.

I passed the common entrance exam and was sent to a junior high school in my area. I was so disappointed because I didn't get my first choice. But I give it everything I had. When everyone was having fun and going on excursions, I remained at home studying hard because I knew having an education was the only way out of this poverty-stricken lifestyle. We didn't have electricity, but we had a small pitch oil lamp which I used at night to study. I tried to do as much of my studying as possible before nightfall because the lamp would be dim, and studying would hurt my eyes. My mother said I was always in my books; she never had to tell me to do my homework. I know she felt saddened sometimes when she saw me struggling, but she couldn't help me because she couldn't read.

Sometimes my mom would reach home very late having missed the bus and with no money to take a taxi. Often the bus would be so full, and there would be so much pushing and shoving, that she couldn't get in. One time someone elbowed her so hard, she even blacked out. Luckily, strangers helped her to a bench and sat talking with her until she was back to herself.

I performed quite well in junior high and won a number of academic awards. At 15, the school I attended, Carapichaima Junior Secondary School, recommended me and another top performer to attend Holy Faith Convent in Couva. At Holy Faith, my home economics teacher realized my circumstances and would give me the edges of the bread we cut off from sandwiches and other leftovers to take home. I looked forward to my home economics classes for this reason, and my family was always anxious to see what I would bring home.

One morning, my mother returned early from work; the elderly woman she was taking care of had died suddenly over the weekend. My mother was without a job. One month later, she got a job babysitting, but she slipped and fell, breaking her ankle. Once again, she was without a job — a very tough time. I remember writing my form six exams with nothing in the house to eat except rice. I boiled it, picked a green mango in the backyard, grated it, added salt, and that's what I ate.

> *"Our heavenly Father has a thousand ways to*
> *provide for us, of which we know nothing."*
> ~Ellen G. White

At this point my mother could no longer make ends meet, and she sought help from the church. When they visited our home and saw the deplorable conditions we lived in, they vowed to offer as much assistance as they could. We were given groceries on a monthly basis as well as clothing. They not only dropped off the groceries but the group leaders, Mr. Willis Manwaring (deceased) and his wife Patricia (Ms. Patsy), would take the time to chat with my mum, inquiring how we were progressing and offering much needed advice. Thank God for their assistance. They provided much-needed food and clothing. They even give me a study desk and chair and paid for my after-school lessons. But this was for a limited time as they had so many more people to help. We would be expected to stand on our own.

Things were still tough when, one day, my Godmother came and told my mother she wanted to adopt me. My mother was tempted but declined the offer. My mother was determined she would keep all her children. She did not grow up with her mother, and she didn't want the same for us.

However, when I finished school, my dreams of attending college were dashed. My mother couldn't afford to pay my college tuition fees. Our lives were so difficult that I had to go out and work. My mom was suddenly hospitalized; she needed a blood transfusion. It was nerve-wracking waiting for the blood tests. I gave blood, but I clearly remember my siblings' blood samples floating in the little containers because their hemoglobin levels were too low. They could not give, but thankfully members of the church stepped up and donated blood. My mother had "run her blood to water" working so hard. It was scary. My mom didn't think she would make it, so she put all our important documents in sealable bags before she left for the hospital so we could easily find them. Thank God she recovered.

From an early age, my family members saw me as the one with the brains, and they focused what few resources we had on helping me complete school. My older brother Gavery worked in the supermarket, and when he got tips, he would buy groceries. When he brought them home, we would be so happy. This is why I believe in tipping people well. You never know the impact your small deeds of kindness may have on others.

My first job was actually at a chicken farm, and it was difficult for us, my younger sister and me. At the end of our first day, the owner paid us and said," Don't come back." She wasn't being mean. She just saw how much we struggled. I felt like an absolute failure.

After a couple of weeks, I got a job at a seaport. It was very hard. I worked in the field as a tally clerk, tallying containers and cargo when ships came in. But I also met people from all over the world, and this fueled my dream that one day I would be traveling all over the world. I collected one-dollar notes from each country that visited our shores; I still have these old bills from Nigeria, India, Morocco, Germany, Finland, etc., all of which I have been to. Today, I am a global traveler. But the seed was sown long ago in hope, faith, belief, and persistence.

Many times, I had to encourage myself. I would look out at the harbor as the sun set and say, "By God's grace, one day I will get my degree." I worked very hard, sometimes working double shifts evenings and nights. On the night shifts, I was always a little frightened when a sugar truck came in. It would just be me and the guy who was doing the offloading. On my break, the walk to the office took me through the container yard past loads of containers stacked up in dim lighting. Pretty scary — a long, lonely walk. I would recite Psalms 23, "Yea, though I walk through the valley of the shadow of death, I will fear no evil; for thou art with me."

I was intensely focused on saving enough money to attend college. I once worked double shifts for three days straight, 3 p.m. to 11 p.m. and 11 p.m. to 7 a.m. On the fourth day, my mother told me, "You are not making that fourth one." I am so glad that she stopped me that day because physically, I was in no position to go to work. In my sleep deprived state, I could have gotten hurt.

The girls in the office often looked down on us. They would often tell us we smelled like steel. It was the cargo that was being offloaded. We were working out in the sun and the dust, the rain, the mud, the wind. It was not easy.

When I had saved enough, I started attending college while working part time. It was a dream come true; it certainly was my dream come true. I was older than the other students, but I didn't care. I went on to earn my associate degree and won a partial scholarship to Munroe College in New York. I was forced to decline because I wasn't able to raise the funds to attend. This was a very difficult and frustrating time for me.

I tried to use the pain of this to motivate myself to keep studying. These obstacles, though daunting and nagging at times, didn't deter me from following my path. I signed up for my master's degree. I didn't have much money, but I signed up anyway. Then the government implemented a program whereby they would pay half of my tuition. That was indeed God sent. I didn't even own a computer, a printer, or any sort of vehicle, so there was no way I could have paid for my full tuition. During this time, I would practically live in computer cafes to complete projects and print assignments.

Classes were in the evening and finished at 8 p.m. I would have to cross the highway (bus route) and take three taxis to get home. Sometimes, when I saw the other passengers in the taxi, I would pray they weren't criminals. My area was known as a crime hot spot, but my oldest brother Troy would always be waiting for me at the main road and walk me to our home.

It makes me sad that there were so many people in my neighborhood who have passed away from being murdered or from being killed by the police — some because of the choices they made, and others who were just in the wrong place at the wrong time. My little brother Che Hyacinth was killed on September 9th, 2006. He was in a village parlor and someone called out to him. That was it. My little sister Cheron came on the scene and was with him as he took his final breath. His murder is still unsolved.

It was normal for us to sit in the back yard and hear gunshots. We would often see police running through our yard chasing after criminals. One evening, after a neighbor had given my mother some money to help out, she went shopping for the ingredients to bake us a cake. We were so excited sitting on our front step waiting for her. But she came back shaking and huddled us into our small house. She had just passed two men with machetes. They stopped her; she was so frightened her knees started knocking uncontrollably. They did let her go, but we never came out at night after that.

While most of the people in my community accepted being victims of circumstance and floated downstream, I instinctively paddled upstream against the prevailing currents. Was it hard? Was it lonely? Did I get depressed? Yes, to all of those, yet I was compelled to keep moving forward.

So strange that within these dark moments too I would learn the value of hard work, learn to keep fighting for and working on my dreams. And it wasn't just my struggle that taught me valuable lessons. My mother showed me that no matter how bad things may be, even if you don't see a way, God has made a way for you. You will overcome every obstacle in your path. "Never stop believing. Never stop trying. Never give up."

The day I graduated with my MBA, my mom was overjoyed. I was actually the first one of all my relatives to have attended a university. My mother was so inspired that she took literacy classes. I am so proud of her. Although I volunteered to teach her, she refused as she wanted the actual experience of attending school and having friends. I feel so happy that she got that experience.

FROM CAREER TO CALLING

Fast forward. After working relentlessly and climbing the corporate ladder, I left my job to start my own company. This is exactly where I dreamed, I would be one day: traveling the world, sharing my knowledge, meeting and helping people, and experiencing different cultures.

I was helping my mom clean up not long ago, and I found my first report card. In the comments, my teacher stated, "Brigette is a bright child but she talks too much." Wow! And today I speak for a living. Chin up, Buttercup. You have everything you need to succeed.

This has been a hard road to success. But today, I do a lot of charitable work. My leadership purpose ultimately comes from a desire to help others. I often say I am a product of people giving back. I could not be where I am today without the help and support of others. I run for a higher purpose. My greatest joy comes from hearing the words, **"You have helped me."**

I use my leadership influence to inspire my team as well as bring awareness and support to charitable causes. Giving back is natural for me because of my humble beginnings. Along the way, people were moved to help me and my family. And it's my duty to do the same. In the words of one of my favorite hymns: "If I can help somebody as I pass along, then my living shall not be in vain."

Who are you? What's your story? We all have a story. Maybe yours has not been as tough as mine. Nevertheless, it paved the path to where you are today. I hope telling my story finally sheds some light on the very REAL me!

Sometimes it feels like I have a sixth sense because I feel people's pain. If someone is going through something negative, I feel as if it is resting upon me. I rarely watch the news. Seeing people crying, going through grief — these things hurt me deeply. I always try to help as much as I can and take the time to encourage others. I hate seeing people being treated unfairly. And this is why I am so passionate about helping others and making a difference. **I lead with my heart.**

In a world of artificial relationships, people are looking for human-centered leadership. If you stood in front of a crowd and started telling people how perfect and talented you are, this will quickly turn people off. On the other hand, if you started off saying, "I am flawed, imperfect and I have faults", people will automatically tune in. Why? Because you are showing your human side and people can relate to this.

This is why it's so important to: Be authentic. Be transparent. Be vulnerable. Be you. Ultimately this is what will draw people to you.

CHAPTER THREE

PERFECTING YOUR LEADERSHIP STYLE

SELF-AWARENESS

While leadership is about execution, getting things done, and action, it also requires time to pause and reflect. Self-awareness has been cited as the most important capability for leaders to develop. Self-awareness helps you to become the leader your team needs you to be. A study also found that self-awareness impacts companies' bottom line; companies with strong financial performance tend to have leaders with higher levels of self-awareness. Yet self-awareness seems to be in short supply among leaders.

The primary responsibility of leadership is setting a vision and enrolling people. Emotion is central to this; emotions influence people. Successful leaders get to where they are by achieving results through others. They connect with the people they want to influence. They understand their own emotions, which gives them the ability to understand other's feelings and to adapt themselves to the people around them. The greater the ability to understand themselves and their people, and to receive feedback in the light of that understanding, the more likely they are to choose an approach that will create the best result for their organization. Although there are exceptions, most great leaders succeed because they have a high degree of EI (emotional intelligence). The "human" touch makes managers better leaders. Until a few years ago, the intelligence quotient (IQ) was considered to be the major indicator of success. Companies were looking for leaders with a high level of hard skills, even when candidates lacked soft skills. Today, however, it's quite the opposite. EI taps into a fundamental element of human behavior that is distinct from your intellect. There is no known connection between IQ and EI.

...ness is the keystone of EI. EI refers to the collection of ... used to identify, understand, control, and assess the ...tions of oneself and others. Numerous studies have shown a positive relationship between emotionally intelligent leadership and higher levels of employee engagement and performance. EI can't be mustered up by machines. Yet a majority of managers undermine the importance of people skills to their success. Empathy, even vulnerability, are purely human, and the real key to moving forward in any endeavor.

Self-awareness is the skill of recognizing and understanding your emotions, motivations, and thoughts. It is the capacity for introspection and the ability to know your psychological state. It is having a clear picture of your strengths and weaknesses. Knowing your areas of weakness allows you to delegate to others who are proficient in those abilities in order to achieve a common goal. Great leaders are aware of their limits. That's why you'll often find them surrounding themselves with individuals who complement, rather than supplement, their skills. Working on your areas of weakness will improve your leadership ability.

Self-Awareness Begins with Self-Assessment: This can be defined as having the ability to recognize one's own emotions, values and drivers, strengths and weaknesses, and understanding how your emotions can affect others around you. It's being aware of your own reactions to people, things, situations, and events. The first step in improving your EI is to recognize your emotions, understand their root causes, and become familiar with your reaction patterns and the consequences of your reactions. Keep in mind that your emotional state is a dynamic condition, and it can vary considerably from moment to moment throughout the day. Your reactions may not always be immediately clear or obvious, but it is important for you to understand why you have a given emotional reaction to something. Especially when you are feeling a strong wave of emotions, pay particular attention to being "in the moment" and attentive to the "here and now," and ask yourself why you are feeling the way you are.

As a goal, the development of self-awareness is to gain an understanding about the nature and "internal source" of your gut reactions, as well as how to manage and harness these reactions to maximize positive outcomes. It entails being completely honest with yourself; it also requires that you be totally objective as you assess and evaluate yourself. Once you identify this, you can start working on improving your self-regulation. Without reflection, we cannot truly understand who we are or why we make certain decisions. Self-awareness helps you to identify the traits that serve *you* well and the ones that work against you. Those who strive to develop a strong understanding of who they are, and what their values are, can improve themselves on a regular basis.

Consider that your psychological state can impact your emotions as well as your ability to reason, make decisions, and to execute other cognitive processes.

Our early life experiences teach us how to lead. We might also adopt a style of leadership that we've experienced from someone else, or that we've read or heard about. If it seems to work, we'll likely stick with it – in effect, it becomes "our" style.

Even with the millions of books on leadership and billions spent in management training, employee engagement is still at an all-time low. It is a manager issue. The reason why it hasn't been improving is because most bosses don't care to look in the mirror. Is our deep-rooted leadership style so difficult to change? I believe it's because our earliest examples of leadership were our parents, and since so many of us came from dysfunctional homes, our ability to lead will be distorted. The problem starts when we don't have a good role model from early on, whether a parent, our first boss, or a particularly effective team leader.

Our leadership styles are entrenched in our personalities and life experiences. Unless you accept and understand this, you will likely not be able to move forward, to learn and grow into the leader you were meant to be.

Researchers have found that the relationship between employees and managers is one of the most decisive factors in the decision to either look for another job or stay put. Clearly the type of manager an employee has matters a lot to the employee since it's often the determining factor in their growth in a role or in a company, as well as their happiness and fulfillment day-to-day.

According to the Society for Human Resource Management, which reported on the Randstad study, unhappy workers admitted that while on the job, they:

- Drank alcohol (5%)
- Watched Netflix (11%)
- Took naps (15%)
- Played pranks on co-workers (40%)
- Shopped online (55%)
- Checked or posted on social media (60%)

Before you judge these employees, let me be clear — that's a dead end. Judgement and blame won't increase your effectiveness or move your team forward. These results are part of a trend of burnout and job dissatisfaction — common human reactions to stressful environments — and *managers,* not employees, can mitigate these behaviors at the source.

The future of leadership mandates new levels of self-awareness. Recently I was speaking with a manager of a large manufacturing chain. He thinks of himself as a "results oriented" kind of guy. I asked about his leadership style, and he said he was assertive and clear in making sure his employees know what needs to be done. If his team doesn't meet performance targets, he knows it is because his staff didn't do their work properly, not because of his leadership. I asked this manager's staff about him and heard a very different story. What the manager considers "assertive," his staff considers demanding. "He's great at micromanaging." It's not a compliment.

It's no secret that technology and automation are transforming the workplace, leaving many workers worried about their future employment and job security. And unfortunately, morale is only getting worse.

Many companies claim to be a great place to work. But somehow, when employees actually start working there, they find this is not the case. Employees spend over half of their lives at work. They want to be in an environment where they feel valued, appreciated, like they belong and are making a valuable contribution. These are basic human needs. Sadly, these needs are not being met, and this is why engagement continues to fall. The only way to bridge this gap is to start looking in the mirror. It starts with self-awareness.

WHO YOU ARE IS HOW YOU LEAD

If you fit into any of the four following categories, you need to start making changes to become the leader your team needs you to be.

Narcissists are typically self-serving. They will cut down anybody who challenges them, and readily take credit for other people's work. A complaint I hear from many employees is: "I presented an idea to my manager, and he immediately made it out to be his own." Narcissistic people intentionally put down others to maintain a high positive image of themselves. A narcissist won't accept even the smallest piece of criticism.

Statements that best describe a Narcissist:

1. People sometimes describe me as intimidating.
2. When people hurt me, I write them off and end the relationship.
3. Growing up, and even in my early career, I did not see humility as an effective leadership trait.
4. There should always be a clear distinction between management and employees.
5. The end justifies the means.

6. I find negative feedback, even when reasonable, to be a personal attack.
7. I feel threatened by intelligent and high-performing employees.
8. I often criticize more than I praise.
9. Great leadership is about exercising authority.
10. One of employees' main functions is to make me look good as their manager.

It's time to think less of yourself and more of others. Leadership is not a right, but a privilege given by followers. You are in that position primarily to serve others, not yourself. Be vulnerable. Don't be afraid to show your human side. Don't take things personally. You should be thinking about how you can help others better themselves. How can you make employees' jobs easier? If you continue down that dangerous slope of selfishness, it will eventually lead to your downfall. "We rise by lifting others." —Robert Ingersoll

Formalists are micromanagers. This person micromanages to the last detail. The work environment is overbearing and stifling because they want control over nearly all decisions; they distrust the team and rarely delegate anything meaningful. In such a scenario, there's hardly room for group discussion or input because the management style is autocratic. Creativity is absent under this dictatorship. Loyal workers trying to find meaning in their jobs or find scope for their creativity are left with nothing but their marching orders.

Statements that best describe a Formalist:

1. I believe systems and procedures comes first.
2. I am not a risk taker, and I like things to be predictable.
3. Things must be done in an orderly, specific way, or I get angry.
4. When people around me become emotional, I don't know how to deal with it.

5. I feel powerless in my personal relationships.
6. Life has taught me to either "be in control" or "be controlled."
7. One or both of my parents were irresponsible.
8. I don't fully trust employees to complete tasks on their own.
9. I've been told I am distant and don't show much affection.
10. I get anxious when I am not in full control of certain situations where I am responsible for the outcome.

The more tightly you hold on to employees, the more you will push them away. You need to let go. You can't control everyone and everything. Focus on building relationships. Trust is a two-way street. If you hired someone, it means you believe they are capable of doing the job. Then trust them to get the job done. You don't need to be constantly monitoring their every movement. Micromanagement breeds resentment and disloyalty. Delegate responsibilities. Give your employees wings to fly, and watch them soar.

Individualists are credit-hogs. The team puts together a wonderful product and rolls it out on time. The client is giddy with joy about how much money and time the new system will save. And then it happens: The manager takes all the credit for the work. There's little or no praise for the team members, or celebration of everyone's successes. This type of manager will hog the spotlight, and when that happens, team morale plummets. This is the same manager who emails you at 10 p.m. on a Sunday night and expects an answer back immediately, the same one who emails you, then follows up almost immediately with an instant message to see if you've checked your email yet.

Statements that best describe an Individualist:

1. I take responsibilities seriously and would describe myself as a high achiever.
2. I am not good at anticipating the needs of others.

3. I felt a lot of my childhood was based on competing to outperform siblings or friends.

4. I rarely show emotions because it doesn't solve anything.

5. I have been told that I am hard to please.

6. I try to avoid long conversations, especially if I think someone will get emotional.

7. I get upset when others don't meet my expectations.

8. I would describe myself as independent and self-reliant.

9. Friends or family say mean things to me, and it makes me feel helpless.

10. I prefer to solve problems on my own rather than ask for help.

Your success can only be a result of teamwork. Use more of the word "We" instead of "I". Set your team up to succeed, and you will also succeed. When we work as one, great things happen. Learn to live in the colorful world of your emotions. Take a risk and challenge yourself to share one emotion per day rather than always saying, "I'm fine." You don't have to do it alone. Together we fail and together we succeed. Being vulnerable is okay. Show employees you genuinely care and are interested in them.

People Pleasers are insecure. Managers with this attitude are concerned about how they look to their superiors. They don't like to rock the boat. They seek to avoid personal interaction, especially when things are going south. You'll note they are conveniently "busy" at crucial times when their input or direction is needed, and often take shelter in incessant meetings that are really façades to mask their insecurity or fear of facing conflict. They are only interested in good news, because they're not able to handle anything more. Got a problem? Talk to someone else.

Statements that best describe a People Pleaser:

1. I have difficulty saying "no" and find that I often over-commit myself.

2. After meetings, I can't stop thinking about how I was perceived, and I am consumed with figuring out how to impress others or make them like me.

3. My parents would describe me as an obedient child who never caused problems.

4. I am dishonest at times in my leadership role to avoid conflict.

5. I want more connection than my friends, family, or significant other(s) want, and I'm always the one trying to make it happen.

6. One or both of my parents was critical or fearful, so I tried hard to keep them happy or gain their approval.

7. If I think someone is mad at me, I would rather do something nice for them than confront them directly.

8. I feel very anxious if someone is upset or annoyed with me, so I am good at "keeping the peace."

9. I rarely get angry, but when I do, I usually hide it rather than show it.

10. I don't question decisions from the top. I just obey instructions.

11. I let employees know they must accept things as they are.

Growing up with an unpredictable parent, People Pleasers get connection when a parent is available again. As adults, people pleasers tend to observe the moods of others around them to keep everyone happy. They are in pursuit of the consistent approval they never received growing up. They are concerned about how well they are liked. Being in a leadership position means you will never be the most liked. It's about focusing on what you're there to accomplish. Ask directly for what you want rather than assuming people know. Turn your complaints into requests. Learn to live in the present moment. Your preoccupation about not being seen or understood is holding you back. While taking care of everyone is all well and good, it's likely that you are neglecting yourself in the process, which can eventually lead to resentment and an emotional or physical breakdown.

Some styles may overlap. While most people will have a single, dominant style, it is possible for you to have multiple styles, especially if you didn't have good role models while growing up or in the world of work.

Then there is The Leader: This is the level you want to reach

- I put the needs of my employees before my own.
- I am quick to recognize and appreciate employees for their hard work and efforts.
- I like to be honest and transparent with employees.
- I often let my employees know how important they are to me.
- I would gladly take a pay reduction in a downsizing strategy if it meant no employee would be laid off.
- I do not ask or expect employees to constantly work beyond regular work hours and leave the office late.
- When an employee is dealing with a personal issue and requests time off, I try my best to accommodate them.
- If an employee performs badly, I feel partially responsible.
- I am willing to say, "I am sorry" if I am in the wrong, or "I don't know." Because I do not know everything.
- I am concerned about achieving goals but not at the expense of the well-being of my team.

A leader **coaches, supports and inspires**. He/she puts the interests of their team before their own. Leaders develop a safe atmosphere where risk-taking and feedback are welcomed. They take care of their team. The focus is on helping everyone around them succeed. They push their team to grow and become their very best. A leader never leaves any of his team members hung out to dry. When a leader is at the helm, employees feel valued and appreciated. Employees long for managers who are authentic leaders.

PERFECTING YOUR LEADERSHIP STYLE

It is not a label: Your leadership style doesn't describe who you are.

It is not your personality: These styles explain how you were shaped by your early years or leadership experiences to relate in certain ways with people in your life, especially those you lead.

My early childhood affected my leadership style in the beginning. I was more self-reliant and didn't know how to say "no" because I wanted to be accepted. Getting to know myself better and becoming more able to let go of disappointments helped to make me a better person and leader. From my mother, I had learned resilience, but from my father's many broken promises, I had learned not to trust people. For far too long, I harbored unforgiveness and resentment towards my father because I blamed him for our rough childhood. But when I let go and forgave him, I was able to trust people more often and more deeply. Today, my father and I now have a good relationship and I am thankful for this.

There is something that is holding you back; you need to figure it out and deal with it. It could be something that happened in your childhood, from bad relationships, or even from having worked under a bad boss. You can heal. And figuring out what negative patterns you have and where they come from is a giant step on that journey.

Relationships have a bearing on who we are and how we lead.

Think of your leadership style as a diagnosis of an injury; one that keeps you from making the greatest impact. It can't be mended without an explanation of the problem and an appropriate solution. Until you take a good long look in the mirror and fully accept where you are, you cannot achieve your maximum potential. We all have baggage or behaviors we aren't proud of. It just takes being truthful with yourself and constantly working to improve yourself to become the leader your team needs you to be.

CHAPTER FOUR

IN PURSUIT OF SUCCESS

How Do You Measure Success?

The world views success for the most part as wealth or fame. But how do you define success? **Can one be rich and still poor?** To a great degree, we are all products of our environment. The values we hold come to us from what is around us — our home, our education, our culture. From infancy, we are impacted by what we see and hear.

In the mid-1800s, the ship Chanunga, on its way from Liverpool to America, had a massive collision with a small vessel from Hamburg. Crowded with more than two hundred passengers, the ship sank a half hour after the crash. The Chanunga's lifeboats were lowered in order to reach the shipwrecked persons, but only 34 were saved. Why such a small proportion? Almost all had seized their belts of gold and silver and tied them round their waists. Refusing to lose their money, they lost their lives. and their money as well.

Compromising the essence of who you are to find success can be likened to holding onto grains of sand. It will always slip through your fingers. Allow your reason for being here to lead you to do the amazing things you were destined to do. Focus on your strengths and work on developing your shortfalls.

Once you become who you truly are (self-mastery), you will make the most of this life that you have been given.

- What is your definition of success? Is it feasible?
- What are you searching for?
- What would make you happy?
- What do you really want?

Wanting something that you don't have sucks the joy out of life.

"Be willing to sacrifice everything, but compromise nothing in your quest to be the best."
~Kobe Bryant

IMPORTANT CAREER LESSONS MOST PEOPLE LEARN TOO LATE IN LIFE:

1. Don't stay in a job you hate.

In 2015, I resigned from a job because of the toxic work culture. Yes, the salary was great, but the job was consuming all my time. Money isn't everything. Always remember: You need to get a good return on time, because even the biggest salary cannot buy your youth or time lost will loved ones back. There are things in life you cannot buy or replace. Don't learn this the hard way. Money can buy a lot of things, but it cannot buy peace of mind. Never give up the permanent for the temporary. Don't lose sight of what matters most. In the short term, it may seem you are giving up a big opportunity, but in the long run, you will realize the cost far exceeded the benefits. Staying in a toxic work environment is never worth it.

We spend over half of our lives at work. We all want a job that gives us a sense of fulfillment at the end of the day. Life is too short to put up with a job you dislike or a boss who treats you poorly. No amount of money can compensate for a toxic culture.

Too many of us are hanging around in places, relationships, jobs where we are not being valued - where the life is literally being sucked out of us. Why? Because of fear or lack of confidence in ourselves and in our abilities. We convince ourselves that we can stay in a job that makes us unhappy because we need the income or because we don't believe we can find another job. But the truth is that spending too much of our lives, our energy, our time on this Earth in a bad situation will make us miserable and, along with wreaking havoc on our mental well-being, possibly impact our physical health.

Working in an environment that you are merely tolerated will only hold you back. Instead, try to find loyal employers who appreciate your talents and who give you opportunities to grow and develop. If you dread Mondays, and the high point of your working experience is either Friday or payday, then perhaps it's time to start looking at other companies. The biggest challenge we all face throughout our careers is to be brave enough to walk away when our loyalty and hard work are taken for granted. Speaking from experience, it's a scary decision.

That's because change is scary. But there are really great positions/great companies out there. Know your worth. Even when your current situation makes your self-esteem take a nosedive, remember your worth.

Life is supposed to be enjoyed, not endured. Although the job market is tough, take small steps every day. Send out resumes, take courses online, learn new skills, and make sure to network. There's always a step forward open to you. Maybe it's even time to start your own business. Work for someone who values your hard work, talents, and loyalty, even if it means working for yourself.

It's been just over five years since I left my job to step out on my own. Someone asked me to describe the jump from corporate world to entrepreneurship. I told her it's like leaving a pool to swim in the ocean. Even the best swimmers can drown. You are open to the elements, the water can be cold, you may get snagged by the undercurrents, and you have to watch out for sharks in a bad mood. If you are heading down that road. I would advise you to plan and prepare carefully.

I didn't just get up one day and take the plunge. I was developing my business part-time, so I was already testing the waters. I also set aside emergency funds and took care of major debts. Entrepreneurship is not a walk in the park. And it's not for the faint of heart. I have faced many ups and downs in my journey, and at times the downs seemed to be more often than the ups. Growing a business can seem overwhelming.

But while entrepreneurship can be challenging, it can be incredibly rewarding. Every day, you have fresh, new opportunities to invest in your dreams. And there is no more deeply satisfying harvest than seeing the seeds of your labor bearing fruit.

> *"Your life is like a balloon...if you never let yourself go,*
> *you will never know how far you can rise."*
> ~Linda Poindexter

2. Take care of yourself.

"If you want to achieve success, you will have to make big sacrifices." I find that many people too ardently heed this advice — they make ongoing sacrifices for their success over a period of years and learn too late that there's more to life than just chasing the rainbow for a pot of gold. Yes, you must make sacrifices, but they should be for the short term, not a way of life. You should be able to enjoy the fruits of your efforts.

Ultimately your well-being is very important to your overall success as a leader. Unless you are healthy, you cannot lead your team with enthusiasm and vigor. It's important to take care of your health, both physical and emotional. Sacrificing your health for success, for wealth or position, isn't worth it in the long run. You need to be well-nourished enough to nourish the people you care about – in all phases of your life. It's important to eat healthy and drink lots of water. If you don't take care of yourself, you will be of no use to anyone.

I had a close friend who worked non-stop. He was always "plugged in," to the point where he wouldn't even take a vacation. Sadly, he was diagnosed with cancer and had to take early retirement. He died shortly thereafter. After years of working like a jackhammer, he never got to enjoy any of his retirement earnings. Our bodies are not machines. You can't keep going 24/7 for years without paying a price. The lights won't always be green. If you don't slow down, eventually you will come to a red light and have to make a complete stop. Don't take your physical health or emotional well-being for granted - no amount of success or money can replace them.

Finding balance is an ongoing process and a lifelong journey. We must balance our jobs with other important aspects of life. A good work-life balance is one in which you work to live, not live to work. Many people don't know how to set the boundaries needed for a work-life balance that works well for them. They don't say "This is too much for me," because they feel they have to prove themselves — maybe to make the list for that promotion, or maybe driven by a pattern they formed earlier in their lives.

In order to be truly successful in life, we must set boundaries. If your employer does not support work-life balance, it's time for you to set your own boundaries. I had a manager who would call me after 9 p.m. as a routine to remind me of tasks for the next day. I realized this would never stop, so I started taking off my cell phone after work hours. We need rest and relaxation to perform at our best, and requiring that your staff be on call 24/7 will inevitably produce resentful employees. Give your employees time to recharge and enjoy their private lives. We used to have a saying: "I have one nerve left, and you're getting on it!" Don't drive your staff to that last nerve.

Balance is a gift you can create for yourself; no one else can do it for you. You have to make it a priority. Some people take long runs or walks to relieve stress, while others find solace in prayer and in developing their relationship with God. Still others find relief through music, television, exercise, arts and crafts, cooking, reading or hobbies. I find disconnecting and enjoying the Sabbath to be essential for my well-being. Get some sleep. You need time to recharge. Rest is so important.

Take time to reflect on your interests. What you are passionate about? What helps you restore your energy? Where can you find that sense of peace and renewal? *Try to create some mental space where you can relax, turn off distractions, and let yourself go.* Additionally, keep in touch with those closest to you - your spouse, your children, your friends, and your extended family.

If you answer yes to any of the following statements, you may need to prioritize your work-life balance:

> Does your job keep you so busy that it hardly allows you to spend time with your family? Then it's not worth it. Who or what are you working for?

> Do you often have to work longer hours, e.g., leaving home at 5 a.m. and returning at 8 p.m.? Do you work weekends as well? That is not working but drowning.

> Is your health consistently threatened due to stress and an unhealthy work environment (bad boss)? Maybe it's time to look for a new job. The truth is, no company will take care of you if you don't take care of you first.

What are you doing for yourself and your life OUTSIDE of work?

3. Take time to listen.

Listening is a great time and money saver. It can solve a host of problems, enhance creativity, encourage insights, and most especially, show people that you care. Listening is crucial to gaining a comprehensive understanding of any situation. Without this full understanding, we can easily waste everyone's time by solving the wrong problem or addressing only a symptom, missing the root cause. I would like to challenge you to make a concerted effort to listen more than you speak. I think you'll be surprised at the benefits.

We have become so connected that we can lose ourselves and our purpose in the process. I always remember a story my pastor once told. As he was rushing to get to a board meeting (for which he was already late), a gentleman approached and asked to speak with him. My pastor took down the information and promised to meet with him when the board meeting was over. When he was finally able to visit the man's house, he saw a large white tent in the yard. He was told the gentleman had committed suicide. This man's mother had sent him to the pastor as a last resort since he was suicidal. Sometimes in the midst of fulfilling our duties (procedures, processes, systems), we can lose sight of what truly matters. It's people. You can apply this to your personal life. If you are in a rush and someone asks to speak to you, stop and listen. First hear them out, at least to the point where you can be confident the situation is stable. You don't want to live with a lifetime of regret.

4. Rejection and failure will strengthen you.

Failure is not the end. Few things in life are certain, but failure certainly is. Although it leaves a sour taste, failures are the pillars of our successes. You gain experiences you could not get any other way. Additionally, rejection is unavoidable in a creative life. Learning how to deal with rejection early on will keep you from plummeting to a place of immobilizing despair. Rejection hurts, but don't dwell on it. If you do find yourself dwelling on your failures, sometimes it helps to think of all the successful men and women who failed repeatedly at various point in their careers. Just Google "successful people who failed."

I worked for a company for three years and never got promoted. In those three years, I only had two interviews for internal jobs (after applying for quite a number). In one case, I was the top candidate and aced the interview, but I was still rejected. Even when I was the "Acting" in a higher position. I later learned they hired a friend of my boss. When I got tired of the internal politics, I started applying externally and was offered an amazing opportunity. My old boss asked me to come back for the same promotion. I have to admit I enjoyed telling him, "Thanks, but no thanks."

Lessons learned:

1. You can be the best candidate and still not be selected.
2. If you didn't get the job, it was never meant for you.

3. You weren't rejected, you were redirected.

4. Your value does not decrease based upon someone's inability to see your worth.

5. Believe in yourself and keep trying - the right door will open for you.

Challenges and roadblocks bring out the best in us provided we have the courage to face them and not give up. If you focus on positive thinking, even the harshest defeat is only a stepping stone. **Not every open door is a blessing.** The test is overcoming the fear behind saying, "no" and maintaining the faith that closing one door will open a new one to an even better opportunity, far better suited to you. In my experience, it's worth that risk.

When I was younger, when my mother would cook beans. She would wash the beans and throw the odd-looking ones outside. However, when the rains came, those odd-looking, rejected beans would grow and produce so much fruit. Moral of the story: People may reject or discard you because you don't seem valuable (to them). But the day is coming when they will see the greatness inside of you. So, don't let any job or organization steal your joy. Keep believing, and speaking, that things are turning around for you. Sooner or later, it will turn in your favor. Remember, it's not about how many NOs you get. It's about that one YES. Shake off rejection and disappointment and keep going. Just keep pushing, and the doors to your goal will swing open to you one day. There is a season and time for everything. Don't worry. Your time will come.

5. Don't let money or your job title define you.

Never let a job define your self-worth or dictate your level of happiness. Most people define success around money or fame. They get their self-worth from these things. This gives money way too much power over your life. These things can be lost in an instant. **You need to be able to separate who you are from what you do**. I have seen too many people give everything to their jobs. Their identity is wrapped up in their jobs. They give up relationships and hobbies. And when the job is gone, whether it's due to retirement or being let go, their lives are empty.

Maybe it's time for you to re-define success. Enter the race you are designed to run. **Focus on a higher purpose,** and you'll bring out the best in yourself and others. Only by using your gifts and talents in the service of others can you live a life that brings lasting fulfillment.

6. Surround yourself with people who will motivate you and push you to grow.

Part of your success is dependent on the people you surround yourself with. Social networks matter. Teamwork and networking are key. I am not saying you should surround yourself with sycophants. Listen for the positive voices. Look for those who can see the greatness in you, believe with you and encourage you. Many of us have stifled our dreams because of doubtful and negative colleagues and friends. **Form alliances and strategic partnerships**. If you can't seem to win in the individual races, try joining a relay. Find a mentor or coach. It doesn't matter how naturally talented you are, you may still need a coach to help you achieve your full potential. Seek out those who have traveled the path before you, and align yourself with those whose skills complement yours. Surround yourself with the "movers and shakers," the leaders in your field. **Run with the leading pack;** those who will champion you and encourage you to keep running.

7. Spend more time away from the office and more time with your family.

I can't tell you the countless times I have heard an employee say, "My job is my life." What happens then if you lose your job or you retire? Your job is not your life. It is a means to live your life. Even if you don't want to believe it, you are expendable. Most employers are only loyal as long as you are fulfilling their self-interests. We sometimes attach to our work environments as if they were quasi-families, and it can be a kind of shock when we realize our employers don't feel the same way about us. You do owe your employer your best work every day, but you don't owe your employer your:

- Personal life
- Health
- Integrity

Work is a never-ending process, and it can be an important and fulfilling one, but life is not only about work, office, and clients. Sometimes in our effort to provide for our families, we miss a key point: **precious time with them**. The interests of an employer or a client are important but so is your family. No one taking their last breaths in this life thinks "Darn, I really wish I'd done a better job keeping up with my email." Disconnect regularly and experience real life with those that matter most to you.

"What consumes your mind controls your life... What's on your mind?"

8. Worrying doesn't solve anything.

It just magnifies fear and creates anxiety. The antidote to fear is action. Don't let fear hold you back. You won't achieve your goals if you're afraid to pursue an idea or are worried what others will think of you. If you push through the worry and the fear, you'll almost always find that you were worried about nothing – at least, nothing that you can't handle. Have faith. And as much as you can, use the energy that worry and fear generate to take action. That way, you shift your focus from "What will happen to me?" (the world is out of my control and I'm afraid) to "I will achieve the things I set my mind to!" Patience and persistence will open the right doors. "I've had a lot of worries in my life, most of which never happened." —Mark Twain

9. Never stop learning. Never stop growing.

No matter how good you are, there is always room for improvement. **It's important to keep learning; keep growing. You can never reach**

that perfect state. Never get too comfortable and think you know it all. Make it a lifelong mission to perpetually improve yourself in any way, shape, or form. No one is perfect, and you need to understand that. Perfection isn't even a useful goal; no matter how bland it sounds compared to "perfect," "better" is the "better" goal. However, make it a priority to constantly keep working towards being the best version of yourself.

Personal development is continuous. Learn everything about the field you are in and look into related fields. Become the expert others look to for advice. With the rate at which technologies are changing, if you decide that you are done with learning, you will be left behind. By continuously learning, you'll be able to keep on top of things, make better decisions, and remain "relevant" in this digital era. Try as well to **diversify your skill set** so you can have income from more than one source. Even though my schedule is quite hectic, I try to read at least three books a month, along with articles. I also take courses online. The world is constantly changing, and you will have to keep upgrading your skills.

10. Happiness is in the present moment.

Many people say, "I'll be happy when I achieve..." Happiness seems to be somewhere in the distant future where you will find that pot of gold at the end of the rainbow. None of us knows how long we have on this earth so you can choose to be happy now. The truth is that the rat race is never ending. It sucks you in and has its jaws fixed so tightly on you that you forget to enjoy the journey and those around you. Life is full of moving targets. The bar is constantly being set higher and higher. It's time to change your mindset. **Have you considered that you are already successful?** Maybe you don't have a big bank account but no matter what your situation, if you can approach it with a balanced attitude—facing your struggles head on and helping others along the way—you are already successful.

Crossing the finish line: The finish line is just the beginning of a whole new race.

I have had to push managers to be out of the office by 7:00 at night, threatening that I would have security turn off the power. I do not endorse anyone staying late at the office. Sadly, in many organizations when you leave on time, you are made to feel guilty, as if you are not committed or dedicated enough. Too many organizations are paying lip service to work-life balance when their sole focus is on the bottom line. If you really believe in treating employees like family, start by encouraging them to leave the office on time to spend time with their real family.

I could go on for hours as this is a subject dear to me. I've heard of employees passing away because of stress at work or working 100+ hours a week. Money should not be the only determinant factor when choosing a job. Work-life balance is very important. Balance means making choices and enjoying those choices. There are three primary aspects to our lives - personal, spiritual, and professional - which need adequate attention. A fine balance needs to be maintained between those three elements to lead a satisfied and contented life. Too often it is the professional aspect that takes over, crowding the others out. Life is too short to live with regrets. It's time to stop enduring life and start living it.

In November 2019, Bernard J. Tyson, CEO of Kaiser Permanente, who was a well-known and admired healthcare executive, suddenly passed away in his sleep. Within a few hours of his passing, I checked out the company's website. They had already issued a statement with the name of his replacement. I thought that was quick. Life is short and unpredictable. Within hours he was an ex-CEO, and within days, LinkedIn removed his 'Influencer" badge.

Everything you fight for on this earth you will eventually leave behind. Focus on eternal things. "Whereas you do not know what will happen tomorrow. For what is your life? It is even a vapor that appears for a little time and then vanishes away. -James 4:14

It's important to build quality moments and build great relationships and memories. Yesterday is gone, tomorrow is not promised, and that leaves only one day in which life is real, one day in which life is actually being lived: today. The lesson? Be humble, be kind, and don't spoil your present to make your tomorrow. Plan for your tomorrow, have goals, even aim for the stars, but don't stop living your present. We are all replaceable. Years ago, one of my co-workers died in a car accident on Friday night. By Monday morning, there was already a replacement at his desk. Your family will miss you, but work won't. So invest in what really counts. As much fun as it is to fantasize, never think you aren't replaceable, or that the company will fall apart if you are not there.

So often, we forget that existence is temporary. We fail to focus on what and who really matters in our lives. Life is truly short, and the best way to live a meaningful and purposeful life is to focus on what truly matters. Hint: people matter most. We are born with a need for human connection. We come into this world empty-handed and we leave the same way. Our positions and job titles are given to someone else. And we can be replaced on any day at any time. It doesn't matter how many degrees or accolades you have achieved, how much money you make, and or how big an influencer you are on this earth. Bottom line, you're here for a time and then you're gone.

I was so shocked and saddened by the passing of basketball legend Kobe Bryant and his daughter Gianna in January 2020. I was in tears. It was tragic and heartbreaking. Kobe has been a positive influence on my brothers and on so many of the young men in the community where I grew up. My younger brother, Brent, really admired Kobe, and I had to sit through so many basketball games watching him play. He was not only a great basketball player, he was humble, generous, had an amazing work ethic, and was a family man. People are trying to understand how this could have happened. It's sad, but we are all mortal. When your number is called, you have to go.

Don't be impressed by:

- Money
- Degrees

- Job titles
- Connections

Be impressed by:

- Kindness
- Integrity
- Humility
- Generosity

As a materialistic society, we have fixed metrics for success based on externals which are not a true indicator of real success or happiness. The things that really matter in life don't have a price tag attached to it. Focus on these. In the end, all we take with us is our character.

What kind of legacy are you leaving behind? Legacy is about building for the future, but it also requires learning from the past. Leaving a positive legacy is to participate in creating a better society, a better world. What kind of society am I creating now? What are we passing on to future generations? And what kind of world do I want my legacy to help create?

The whole issue of leaving a legacy may remind us of death, but it's not about death. It's about life and the choices we make. However, being reminded of death may not be a bad thing, because it gives us a perspective on what's important. Thinking about our legacy helps us decide the kind of life we want to live and the heritage we want to leave behind. It means developing and passing on a timeless part of ourselves. The idea of leaving something meaningful behind that will live forever is appealing. We all hope to be remembered in some way after we're gone, to have what we've done and held dear live on after us. We also want to feel that our lives matter, that somewhere in the many trails and pathways of human development, we might leave our own footprints. Most of us will not be a Nelson Mandela or Mahatma Gandhi, with our name and achievements preserved in the history books. In reality, if you don't pass on your life experiences, the wisdom you've gained will disappear after you leave this earth.

Your legacy does not live on in systems and processes but in the hearts and minds of people. I had a supervisor who had poor people skills. Her sole fixation was on results, and, sadly, when she retired, none of the staff chose to stand up and say anything about her. It was a very short retirement program.

5 THINGS TO STOP TOLERATING:

1. **Negative self-dialogue**. Are you hard on yourself? Do you point out your flaws, criticize yourself or beat yourself up when things go wrong? Negative self-talk is detrimental to your emotional well-being. Start talking kindly to yourself.

2. **Holding on to the past**. Living in the past does no good. You can't start the next chapter, if you keep re-reading the old one. We all make mistakes. Learn from it and move on.

3. **Comparing yourself**. Nothing robs you of your happiness and peace of mind faster than comparing yourself to other people or what they have. Trying to keep up with the Joneses will make you miserable. Value, appreciate and love yourself.

4. **Believing in perfectionism**. Life is not perfect, and no one is. Trying to be perfect will frustrate you and impede your efforts to move ahead. Focus on doing and giving your best and that is more than enough.

5. **Wasting time**. While it is true that time is the most precious of all commodities, it is more important to remind yourself that time is also a depreciating asset. It must be cherished and made the most of. Stop procrastinating. Use your time wisely. Take small steps daily to get to where you need to be.

We often equate success with talent. But the reality is, talent and technical skills alone are not enough. We have all seen talented people squander their success by making poor decisions.

HERE ARE 10 BEHAVIORS THAT REQUIRE ZERO TALENT YET HAVE A HUGE IMPACT ON OUR SUCCESS:

- **Being on Time** - Many people have a habit of being late to meetings, work, and appointments. Most people hate to wait for someone else (even chronically late people hate to wait for someone else). Being on time takes zero talent and shows discipline. It gives a good first impression.

- **Work Ethic** - Cutting corners may seem like the easy way out but it always leads to dead ends. Doing your work with honesty and dedication will take you to new heights. Take pride in the quality of the work you're doing.

- **Effort** - Give your everything when you do something. You don't want to later regret a half-hearted effort. Make the strong and realistic effort you need to make things happen. Always do your best.

- **Body Language** - Your body language speaks volumes about you. Be aware of your body language; make sure it is conveying the message you want to communicate.

- **Energy (Motivation)** - There can be days in which our energy levels are low; we don't feel motivated; maybe we don't even want to get out of bed. That feeling may have a message for you, but don't let that feeling dictate your behavior. Stay as focused as you can. Crank up that little laser in your head and focus it on your goals. If you know your "why," it will be easier to stay motivated.

- **Attitude** - A positive attitude can go a long way in a workplace. Having a positive attitude is essential to do creative work. Your attitude determines the course of your life. When you're negative, you act as a roadblock in the path of your own success.

- **Passion-** The enthusiasm you show when you are passionate about something is easily noticeable and can rub off on others. Being passionate about something also gives you the ability to endure in times when things may not be going your way. And it makes life so much fun!

- **Being Coachable -** Be always open to learning. You can never know everything. To increase your chances of success, you need to be a continuous learner.

- **Doing Extra -** Doing something extra will not cost you much but it will definitely add a lot to your character and make you stand out from the crowd. "There are no traffic jams along the extra mile." –Roger Staubach

- **Being Prepared -** "Failing to plan is planning to fail." Always be prepared, formulate a plan before you do something. Being prepared **significantly** reduces the risk of failure.

Which skills are you lacking, and where do you occasionally fall short? Most of the big opportunities that we get in life come as a result of the little choices we make every day. Poor choices can potentially harm your future success. In life, your competition isn't other people. It's the negative thoughts you think, the time you waste, the procrastination you allow, the unhealthy food you eat, and the personal development you ignore. Look in the mirror. That's your competition.

Soft skills are absolutely invaluable in every organization, and each will boost you towards greater personal and professional success! We can't control what life throws at us, but we can control how we react to it. Start making wise choices. It will not only help you achieve success, but it will also help you to sustain it.

TAKE SMALL STEPS EVERY DAY, AND EVENTUALLY YOU WILL GET THERE

A four-year degree attained after seven years is still a degree. A graduation at 50 is still a graduation. A business started at 65 is still a business. It's okay to start over. And it's okay to run at your own pace. Everyone moves through life to the rhythm of their own heartbeat. You are exactly where you need to be. Don't let people define you with their timelines of success. They are in their time zone, and you are in yours. You did not miss your moment. You are very much on time. It's never too late to dream a new dream.

Age when these individuals started their company or when their careers took off:

- Reed Hastings (Netflix): 36
- Sam Walton (Walmart): 44
- Charles Flint (IBM): 61
- Colonel Sanders (KFC): 62
- Anna Mary Robertson Moses, better known as Grandma Moses, began her prolific painting career at 78.
- Susan Boyle's debut studio album, *I Dreamed a Dream*, was released in November 2009 and became the UK's best-selling debut album of all time – at the age of 47.
- Harry Bernstein published his memoir called "The Invisible Wall: A Love Story That Broke Barriers" at the age of 96. He died at the age of 101.

IT'S A NEW YEAR, AND MAYBE YOU HAVEN'T SET RESOLUTIONS YET. YOU STILL HAVE TIME. (IN FACT, YOU CAN DO THIS ANY DAY OF THE YEAR. HOW ABOUT TODAY?)

1. Set Goals.

It's never too late to set new goals. Write them down. Speak them into being. If you don't set goals, you will be drifting aimlessly wherever the winds take you. Form a plan and visualize the end result. Eradicate time wasters. Think outside the box. If something isn't working, don't be afraid to try something new. Take risks. Look for opportunities others may overlook. Break down large goals into small ones so you can see progress.

2. Focus on Your Skills and Talents.

Embrace your distinctiveness. Learn from others but don't try to imitate them. You will be a poor replica of someone else when you could be such a fine example of yourself. **Find your gift.** What is your core purpose? What is it you were given that no one else can do better? Allow your reason for being here to lead you to the amazing things you were destined to do.

3. Run Your Own Race.

Gauge the course and **run at your own pace.** Don't look to the left or right to see how others are doing. Look straight ahead to the finish line. Focus on beating your personal best. It's important not to compare yourself to anyone. Sometimes it may appear others are progressing faster than you. Don't worry if others overtake you. Everybody has their day; you will have yours. **It doesn't matter where you start, as long as you finish strong.** We all achieve milestones at different points. Even if you fail, remember it's not the end of the world. Tomorrow is a fresh opportunity, so pick yourself up and head back to the drawing board.

4. Be Positive.

The longer the course, and with no end in sight, the more it becomes a mind game. Don't get side-tracked by people who are not on the track. Stop doubting yourself. Replace negative thoughts of inadequacy with positive affirmations. **"I can and I will!"** Try every option, and keep trying again and again. Where there is a will, there is always a way, and it may be closer than you think. Every day tell yourself, "Maybe if it didn't happen today, it will happen tomorrow." It may be raining right now but just remember: the sun is always shining above the clouds.

5. Work Hard but Work Smart.

It all comes back to working hard. There aren't any shortcuts in life, and ones you seem to find will lead to dead ends. Give it 100%. Be persistent. It takes a huge commitment, and you will likely have to make some sacrifices. How badly do you really want this?

"Take pride in how far you've come. Have faith in how far you can go. But don't forget to enjoy the journey." -Michael Josephson

6. Be Patient.

We live in a culture that is daily upregulating our need for "instant gratification." **Everybody wants everything now. But if we calm ourselves and watch, listen, feel, nature teaches us that everything happens in seasons and cycles.** A little patience, my dear. Don't be too hasty. You can't expect to plant a seed today and reap a harvest tomorrow. Growth takes time. Keep sowing seeds; your effort will bear fruit. Your day is coming. Prepare and position yourself for it.

7. Enjoy the Journey.

Enjoy the off seasons. Breathe! Life is not a 100-meter sprint but a long-distance race. Prioritize; it's important to take time to stop and smell the roses. Take breaks. Spend time with those closest to you. Show them how much you appreciate them. **These are special moments that you don't want to miss, that may not come around again.** And don't wait for huge victories. Celebrate your small successes and help others to celebrate theirs.

DEALING WITH TROLLS

As my following and influence started growing, this has brought on an onslaught of trolls. They have crawled out from under the bridge in larger and larger numbers.

"They see me as a threat of some kind... I think every strong woman in history has had to walk down a similar path, and I think it's the strength that causes the confusion and the fear. Why is she strong?

Where does she get it from? Where is she taking it? Where is she going to use it?" -Princess Diana

It's amazing the lengths some people will go through to try and pull you down for no apparent reason. The more successful you are, the more you will have to deal with trolls. Trolls and naysayers can be very frustrating and annoying to deal with. They can distract and discourage you from pursuing your goals. At every step, you will encounter the naysayers. To be successful in any area of life, we must master the ability to overcome their negative influences on our lives.

HERE ARE 5 WAYS TO OVERCOME THE NAYSAYERS:

1. Ignore them.

They are a distraction. The bigger your dreams or goals become, the more the naysayers will flood in. Don't let their words sink in and take root. Don't give them residency status in your head - redirect them to your short-term memory. People will always have something negative to say, and sadly, there are people who find satisfaction in finding fault. The truth is that hurting people hurt other people. Stay focused. "You wouldn't invite a thief into your house, why would you let negative people invade your mind?" - Unknown

2. Respond - don't react.

If you must engage in discussion, respond politely and respectfully. Let your emotions subside. Never respond in the heat of the moment. If you respond wisely, sometimes you can win them over. However, don't waste time trying to convince them. Additionally, not all criticism is a bad thing. There is a difference between constructive criticism and personal attacks. Decipher which it is and be open to listen and learn.

*"You will never reach your destination if you stop
and throw stones at every dog that barks."*
~Winston Churchill

3. Safeguard your dreams.

We are in the age of oversharing. You don't have to share everything. You don't have to let everyone know what you are planning to do. This is life, and not everyone will like you or want to see you succeed. Don't take it personally. It has nothing to do with your real worth, so don't let it impact your self-worth.

When you are working on your dream, remember these three things:

> ➤ Select the people you talk about your plans to carefully when your project is in the infancy stage. When I was writing my first book, most of the people I told were negative.

> ➤ If you are doing it for money, you may be greatly disappointed. Focus on adding value. This is your unique contribution to the Universe.

> ➤ Stay committed and focused. What you want won't always come easy, but if you work hard, and never give up, you will get there. If you put in the work, the results will come.

4. Take control of your environment.

If certain individuals are constantly bringing you down, it's time to eliminate them. **Pick your battles wisely.** I see so many people - even those whom you'd think would know better - engaging in online battles with trolls. You can't win a pointless battle against someone who's hiding behind a computer and whose goal is to break your spirit. On social media, you can simply block them. If you're tempted to fight fire with fire, remember that the fire department usually uses water. If it's someone you cannot avoid, then reduce contact with them or just tune out when they are speaking.

5. Personal development.

Develop thicker skin. Remember it's not about them. It's about you. They are just an extra in your movie whilst you have the leading role. Seek continuous self-improvement. Negativity offers us a chance to evolve and learn from our experiences. Personal development (spiritual, emotional, mental, social, and physical) is crucial.

> *" Promise yourself to be so strong that nothing*
> *can disturb your peace of mind."*
> ~Christian D. Larson

The 20-80 principle advocates that 20% of the people you have to deal with produce 80% of the problems. Negativity is always a factor in life, but it's important not to let it paralyze us. Don't let them get to you. Stay focused on the prize. Everything in life must be used as a growing experience. If we only receive positive feedback, we would become complacent and wouldn't grow. In order to succeed, we must learn how to recognize and embrace what's beneficial and quickly discard the meaningless. This is your life. Take back the pen and write your own story – and make it a happy one!

EVERYTHING COMES TO YOU AT THE RIGHT TIME.

My right time was when a door that I had been knocking on for so long finally opened. I was heading into unknown territory, and the odds were totally stacked against me. There seemed to be nothing working in my favor, yet I kept pressing on.

The days leading up to my breakthrough were indeed the toughest. As the famous saying goes, "the darkest hour is just before dawn." Well, the storm unleashed its full fury. Everything that could have gone wrong did, and then, of course, there were the dissenting voices.

Life will throw curve balls at you and will attempt to break you down; nothing may happen exactly as you have planned. Just when you think things are starting to turn around, life may smack you back down, but don't despair. You will get disappointed, but don't be discouraged. When life knocks you down, you may need a little time to regroup. And self-pity may be perfectly appropriate – for a moment. But don't stay there for too long. Don't make it a way of life. Get back up and say, **"This is NOT how my story is going to end!"**

"Rejection does not mean you aren't good enough. It just means the other person failed to realize what you have to offer." -Mark Amend

It was then, when all hope was almost gone, everything changed. I **got my breakthrough.** I was amazed! I wasn't expecting anything to happen so soon. I was just so focused on my plan and had mentally psyched myself up for the long bumpy road ahead. Yes, it had been bumpy for quite a while, but everybody has their day. And this was my day.

Don't be discouraged. Don't lose hope. Seasons change. It won't rain forever. The sun must shine through.

Stop trying to open doors that were never meant for you. This will drain your energy and cripple your spirit. The real value of a diamond is generally only recognized by a professional jeweler and not by a farmer, carpenter, etc. You may be barking up the wrong tree. As my grandmother would say, "What is meant for you will not pass you by. If it didn't open, it's not your door." There will be more opportunities. Keep going. Don't give up. It's just a matter of time before things work out in your favor.

Remember, every "no," every rejection, is just a step closer to your "yes." When one door closes, a better one will open. Being knocked down doesn't mean being knocked out of the race. Keep trying. Keep reaching. Keep dreaming. *You never know what's just around the corner.* You will get your breakthrough too. The truth is, it may not happen in the way you had imagined, or come from the direction you expected. **Stop dwelling on closed doors.** Let go of rejection and disappointment. Let it go. Even if things look bleak right now, your future is bright! Your better days are ahead of you, NOT behind you. The BEST is yet to come.

CHAPTER FIVE

WISE LEADERSHIP IN THE AGE OF ARTIFICIAL INTELLIGENCE

When we think of top leaders, we think of individuals who are smart and intelligent. In an era of increasing discontinuity, many leaders find it difficult to reinvent their corporations rapidly enough to cope with new technologies and trends in the marketplace. Leaders will continue to rely on new scientific discoveries to deal with change. However, depending on intelligence alone prevents leaders from successfully coping with disruption. The use of explicit and tacit knowledge isn't enough; leaders must also draw on practical wisdom.

One of the most compelling questions about the rise of Artificial Intelligence is this: Will machines ever be wise enough to transcend our capabilities as leaders?

AI algorithms are capable of looking at vast amounts of data and finding trends that unveil insights difficult for a human to find. AI extends the scope of our vision. It lets us see further, pulls the camera back wider, digs into levels below the surface, and zooms in on the tiniest details. It allows us to connect information too vast for us to process, too deep for us to contain in memory, and too complex for us to fully understand. Still, with a million eyes, a million hands, and an ocean of data, we will find patterns. Those will guide us (and our algorithms) to more significant patterns. It lets us see more patterns - but that doesn't mean those patterns will ultimately be the right ones.

Current AI development has created a conflict between science, business and ethics — what the technology is capable of and where is it going. According to the AI enthusiasts, AI is going to solve every problem and help cure every disease. While this statement is a bit exaggerated, I've often heard people speak as if this was the truth, and not just about AI but about technology. It's what I like to call the "silver bullet fallacy." But I've only ever heard it from people who know very little about the field and can't tell a simple coding routine from a neural network. I'm not worried by artificial intelligence or artificial wisdom. I find them to be far more reliable, predictable, and consistent in its decisions and suggestions than humans. What worries me is human "intelligence." No AI system ever proclaimed that it would solve world hunger or destroy humanity, or that it should distinguish between race, creed, or social status - only people have. The "silver bullet fallacy" highlights how many people are afraid of missing out, while others are afraid of the unknown and often form opinions based on those fears. Which tells me that what I should be worried about is not the artificial form of intelligence, but the real one.

There is this false notion that AI will be similar to a thinking and creative human brain in the foreseeable future. We hardly understand consciousness ourselves, so how can we duplicate it in AI? With AI, we are still talking about the ability to program for various functions and decision-making options based on learned experience for an indefinite period of time. Intelligence will still be solely confined to the parameters of software. AI will have limitations because AI is not equipped with human abilities such as inspiration, emotions, spirituality, and many more. We need to curb our tendency to overrate this tool. The sophisticated neuro chemicals in the human body are impossible to duplicate in a mechanized system and without these, AI will never be able to have true emotion.

I write and speak a lot about leadership. It is my firm belief that wisdom is critical to good leadership. For far too long, we have rewarded leaders for their intelligence. Our modern society is infatuated with intelligence. In today's complex world, however, we need a different approach to leadership that goes beyond this. **We need** wise leadership. Wise leaders are smart - but they know how to adapt their cognitive skills to different situations and utilize them to serve a greater good. They possess understanding, great self-awareness, discernment, patience, and act with humility and ethical clarity. I once heard someone say, "Intelligence is the ability to solve problems, and wisdom is the ability to circumvent the problems altogether." So now we know what to do wisely. Intelligence is the ability to acquire knowledge. Wisdom is the ability to apply what you have learned in a practical manner through reflection on past experiences and through your senses; we might also call it "a high level of common sense."

Another way to distinguish them is that intelligence is knowing what do, wisdom is knowing why - classic strategy and tactics breakdown. The machines struggle with the tactics, and that's going to go on for a while longer - and it will be much longer than that before these systems even get a glimmer as to "why." Right now, they know what they know, they don't know what they don't know, and they are oblivious to the concept of being wrong. We may become intelligent by harnessing knowledge. But when we combine intelligence with awareness, with a wider range of consciousness, then wisdom shines. And wisdom can bring a perceptible shift in humanity. If those developing and executing AI work from that space, it can create wonders.

Wisdom is the reflection on and refinement of previous decisions. AI is still pretty much simple pattern recognition. And while the pattern recognition will become less simple over time, and might even surprise us with its fancy cognition tricks, there's still no contest. Will our brains stop evolving when we detach ourselves from the natural systems and work as extensions of artificial systems that process information and data far beyond human abilities?

We need to motivate humans to keep enhancing our wisdom rather than simply outsourcing our intelligence. Remember the brain is a naturally lazy, energy-saving organ. It's going to be a long, tough swim upstream against our evolutionary biology.

Whether you're a janitor or the CEO of a company, wisdom is not a function of occupation. Intelligence is about reason, the cognitive function that serves to categorize, structure, and order things in artificial ways following human instructions, such as in generating algorithms. AI is an electronic processing which "reads" and "boxes" things faster than people, but it's just mechanics; it just "mimics" reason with no understanding. Wisdom, on the other hand, deals with real responses involving metaphysical and temporal aspects of life: wonder, understanding, insight, joy, truth, motives, creativity, goodness, beauty, happiness, promises, values, virtues.

AI will continue to evolve and permeate the daily aspects of our lives. And as more of this new facet of technology weaves its way into the fabric of our existence, we need to guard against blurring that line between the many faces of intelligence and the authentic power of wisdom.

As much as we are all dependent on technology these days, we seem to forget that we're wiser than any smart device out there. Without the wisdom that drives the smart device, the smart device is just a DEVICE.

Intelligence is the power to know but wisdom is the ability to know how to use the power of knowing in your daily life. While AI can help leaders make more informed decisions, it lacks the ability to factor non quantifiable areas into those assessments.

> "*Wisdom is the principal thing; therefore, get wisdom:*
> *and with all thy getting get understanding*"
> ~Proverbs 4:7

$$W = f(T + E)^y$$

Wisdom is a function of **Time** and **Experience** to the power of **You** (**individual factors**). Individual factors comprise aptitude, motivation, attitude, personality, and cognitive style (the preferred way an individual processes information). Without wisdom, every other part of the leadership equation risks falling apart. Wisdom comprises the foundation of leadership.

Wisdom is fundamental to good leadership. Knowledge will only get you so far. It's wisdom that will give you the edge. There is a great difference between knowing a thing or two and knowing how to use that knowledge for the good of mankind. We humans train and learn, we gather information and become knowledgeable, and then we have the additional capability of selectively choosing and applying what we have learnt. Most current AI systems are basically large pattern recognition systems with statistical and probability analysis; they don't learn like humans (although they have " training" / learning data, which is mostly used to improve the pattern recognition). In a narrow domain, AI is and will become more effective with time, just like machines have evolved to ease repetitive tasks. But wisdom is another path altogether.

We have all the potential to become wiser, but it will take patience, reflection, humility, honesty, and the willingness to learn and grow.

FROM KNOWLEDGE TO WISDOM

Wise Leaders:

- **Appreciate others**: Lead with gratitude. Wise leaders are comfortable in their own skin and can acknowledge the skills and strengths of others. Their motivation doesn't come from their ego's need for credit. Instead, they make everyone feel appreciated and valued. Nothing drains morale from a team like feeling your efforts are unnoticed. Leading with an attitude of gratitude allows one to **appreciate the little contributions.** Even small gestures of gratitude show people that they matter. Such leaders openly praise their team and publicly acknowledge their contributions. True leaders know they are nothing without the people around them, and they are not afraid of showing it. Recognition and reward are important for building commitment and strengthening relationships.

- **Are good listeners:** *"Seventy-five* percent of an individual's time is spent communicating. Typically, forty-five percent of this time is spent listening and thirty percent speaking" (Adler, Rosenfeld, Proctor, 2001). Hearing is not the same as listening. Wise leaders understand the art of communication to effectively get their message across. They truly listen to what is said to them and respond appropriately. Wise leaders are not interested in solving merely to the level of symptom relief - they are interested in getting to the root cause. They don't jump quickly to conclusions. **They welcome feedback** and are willing to listen to all the facts before they make a decision because they know, they don't have all the answers. This takes humility. They listen with the intent to understand. Such leaders think before they speak. **They ask the right questions.** Today many leaders talk far too much and listen too little, when it should be the other way around. The words you speak to your employees and to the watching world define you.

- **Keep their emotions in check**: They stay composed under pressure. Have you ever had a boss fly off the handle when things didn't go their way? It is impossible to deal with such a person. You never know what you are going to get. Wise leaders are slow to anger, don't take things personally, **and don't hold grudges. They** don't become defensive or upset when a team member or client voices a concern or points out an inconsistency or mistake. **They** practice self-control and self-restraint.

- **Focus on uniting, not dividing:** Wise leaders build great teams. They are able to rally people and gain support for their goals. They work by uniting the people they're trying to influence, not by dividing them or playing them off against each other. Building bridges is their primary objective. They bring people together for the common good. They make an effort to understand others, their drivers, motivators, and value sets in order to truly give and get the best from them. **They sow seeds of unity rather than seeds of discord.**

- **Are reflective:** Wisdom is developed by reflecting on experience to gain insight. Wise leaders reflect on their experiences to see what lessons they can learn. They are aware of their limitations - they are not afraid to discover their limitations through self-reflection. They desire to gain the insight needed to understand, and to apply learning to current and future circumstances. When was the last time you paused? No meetings, no phones, just stillness. Regularly take time to be alone with yourself. Set aside time for personal reflection and some deep thinking. At the end of my day, I try to go through what happened, and sometimes I ask myself, **"Could I have been more patient? Am I true to myself and values? Was I too impulsive? What could I have done better?"** I look back on how I have been leading and also look forward to what kind of leader I am trying to become. Only then can I identify the necessary steps to get there. Taking time to reflect allows for information to be absorbed. It will give you a chance to focus which is crucial for effective leadership. Leaders that can appreciate the value of stillness can move forward and sustain momentum after pausing. Our tech-saturated lives lead to too much multitasking. Distancing oneself from the distractions and taking the time to listen to that still small voice is the path to wisdom. This quote from Warren Buffett is worth taking to heart: "I insist on a lot of time being spent, almost every day, to just sit and think. That is very uncommon in American business. I read and think. So, I do more reading and thinking, and make fewer impulse decisions than most people in business."

- **Make decisions for the greater good:** They lead for a cause, not a promotion. **Leadership must serve a higher**

purpose. Wise leaders not only focus on the organization and their employees, but also on the society as a whole. They look at the overall big picture. They make decisions that take into account the larger context. Leadership is about making a meaningful contribution. They are concerned about the future and how their decisions will impact others. Leaders are responsible for fulfilling their civic duty; the actions of an individual must benefit society as a whole.

- **Are fair and neutral:** The best way to lead is to lead by example. Great leaders are known for the ethical principles they stand on, and their actions promote these values. They speak up in the face of adversity and stand up for what is right, not what is popular. They are honest, impartial, and transparent. They are accountable and don't try to blame others when things go wrong. They don't throw anyone under the bus. They are equable: they take failures gracefully and don't let successes go to their heads. People know what to expect from wise leaders and can depend on them. More than ever, we need leaders who will stand on integrity and put people first. It's a wise leader who will walk the talk.

- **Have good intuition:** When leading a team into uncharted territory, wise leaders trust themselves to make sound decisions. They tend to make intuitive decisions using both discernment and information. They appoint the right people to the right positions. Machines are always dependent on the code they have been given or the data they are fed. The value of our gut feeling, as humans, is hard to overstate. Wise leaders draw from past experiences and are willing to ask for help from experienced members of their field when necessary. They go a step further and look behind the numbers to find the real meaning. They read between the lines and exercise good judgement.

- **Inspire those around them:** They work to teach, motivate, and develop those around them. They build solid foundations. No matter the situation, wise leaders keep people's spirits high by generating enthusiasm. They remain beacons of positivity in the face of challenges and failures. Their positivity is contagious, and it shows in the quality of their team's job. Inspiring leadership is about energizing employees, creating a sense of direction and purpose. **Such leaders are capable of taking an organization and people to new heights.** They are able to get higher levels of effort and dedication from their followers. The word "boss" only signifies authority over others. To be called a leader, you must inspire your team through your actions and words to believe in themselves and in the vision. Wise leaders inspire their team members to become the best version of themselves by helping them to discover and develop the unique qualities they have to offer. The key is an authentic connection with each employee based on genuine care and respect. Leaders who can spark the emotions of the heart will have real influence. The greatest legacy a leader can leave is having developed other leaders.

- **Are compassionate:** The word compassion generally evokes positive feelings. We like to think of ourselves as compassionate people who are primarily good and kind. We identify being compassionate with being truly human. We feel offended when someone accuses us of lacking compassion. The word compassion is derived from Latin words meaning, "to suffer with." Compassion requires us to identify with the weak, hurting, vulnerable, and the powerless. It is more than mere kindness. Compassion calls us to relieve human suffering, to answer human need. It means taking action. Being compassionate is not about being extra nice and soft, or avoiding problems. It's about retaining a dignity and respect for humanity. We lead people, not organizations, and our mission is to serve people, not a goal. People are the foundation that make organizational goals happen. Compassionate leadership focus on connection and community. It gets the job done without sacrificing people in the process. **Wise leaders** understand where others are coming from and demonstrate genuine empathy in challenging times. They carefully consider timing - when to make a move or to discuss issues. For leaders to maximize situations, they need to go beyond spreadsheets and routines. It's about taking a genuine interest in the team, including a common respect and concern for each individual.

Artificial intelligence (AI) is a hot topic as it is automating the decision-making process, promising better qualitative results and improved efficiency. The new era of AI will also see the creation of new kinds of jobs and roles in our organizations. AI likely will reshape jobs all the way up to the C-level offices. That doesn't mean, though, that leaders will no longer be needed. They simply need to prepare themselves for shifts in their work responsibilities. Leaders should start developing their social skills, learning how to engage their people if they want to remain relevant in the new reality. Our challenge lies not so much on the technological side of AI, but on the human side.

The impact of AI means human characteristics such as empathy, compassion, and collaboration are likely to become the future high-value skills cherished by leading organizations. It's ironic that the technology that potentially threatens humanity might actually be the technology that forces humans to become more human.

Today, we need technology that works with us, that amplifies our voices and improves the human condition. **Our leadership crisis is due to overestimating the importance of competencies and discounting the critical importance of wisdom.**

More than ever, we need wise leadership. Wise leadership is knowing what to say and not say. You can be the best manager but react poorly while having a bad day, and if someone records it, that one slip can spell the end of valuable career. And once it goes viral, you can't remove it. When you are in a leadership position, you're not allowed to overreact, even on a bad day. As leaders, we are being watched. We have to stay centered in our wisdom at all times. Sometimes I see viral videos of leaders having a meltdown or behaving poorly and I think, "Do they know there are cameras everywhere?" That's the downside of technology. Someone is always watching and listening. Within the past year, we've seen several business leaders making public apologies for inappropriate or offensive words and actions. We always have to think carefully before reacting. If you feel you are at your tipping point, remove yourself from the situation and gather your thoughts. Learn to respond, not react.

The defining difference between success and failure in this highly competitive marketplace comes down to decision-making. The organizations which make the best decisions and end up reaping the benefits of those good decisions, have the best leaders. You can enhance organizational productivity, creativity, and capacity by learning and applying the core values and taking the time to work on becoming a wise leader. We live in a world of increasing division and destruction because we've put too much faith in intelligence. **We already have enough "intelligent" leaders; what we really need are wise leaders.**

SECTION TWO:

BUILDING THE WORKFORCE
OF THE FUTURE

CHAPTER SIX

PEOPLE DON'T QUIT JOBS. THEY QUIT MANAGERS.

Employee engagement is at an all-time low. According to a State of the Global Workplace report, 85% of employees are not engaged or are actively disengaged at work. The economic consequences of this global "norm" are approximately $7 trillion in lost productivity. More than two-thirds, 67%, are not engaged with their work and workplace, while 18% are actively disengaged. Those "not engaged" make up the majority of the workforce -- they are not your worst performers, but they are indifferent to your organization. They give you their time, but not their best effort nor their best ideas. According to Gallup, disengaged employees have 37% higher absenteeism, 18% lower productivity, and 15% lower profitability.

Many organizations underestimate the power of great leadership in increasing employee motivation, engagement, and retention. Over the course of my career, I have only had one good boss. As I think back, this was the single biggest determinant of whether I stayed or left a company. It does not always have to do with the size of your paycheck, the length of your commute, or the everyday tasks you do — what matters most to workplace happiness are the qualities your manager brings to their job. A boss sets the tone of the organization.

Please don't get me wrong. Yes, motivation is intrinsic but dealing with a bad boss for 8-10 hours a day, 5 days a week, can even wear out the most loyal employees. A bad boss can make a good job, even in the best company, unbearable.

An employee's relationship with their manager impacts their level of commitment to the organization's success. People are loyal to their bosses before they are loyal to the organization. People see the company through the lens of their relationship with their immediate boss. Gallup research found that a mind-boggling 70% of an employee's motivation is influenced by his or her manager. It's no wonder employees don't leave companies; they leave managers. In spite of how good a job may be, people will quit if the reporting relationship is not healthy. Nobody starts a new job thinking they will be less than extraordinary, but we keep seeing people demotivated or leaving. In most cases, it's not because they don't like their job but because they were beaten down by bad management.

A bad boss will intimidate, compete with, and micromanage employees. The damage that can result from working for a bad boss involves much more than just being mismanaged. Working bad bosses can erode your self-confidence and increase anxiety and stress. They can even make the work itself seem like drudgery. I worked for a boss who was always hovering over our shoulders to see what we were doing, and even asked for a spreadsheet of our daily activities. It was very stressful, and I felt anxious and defensive all day. I put up with it because I had my college debt to pay off. Once this was cleared, I left that job for one that paid less, but the relief! It felt like 100 lbs. was lifted off my shoulders!

Organizations know how important it is to have motivated, engaged employees, but most fail to hold managers accountable for making this happen. When they don't, the bottom line suffers. You can give employees all sorts of perks and benefits, but if you treat them poorly, they will still leave. With employers in North America alone spending $1 billion every year on engagement, this is clearly a focus area for businesses to work on.

Companies need to take a closer look at their managers and their leadership style. Employee engagement is more of a manager issue. A Gallup poll of more 1 million employed U.S. workers concluded that the No. 1 reason people quit their jobs is a bad boss or immediate supervisor. Three-quarters (75%) of workers who voluntarily left their jobs did so because of their bosses, not the position itself. **They reported their bosses were the worst and most stressful part of their jobs.** How bad are they? Bad enough for 65%

of respondents to say they'd rather have a new boss over a pay raise.

Bad bosses are the No. 1 cause of unhappiness at work. Most of the time, when an employee has an issue with their company, it's boss-related. At the end of the day, we spend a large part of our lives at work. It's akin to being in a relationship. A non-supportive manager can make us feel like we're in an abusive relationship.

Too many managers view their position as one of entitlement rather than one of responsibility. In days past, managers would focus on developing their employees. Today some are more focused on self-promotion and securing their position. A manager's job is to facilitate a good working environment for his/her employees. The focus should be on helping everyone around you succeed. Managers define culture, and culture undergirds the lasting health, success and sustainability of an organization.

There is mounting evidence that happy workers are more productive workers, which translates into higher stock market returns. **Maybe it's time companies invest more effort and resources into management selection and ongoing training**. Few things are as costly and disruptive as managers who kill morale. Many bosses can manage processes, but they are not deft at leading people, which calls for inspiration, vision, and soft skills.

"If management stopped demotivating their employees, then they wouldn't have to worry so much about motivating them."
~Mark Graban

Research shows when your employees are connected and engaged, business booms. There is an economic link between employee satisfaction and company financial performance. A happy workplace culture does translate into better stock returns. Happy Employees = Happy Customers = Happy Shareholders.

We now have a workforce where millennials are fully integrated, and Gen Z is on the way. Millennials gravitate to leaders who are humble, social, and authentic. They thrive on regular feedback, interactions, input. The biggest change in the dynamics of the workplace is the shift from leadership by authority to leadership by influence. The days of a boss saying "jump" and employees responding with "how high" have passed.

According to the Bureau of Labor Statistics for 2016, the average length of time an employee stayed with one company was 4.6 years. And as younger generations enter the workforce, that timeframe is likely to shrink even further; a study by Future Workplace showed that millennials expect to stay in one job for less than three years.

It's not rocket science. If a manager has a foundation of truly caring for their people, it becomes easier to lead and retain good employees. Your staff can tell if you are authentic and want the best for them. When employees have a boss who truly cares and appreciates them, they are willing to go the extra mile to ensure successful outcomes.

> *"The biggest concern for any organization should be when their most passionate people become quiet."*
> ~Unknown

FOR EMPLOYEES, THESE BEHAVIORS ARE SOME OF THE BIGGEST DEAL BREAKERS:

1. **Micromanaging.** This is the primary killer of creativity and innovation in the workplace. It fosters an environment of distrust, as employees feel suffocated and confined. Micromanagers monitor an employee's every movement. To some employees, it feels like harassment. If you hire individuals for a job, give them room to get it done. Your job as a manager is to provide the tools and support an employee needs to effectively perform. Micromanagement sucks the life out of employees. Constantly monitoring an employee's every movement can be disheartening. Sometimes knowing when to step back and let your employees do their work is what they need.

2. **Setting people up to fail.** Such bosses keep tabs on their employees, using what they find against employees in their performance appraisals. They focus more on an employee's weaknesses than on strengths. They can list all the mistakes an employee makes, even those that were discussed and rectified. Often, they strategize to bolster and protect their positions. They don't hire people who are smarter than they are or who share their specific knowledge base.

3. **Picking favorites.** These managers hire and promote based on personal favoritism rather than merit. We know too well about office politics. These bosses only recommend employees in their "inner circle" for assignments or growth opportunities while they keep back other employees. They recognize and reward the same employees repeatedly. They surround themselves with sycophants. Additionally, if an employee stands up to them, the victimization begins — the "offender" is considered a poor team player and treated as an outcast. Always favoring certain employees for promotions and assignments is a sure way to damage team morale. Employees who are not in your inner circle will always believe that you favor the employees who are chosen. This perception destroys team spirit and undermines engagement.

4. **Taking the credit for employees' work or successes.** Bad bosses will do anything to look good, including taking credit for the employee's work or ideas. Self-promotion is their top priority. There are few things more demotivating than working hard to earn something only to have it unfairly taken away. This causes employee engagement to plummet.

5.**Making false promises**. Some bad (and dishonest) bosses will lie to get an employee to accept a job or a responsibility. Once the employee has fallen it, these managers keep changing the goalpost when the target is in sight. They are seen as untrustworthy and inauthentic. They practice the carrot and stick approach for employee motivation, and they use a fake carrot to do it.

6. **Ignoring feedback**. Some bosses only listen to subordinates when the feedback is positive. These managers don't admit mistakes. They take negative feedback personally, and they tend to "shoot the messenger." Employees witness this and learn not to say anything. And if these managers do, somehow, receive feedback, they ignore it. Nothing gets done. Employees know they are wasting their time and stop giving helpful feedback. Such leaders operate in a bubble and set themselves up for failure.

7. **Not standing up for employees**. Throwing employees under the bus rather than standing up for your team in distressing moments is a sure way to lose points. If you want to build loyalty, you must demonstrate loyalty. These bad bosses are quick to point fingers, leading to a culture of distrust. It leaves employees feeling like they are on shaky ground. Good bosses don't dwell on mistakes made by others, hold grudges, or point fingers. They take responsibility and focus on solving problems.

8. **Overworking employees.** They have unrealistic expectations about what is possible from employees. They see celebrating successes as a waste of time, time that could be better spent on more work. Their main focus is on the bottom line. They show no empathy. **They don't care about employees** and don't try to hide it. If an employee is ill, their only concern is when the employee will return to work. It's discouraging working for such a boss as this. They don't want to authorize personal days, they question the need for sick days, and they seem to think that asking to leave a little early is a direct affront to Western Civilization.

9. **Losing their cool when things go wrong**. These types of bad bosses have low emotional intelligence; employees know to stay away when they are upset. They also insult employees, and often use a disrespectful tone. They rely on fear and intimidation. They can make some employees cry. Employees have to walk on eggshells around them. And that's not a healthy environment to be in.

10. **Displaying incompetence**. They keep offloading their workload and responsibilities onto high performers. They view their position as one of entitlement rather than one of responsibility. They fail to give clear direction or provide frequent feedback. These types of managers get promoted based on the "The Peter Principle" which states that the selection of a candidate for a position is based on the candidate's performance in their current role, rather than on abilities relevant to the intended role. Thus, "managers rise to the level of their incompetence."

11. **Treating employees like robots.** Employees want to work for someone who treats them like a human being. They have emotions and personal lives. Showing you sincerely care about employees helps to build relationships and loyalty. I can't emphasize this point enough. If a staff member is dealing with an issue, whether professional or personal issues as illness or bereavement — show empathy. The way you treat them when at their lowest is something they will never forget.

12. **Taking no interest in employees' development.** One of the top reasons employees leave a company is the lack of development opportunities. Employees can interpret an employer's unwillingness to invest in training as a disregard for their professional development. Subsequently, if a team member has informed you that they want to move to another department, support their wishes. Don't become an obstacle to them. Acknowledge and encourage strengths, recognize the different skills your employees possess, and recommend training and development opportunities.

13. **Being inflexible.** They make mountains out of molehills for requests as simple as needing time off or wanting to take an earlier lunch. Employees should feel comfortable to approach you at all times, but when you are inflexible, it creates a wall between you and your team. I am not referring to being unethical or breaking procedure, but putting your team first and using your judgement in certain situations will make people more inclined to trust you.

14. **Letting accomplishments go unrecognized**. No one likes to feel ignored or like their efforts are taken for granted. As Dale Carnegie stated, "People work for money but go the extra mile for recognition, praise, and rewards." Appreciate employees, show them how much you value their efforts. And it doesn't always have to be about monetary rewards. Simple things, such as saying "Thank you" and "Well done," go a long way.

I have seen too many exceptional employees become disheartened, stop caring, and just go through the motions until they find another job. A culture of blaming, punishment, inflexibility, and insensitivity only pushes people away. Employees want managers who will inspire them, who are fair and honest and will stand up for their team.

THE BIGGEST DANGER OF LEADERSHIP: ARROGANCE

According to research from the University of Washington Foster School of Business, humble people are more likely to make the most effective leaders. It turns out, humility offers a competitive advantage.

So why have arrogant or narcissistic leaders become the norm?

It has been historically perceived that humility is a sign of weakness and an antithesis to leadership. There is still an expectation that successful leaders are more arrogant than humble. Narcissism is mistaken for self-confidence, and toxic leaders seem to be "in control." They are able to provide short-term results, but the truth is, they leave a trail of destruction in their path. Organizations pay heavily for such managers with low engagement, high turnover, and reduced productivity. Arrogant leaders have a shelf-life within their organizations. They may "rule the day" at first. But eventually people tire of them and their tactics, which lessens overall commitment from the team. Intimidation, threats of punishment, and consistent selfishness can only work for so long.

THE POWER OF HUMILITY IN THE WORKPLACE:

Leading with humility means focusing on others and practicing servant leadership. Humble leaders:

1. **Put people first.** Their focus is on serving others. They do not get consumed by grasping for more power. Instead, they seek more ways to help others.

2. **Admit their mistakes.** All leaders make mistakes. Humble leaders own up to them. They don't play the blame game when things go wrong. Instead they hold themselves accountable. Vulnerability builds trust.

3. **Share** information and delegate some of the work. Humble leaders are aware of their strengths and weaknesses. They realize that they cannot do everything. They delegate because the work is more important than their egos.

4. **Listen. Employees can approach them.** This allows them to create an environment of open communication and effective feedback.

5. **Do not hesitate to give credit** where credit is due. They appreciate the contributions of others. They are quick to recognize and reward the efforts of team members.

6. **Are empathetic** to those in their charge. They genuinely care about employees, and employees can feel this sincerity. Empathy allows them to build healthy relationships and bond with team members.

7. **Are authentic.** They are the same person in every situation. This makes them trustworthy. Authenticity goes hand in hand with integrity. They are individuals of integrity.

"THE EMPEROR'S NEW CLOTHES"

Many people think humility is a weakness, but it actually takes strength. Humility reassures people and gives them the sense that you won't judge them or look down on them; team members will be motivated to share their suggestions and recommendations with you. One of the best employee engagement tools is transparency. To be transparent requires two-way communication, so feedback from employees is important. Honesty creates a solid platform on which to build a relationship of trust and loyalty. The ego, as with so many things, makes a good servant but a bad master. An inflated ego can blind us with a false sense of ourselves — our indestructibility, our moral rightness, our value as compared to others. It clouds our judgement and leads to poor decisions and a breakdown of relationships. It's not about you. **Build a strong team** and surround yourself with smart, passionate, and highly competent people. Researchers in a study at the University of Michigan and North western University's Kellogg School of Management in Illinois stated, "flattery and opinion conformity" make leaders overconfident, resulting in "biased strategic decision making" and an overall disconnect from the execution on the ground.

Humility doesn't mean that leaders can't make tough decisions. A humble leader should not be mistaken for a weak one. It takes strength, courage, and wisdom to practice humility. I have learned that the best leaders are selfless and more concerned with the well-being of their team than with personal titles or status symbols. Easily offended managers with inflated egos don't build strong teams. You cannot be an effective leader if you feel that you are better than your subordinates. No one likes dealing with egomaniacs. Arrogance is off-putting; it destroys relationships and lowers employee morale, whereas genuine humility has a way of winning others over.

Good leaders empower. Bad ones micromanage. It is dreadful to work under a manager who is more worried about pushing their weight around than building relationships. The role of any leader within a corporate framework is to build up the team and to encourage growth. If we want employees to feel committed to the organization, we need to show that we respect and value them. This takes humility. Once people trust you, they will follow your lead. You won't need to flaunt your title to get them to do the best possible job.

People might tolerate a boring job or long commute, but they are more prone to leave if their boss treats them poorly. Humble leaders get the best from people. They have more influence, they retain top talent, and they earn more respect and loyalty than those who rely upon ego and power. Want to be a good boss? Start by taking a slice or two of humble pie.

The corporate world is full of "mere managers" and lacks leaders. Leaders build people up. Those who settle for being "mere managers" pull people down. Leaders are those comfortable and secure in who they are while "mere managers" are competing with their subordinates. Our system has fallen into a self-reinforcing command loop constructed to increase shareholder value at all costs without regard for the human factor. Sadly, if you do not cure the cancer in the root of the tree, not only will the branches and leaves die, but so, in due time, will the tree.

Leadership is about people. Your business is nothing more than the collective energy and efforts of the people working with and for you. Building loyalty means developing a relationship between employee and employer over time. And one crucial factor in that development is building trust. **Transparency, authenticity, and walking the talk are essential for building and sustaining trust.**

Being open with employees promotes an engaged workforce. Threats and intimidation only yield temporary results. You can't keep throwing your employees under the bus and expect them to give their all. Show people that you care about them and are interested in their welfare. Loyalty is a two-way street. If you want loyalty from employees, you must first give it. If you want employees to go the extra mile, you have to be willing to go the extra mile for them. It works both ways. People want to work in an organization where their ideas, loyalty, and hard work are appreciated. You can't buy employee loyalty. It all comes down to how you treat people. It's not the highest bidder, but the company that treats its employees well that EARNS their loyalty.

Employees know when they are on shaky ground. If a company has no loyalty to its employees, why should they be loyal in return? If we treat people only as the means to an end, we will never have their loyalty. Don't just consider them as a robot in a production line. Demonstrate that you value people, and they, in turn, will take care of the business.

When it comes to keeping employees motivated, there are a number of factors to keep in mind — from communicating goals and expectations to showing interest in your employees' professional aspirations. You can offer all sorts of team building exercises, engagement programs, and perks, but the number one incentive to keeping employees engaged and productive is having a good boss. A good boss is the best incentive of all. It's time that companies realize that money and perks will not retain good staff if they have a bad boss who makes their time at work miserable.

Many managers assume once an employee is receiving a salary, they should be loyal. Little do they realize compensation is a satisfier, but generally not much of a motivator. It all comes down to how you treat people. Employees want to be treated like human beings. They have feelings, emotions, and personal lives. When an organization treats its employees like objects, they feel disrespected. When, on the other hand, an organization appreciates its employees, shows empathy and is flexible, they'll have to think twice about leaving.

APPRECIATING EMPLOYEES

As I said earlier, "People don't leave companies. They leave managers." More often than not, it's not because they are underpaid. Rather, it's because they feel undervalued and unappreciated. I once stayed in a job where I was underpaid, but my manager was so fantastic I found it hard to leave. "A truly great boss is hard to find, difficult to part with and impossible to forget." What can a boss do to make employees happy? Lots of managers think that they've fulfilled their duty by providing a pay check, but that's not enough if you want engaged and productive employees.

All great bosses know that employees need to feel appreciated. **Nothing works better than positive reinforcement.** Research suggests you need to praise at least three times as much as you criticize to keep employees happy. Instead of being quick to criticize, be quick to point out some of the great things you see your employees doing. This will not only reinforce these positive actions in the employees that performed them but also encourage other employees to do the same. And when you start looking for reasons to compliment your employees, you'll likely start seeing them in a more positive light as well.

Employees are our greatest asset. Then why do most companies treat employees poorly? **Any strategy or business plan relies on motivated and engaged people to make it happen.** If an employer treats people poorly, they aren't going to put the same level of effort into what they do. When you have a bunch of employees who refuse to go the extra mile to help a customer or to help the business grow, your company is in trouble. Worse, they will tell others about their negative experience working for your company.

I once had a supervisor tell me that the company we worked for, could not find good talent. Yet this was the same person that blurted out to me in a meeting. "Brigette, if you think you want to take my job, walk to HR and tell them to give you this position!" All because I'd innocently asked for clarification. If a company seems to have trouble hiring good personnel, it may be time to evaluate the screening/hiring process in addition to how employees are treated after the hire.

Research conducted by Globoforce found 78% of workers *said they would work harder if* their efforts were better *recognized* and appreciated. Authenticity, respect, and being a people builder gets noticed and respected by employees.

I used to ask managers to name three things their employees needed to improve upon and three things they did well. They struggled to come up with the positives but had no trouble identifying the negatives. Focusing on the negatives feeds into a culture of blaming and fault finding. It's demoralizing and demotivating to work for a manager who looks for and remembers your mistakes, large and small, to use them against you. Mistakes aren't weapons — they shouldn't be used to punish. They should be viewed as learning experiences.

And instead of spending so much time looking for what people are doing wrong, just think how encouraging it would be if managers spent as much time and effort to catch employees doing something right! Mistakes need to be corrected, but let's focus on the positives and uplift our team. Nitpicking is disheartening. **Magnify the positives and you will get better results.**

Don't take your employees for granted. No one likes to feel undervalued. However, this must come from a root of authenticity; otherwise employees won't buy into anything you do. It starts with treating employees well. Always acknowledge employees' efforts and contributions openly. Let them know how much you value them.

I stood in the back of a Reward and Recognition program in an organization I was consulting with. They had called me to sit at the front with the management team, but I preferred to stay with the employees. You really get key insights when you do this. To the employees, this reward and recognition was a ritual and not a motivation. They grumbled that the same people were being recognized every month. They could call out the names of all the awardees for each category before it was announced. This program was doing quite the opposite of what it was meant to achieve. It left most of employees feeling unappreciated.

A Maritz study in 2010 showed more than 84% of employees viewed their company as a great place to work if it had three or more reward and recognition programs in place. **Companies that truly care for their employees get a ROI that is immeasurable.** The ROI is not only increased productivity; employees become great brand ambassadors. This is priceless.

There are numerous ways to compensate excellence. Timely recognition and acknowledgements of a person's behavior, effort, and accomplishment is sufficient motivation for the person to support the organization's goals and values beyond expectations. Companies should look to reward motivated employees who put in the extra effort and deliver results. If they don't, those great employees will soon be somebody else's valuable human resource. It feels good to do a great job. It feels even better when it is noticed by the boss. Internal motivators are wonderful but praise by someone who is respected means more than we've realized.

Employee recognition methods should of course be tailored to the type of company and the personality of the employee. **Special rewards are less effective if they're just given out of habit or to the same individuals.** Don't only recognize the same top performers but also those who offer support, have improved, or give their best. Every contribution from each team member matters, whether small or great. Let them know this. Appreciation coupled with incentive rewards is a great morale and productivity booster. Even the slowest employee will work to the best of their ability if they know their efforts are appreciated. When people are commended for doing something right, they get inspired to do better.

It does not cost much to show employees how much you appreciate them:

- A personalized thank you giving specifics on how the employee has helped.
- Recognition in meetings.
- Remember to cc people's supervisors. "Don't tell me. Tell my boss."
- A random breakfast or lunch.
- A relevant gift. Even something that can help them do their job better.

- Time off.

I once took over a project where I asked for weekly status reports. When I sent back thank you notes, one employee said that was the first time in his entire career he had ever been thanked like this. This should have been the norm, but sadly it wasn't. Always reward staff for good work. Show employees how much you value and appreciate them. Be generous in saying "thank you."

Actions speak louder than words. "Thank you" can only have real meaning if employees know you are an authentic person, **a leader who genuinely cares about employees**. Other great phrases that go hand in hand with "thank you" are:

- Great job.
- Well done.
- I'm sorry.
- How can I help you?
- What are your thoughts?
- I am glad you are on our team.

It's also important to recognize the efforts of your employees even when things don't go as planned. We shouldn't automatically assume that a missed objective means that the team members haven't done their utmost to achieve it.

Two of the most basic human desires are validation and appreciation — we need to feel like we matter. People want to feel appreciated, respected, and included. The good news is that even if you invest only a small amount of time into appreciating your team, you can save yourself — and your bottom line — a lot of grief. Waiting too long to appreciate employees could result in those you lead feeling resentful. Not only do underappreciated employees cost more when they (inevitably) leave, but they can cost a lot more if they stay (faulty work, poor customer service, reduced productivity).

Choose to see the best in others. Choose to see what makes them amazing, and let them know the amazing things you see. Play to your team's strengths and everyone wins.

LEAD WITH LISTENING

My new boss told me to never be afraid to give feedback. In the following Monday meeting, I happily shared my viewpoint on a new policy. Thereafter, I noticed my boss's disposition towards me change. He stopped talking to me. I was shunned. I even felt the effects of this in my monthly performance appraisal, where he noted I was not supportive of the organization, and I needed to be a better team player. The picture was quite clear — despite the pro forma invitation, truthful feedback was not appreciated.

Listening is the most important skill a leader can master. It is the basis of many other leadership skills. However, it is a tough skill to master as it requires us to be more present, attentive, engaged, patient, and flexible. "Silent" and "listen" contain the same letters. Only when one is silent can they truly listen. In this digital age, good listening skills are fast becoming a lost art due to information overload and shortened attention span. **There is a difference between hearing the words someone is speaking and actually listening to them**. Listening involves paying attention and responding with appropriate nonverbal cues. Listening means you are taking the speaker's perspective into account and truly considering what they have to say.

Many of us are guilty of starting a conversation or putting a thought or question out there without giving ourselves a chance to listen to what others have to say. It may be because we never stop talking, but more often it's because we are so busy formulating our reply to what we assume they will say. It's not enough to listen with your ears; listen with the intent to hear and understand.

The four foundational skills of language learning are *listening, speaking, reading*, and *writing*, in that order. We get extensive training on the last three in school but listening, which is the most important in developing our social skills, is often overlooked. When communicating, it's important to listen, digest, pause, reiterate, formulate, and then respond.

On average, we retain just 25% of what we hear because of our lack of listening skills. What is your speaking-to-listening ratio? Listening is crucial to gaining a comprehensive understanding of the situation (and a better understanding of the speaker). Without this full understanding, one can easily waste everyone's time by solving the wrong problem or mistaking symptoms for root causes."

> *"Leaders who don't listen will eventually be surrounded by people who have nothing to say."*
> ~Andy Stanley

Developing leadership skills is a lifetime project. It's too easy, as a leader, to feel like you have to be the one who knows everything. Great leaders recognize that they need to keep learning. Leaders need to be willing to learn and be open to seeking input from both inside and outside their organizations. Feedback allows us and the organization to grow. Additionally, treat everyone you meet with respect, from the janitor to the CEO. Great business tips may come from the most unlikely sources.

Listening forms the foundation of good relationships. It shows you care. You can't convey empathy or emotional intelligence if you do not listen. The quality of our listening determines the quality of our influence. Employees want to be heard, and they want to be respected. Listening transmits that kind of respect and builds trust. This leads to more motivated and committed team members.

Titans such as Blackberry, Kodak, and Nokia have paid the price for leaders who refused to listen. Their leaders operated in a bubble and engaged in group think. *The greater your success, the more you need to stay in touch with fresh opinions and perspectives and welcome honest feedback.* Listening is the best way to understand the needs of your clientele, a must in creating a successful strategy. Raw truth is needed to make well-informed decisions and steer the organization in the right direction. Good leaders are active listeners.

It's no secret that knowledge and wisdom are not gained by talking but by listening. Listening includes listening to that **"still small voice."** If something is wrong, don't simply try to justify it. That's just mindless (and generally fear-based) reacting. Even if you get away with it for a time, remember: the piper must be paid. True integrity starts with listening.

As a leader, your job is to encourage others around you to be open and honest without worrying that they might be letting themselves in for a negative consequence. Listening leads to personal awareness and growth. If you do not listen, you will not grow. Additionally, when employees offer their ideas and differing opinions, be open-minded. Again, don't react. Consider and then respond. It is always valuable to listen to your employees. **The reality on the ground is very different from what you may think.** It's more realistic and practical. Provide your team with an atmosphere where employees' ideas and suggestions are valued. Employees who give you feedback are doing you the honor of taking a chance. They risk negative consequences or the frustration of being ignored. Be worthy of their trust.

When you receive feedback, seriously consider it. It may not be something you want to act upon directly, but it will give you a greater understanding of both the subject and the source. This helps improve employee morale.

Poor communication comes with a high price tag. It accounts for businesses losing millions of dollars each year. As a leader, your job is to encourage others around you to be open and honest. Companies that remain strong in this competitive market are those that understand the need to embrace change and continuous improvement. The success of your business depends on mastering the skill of leading with listening!

LEADERSHIP IS REALLY SIMPLE BUT WE MAKE IT COMPLICATED:

Simplicity is sometimes the most difficult thing to find in management. It's difficult working in an environment where complexity is the gold standard. It can even wear out the best employees and cause them to start planning their exit strategy.

7 SIGNS OF A MANAGER WHO LIKES TO MAKE THINGS COMPLICATED:

1. They waste employees' time on multiple useless meetings.
2. They don't delegate or empower employees. They prefer to micromanage.
3. They protect silos and uphold the organizational hierarchy. They emphasize the distinction between staff and management.
4. They are inflexible and focus on the red tape. They always go by the book.
5. They take a well-functioning system and turn it into chaos for the sake of improvement.
6. They withhold information to ensure they are always the smartest person in the room.
7. They don't train, mentor, or coach employees for fear they may surpass them.

Keeping things simple means keeping them effective and efficient. Always complicating things can be mentally and physically draining for employees. If you ever worked for such a boss, you know how stressful it can be. They make mountains out of molehills for simple things requests (e.g., time off). They make the process harder than it needs to be. They go around in circles to explain a point. Ask them to pick a letter, and they'll go from A to Z to show how much they know. They are poor communicators. Being able to share complex things in a simple way requires maturity, wisdom and a clear understanding of the situation.

You've probably heard the saying, "If it isn't broken, don't fix it!" Of course, in this technological age, we need to continuously embrace change, but bad managers can ruin a good system. At the same time, if an employee develops a better method of doing something, they refute it. Things should only be done their way. They see less need for a two-way dialogue because they believe they have the solutions. They review things over and over again, adding a lot of unnecessary work for their employees. In the end, this only leads to confusion and reduced productivity.

Leadership is really simple, but we make it complicated. Simplicity comes from putting people first. As Richard Branson stated, "Take care of your employees and they will take care of your business. It's as simple as that!"

Your employees are your most valuable asset. Don't take them for granted or treat them poorly. They use your internal tools and systems and interact with customers. They are your best brand ambassadors. You can't buy loyalty, but you can certainly foster and nurture it. Employees who have been pushed to the point where they no longer care will not go the extra mile. They will not take the initiative to solve problems. They will end up treating customers the same way you treat them. **Employees are the heartbeat of the company. And if the heart stops beating... what will happen?**

THE GREATEST INVESTMENT YOU CAN MAKE IS IN PEOPLE.

The long-term success of any company depends heavily upon the commitment of its employees. Sadly, most companies don't think critically about how to increase employee retention. They think a paycheck with a few perks is sufficient. Years of experience are hard to replace.

When a loyal employee leaves, it costs the company. The impact on the organization's culture is also severe. Beyond the more tangible losses, costs of hiring and training as well as the time the role is unfilled, it affects team morale and causes other employees to reconsider their loyalty towards the organization. And poor employee loyalty can damage a company's image. Sites like Glassdoor and Indeed offer employees a platform on which to air their true feelings about their employer. Fortune bases its "100 Best Companies to Work For" ranking on employee reviews of company culture.

What do employees want? Autonomy, flexibility, appreciation, and opportunities for growth and development. When people feel undervalued, they leave at the first opportunity that comes their way. The ones with the most marketable skills and talents — a company's best people — are the ones that companies can least afford to lose.

Frequent turnover has a negative impact on employee morale, productivity, and company revenue. Every time a business loses and replaces a salaried employee, it can cost between six to nine months' salary.

Loyal employees are a major asset for a strong business. When a company loses a great employee, it causes the other employees to start thinking, "Why would that person leave the organization? Why would the organization let them get away? Perhaps I should start looking elsewhere myself." Not only will other employees question it, but clients often question it as well. When clients trust an employee and that employee leaves, the clients begin to feel a sense of loss. The ripple effect of losing a great employee is tremendous, and it goes well beyond what is easily quantified.

A lack of loyalty isn't only reflected in the loss of employees. In many cases, disaffected employees stay on and show disloyalty through their attitudes. In a way, that's worse than if they left.

If companies are going to excel, they need two things: **loyal employees and loyal customers**. The link between employee satisfaction and productivity is long-established. Research has found that happy workers are 12% more productive than their less satisfied counterparts. Loyal employees = loyal customers. Loyal employees are worth more than their weight in gold. They uphold your brand and ensure the sustainability of your business. They make it possible for you to win.

GIVE YOUR EMPLOYEES REASONS TO STAY

Leadership is about people. If you put people first, everything else will fall into place.

Building an organization of committed, loyal employees ultimately comes down to demonstrating to employees that the company deserves their loyalty. You need to provide a reason for your employees to be loyal. Employees want challenging work, recognition and respect, opportunities for advancement, professional growth and development, and a flexible work environment. Studies abound showing that when your employees are connected and engaged (i.e., loyal), business booms.

In the present environment, it has become a necessity for the organization to have a strategy for retaining their best employees. **Your competitors are waiting at the door with "treats" to lure away your top performers.** If you keep treating employees like they are easily replaceable, you will be paying the price for this. According to data drawn from 30 case studies taken from 11 research papers on the costs of employee turnover, it costs at least 20% of their salary when an employee leaves. These costs reflect the loss of productivity from the departure, the cost of finding a replacement, and the reduced productivity while the new employee gets up to speed.

When employees feel disconnected, undervalued, and unappreciated, it doesn't take long for them to jump ship and look for another job that will recognize their contributions. The only thing that can lower employee turnover is to give employees a reason to stay,

Ultimately having a culture that promotes open communication, fairness, teamwork, camaraderie, and a family atmosphere helps to retain good employees. Focus on building quality relationships. Employees with strong bonds to those they work with are usually the most engaged and tend to stay with a company longer.

Furthermore, when people leave your organization, find out why **(Exit Interviews).** Your organization may have morale weaknesses you are not aware of or have been underestimating. In one study, 89% of managers surveyed said they thought most employees leave for better pay. However, another study found that 88% of employees who quit did so for something other than money. Clearly, there is often a disconnect between managers and employees about what motivates an employee to leave. The reason for leaving is not always salary, and exit interviews are not always accurate. HR needs to dig deep to find out the underlying reasons for staff turnover. And most importantly **"act."** Take action; let employees see you are genuinely committed to enriching their work experience.

Consequently, when people stay with your organization, find out why **(Stay Interviews)**. Here's the reality: employees are only as loyal to the company as they believe the company is loyal to them. Stay interviews give employees an opportunity to share their concerns and what they like — and don't like — about their current role with the company. They act as a good retention tool. When companies understand why employees stay, those important factors can be reinforced. For this to be effective, make sure you follow through with suggestions. And when you make changes, inform employees these resulted from their suggestions and responses in stay interviews.

I read in the newspaper recently about how former France Télécom bosses were given jail terms over workplace bullying. They were found guilty of "institutional harassment" and creating a culture of routine workplace bullying that sparked a number of suicides at the company. Employees suffered psychological abuse as bosses focused on cost savings and job cuts. The court examined 39 cases of employees, 19 of whom had taken their own lives and 12 of whom had attempted suicide. In July 2009, a 51-year-old technician killed himself, leaving a letter accusing bosses of "management by terror." The ex-chief executive Didier Lombard denied management bore any responsibility for the deaths. He told the court: "The transformations a business has to go through aren't pleasant, that's just the way it is, there's nothing I could have done."

The landmark ruling is first time managers have been held criminally responsible for implementing a general strategy of bullying even if they had not dealt directly with the staff involved. We must always ensure we treat employees with empathy and in a fair manner in the wake of restructuring and downsizing strategies.

It's time we start holding bad bosses accountable for the poor decisions they make and the callous way they treat employees. If managers know there are harsh consequences, they would be more prone to consider the humane side of decision making. You're dealing with people's lives, and generally, the sense of self-worth they attach to their jobs. A little empathy goes a long way.

I lost one of my managers a couple of years ago and I can't seem to forget him or the legacy he left behind. He was one of my earliest examples of true leadership. I often refer to Joseph as "The Memorable Leader."

HERE ARE FIVE QUALITIES OF GOOD BOSSES:

1. **Integrity** & Authenticity go hand in hand. Joseph was honest with employees even though this trait was sometimes unpopular with top management. He often took up the slack for his team. If leadership is not authentic, then what is it?

2. **Humility**. True leaders always aim to serve rather than be served.

3. **Empathy** plays a critical role in one's ability to be a successful leader. It sharpens your "people acumen" and allows leaders to develop and maintain relationships with

those they lead. Leaders that possess this trait always make time for people. They possess high emotional intelligence (EI).

4. **Communication Skills.** Great leaders are able to communicate their vision in a way that motivates their team. They are great communicators: quick to listen and slow to speak. We never heard of upcoming changes via the grapevine. Joseph always kept us in the loop.

5. **Inspirational.** Joseph didn't need a title to get us to complete tasks. He had our full support. Words such as "Good work team," "You are the best," "I trust your judgement," were at the top of his phrasebook. Team spirit was high during his reign.

"If you want to build a ship, don't drum up the men to gather wood, divide the work and give orders. Instead, teach them to yearn for the vast and endless sea."
~Antoine de Saint-Exupéry

Good bosses are few and far in between. Employees are not asking for much. They just want to be in a healthy environment that supports them and helps them develop. Build up employees and you build up the company. **A great manager makes all the difference. Be kind, consistent, and help others grow.** Employees leave jobs because of toxic management. If they feel valued, they will stay. If they feel belittled or poorly treated, they may leave no matter the amount of money they walk away from.

True leaders live on in the hearts and minds of followers. Sometimes I can still picture Joseph walking through the office greeting staff in the morning. He might even give me a little nod or pat on the back. Those are the special moments I still hold dear. It doesn't take much to create those special moments with your team.

Can you become a better leader? Yes. Sometimes it just takes being human and developing your people skills. Technical skills alone do not keep employees motivated. **In this Artificial Intelligence**

economy, the new "smart" is not determined by IQ but by EQ. It's about listening, relating, collaborating, and connecting with your team. This takes humility, authenticity, and empathy. Studies have shown that leading with vision, inspiration, and purpose produces better bottom-line results as well as happier, more engaged employees. If we want employees to feel committed to the organization, we need to show that we respect and value them. The "human touch" makes all the difference.

CHAPTER SEVEN

EMPLOYEE SENTIMENT MATTERS

Many companies invest heavily to improve the customer experience but sideline employees who are responsible for delivering that experience. What some organizations forget is that their employees are their first and most important customers (internal). When employees are treated as "second class citizens," it results in decreased employee morale.

Employees are your best brand ambassadors. Your brand position is determined by the customer's experience, which is delivered by your front-line employees. Your front-line employees know your customers best; they interact with them daily. They may well have much better-informed solutions to improve customer service and your products than you do. They use your internal tools and systems every day. They may have money-saving ideas for improving systems and driving efficiencies. **When you empower employees, you promote their vested interest in the company.** For instance, when an employee sees a problem, they would be more motivated to come up with a valuable solution. The idea is implemented, the employee is acknowledged and rewarded, and the result is a success all around.

Engaged employees feel internal motivation to go above and beyond the call of duty. They willingly go the extra mile. They are the people who will drive innovation and move your business forward.

Unhappy employees cost companies billions of dollars each year in lost revenues, settlements, and other damages. The loss of revenue can send even established companies into financial distress, and even bankruptcy.

Financial losses can result from:

Decreased Productivity: According to research conducted by Gallup, disengaged employees cost companies $450 to $550 billion in lost productivity each year as a result of poor performance and high absenteeism.

Employee Negligence: When employees are put first, they feel a sense of ownership in the business. Such employees will take the initiative to solve problems before they get worse. On the other hand, an unhappy employee will take no ownership as an issue escalates. It is also common for dissatisfied employees to neglect to complete tasks or to make mistakes. This leads to poor quality control standards, unsafe products, and danger to consumers. Cases of serious injury or death caused by company negligence often results in hefty settlements being paid out to those affected.

Tarnished Reputation: Employees interact with customers, and unhappy employees are free to say anything they want, no matter how negative, about the company's culture, products, and services. The actions of one individual can bring down a company or uplift it. In an age of social media, individual employees' actions can have dire effects on an organization.

Imagine this: Video accounts of poor customer service go viral on Facebook, as do hashtags on Twitter calling for a boycott of your company. Mainstream news picks up the story. Maybe lawsuits follow. And even if you don't have to settle, you have a perfect storm of negative press on your hands.

Business success starts with the employee experience. You can't expect stellar customer service from employees who feel distrusted and discounted.

In 2015, *Airbnb* announced that they were appointing a Global Head of Employee Experience. The following year, the company topped Glassdoor's list of the 50 Best Places to Work. When employees are happy (feel valued and respected), they will create remarkable experiences for your external customers.

Employee Sentiment Matters

In a world where customer demands are constantly evolving and business innovation is vital, you cannot afford to have low engagement levels among the workforce. But how do you locate gaps in your employee engagement strategy? Imagine having a real-time pulse on all of your people in your business at your fingertips. Sentiment analytics is the answer.

You might have heard the term "employee sentiment" getting thrown around a lot lately. But what exactly is it? This is where employees influence corporate decision-making by expressing their opinions and views on corporate decisions (customer and product). Sentiment analysis is an effective first step to help businesses get a real-time grasp of their people, performance, and culture. Sentiment analysis involves gathering feedback to capture and quantify brand perceptions. It relates to the way a company is run and how workers perceive it. Sentiment analysis techniques gauge how employees feel about their jobs and workplace by observing their language, tone, and interests in communication via email and other channels. Feedback can be collected using internal social discussion platforms, and these perceptions are monitored over time. This analysis can reveal if workers are happy or dissatisfied with the company. It determines the "why" behind the engagement scores.

Using the results, organizations can create meaningful solutions that boost employee engagement. Recent illustrations of this new "employee sentiment" impact on business decisions include Amazon rethinking whether it should offer facial recognition products to law enforcement and Google backing away from a Pentagon AI software contract.

Employee sentiment can also negatively impact a firm's recruiting abilities. At Facebook, employees openly complained, first internally and then on external social media, about how the firm's hiring practices were damaging the company's business results. There was also an impact on retention. If issues are not resolved, employees might quit and take other top performers with them.

Many organizations are already sitting on a wealth of data. And after all, that data can be analyzed and leveraged to identify risks and opportunities to enhance people and business performance. A good text and sentiment analytics platform blend natural language processing with machine learning and AI to predict whether the sentiment in word combinations and phrases are positive, neutral, or negative, applying a numerical sentiment score in a range of -1.0 to +1.0. These scores are amassed and visually presented to support analysis across multiple dimensions, including the data source, business units, supervisors, and other general workforce demographics. Machine learning algorithms identify words that might be negative or problematic and cluster them into themes.

You may be hearing feedback from staff about how you can improve systems and processes, but until you've quantified all of the suggestions, it's just anecdotal. You can now categorize the data by sentiment or attitude. By identifying sentiment and visualizing it in multi-dimensional real-time analytics, you can unlock powerful insights about employees and their supervisors. Sentiment analysis tools give a visual snapshot as they can heat-map positive and negative sentiment over the entire business.

This will allow you to identify areas of the business that require attention or areas that are doing well so you can improve on those results. Employee feedback typically clusters into topic areas and text that analytics algorithms are trained to recognize, including these themes:

Employee engagement themes identified by machine learning include:

- Management
- Workload
- Benefits & Compensation
- Training
- Systems

- Career Growth
- Work-life balance
- Teamwork
- Appreciation

The algorithms do all the tedious, time-consuming work of reading qualitative feedback and organizing each comment into different buckets. A vast amount of text is analyzed to see if employees are concerned about a specific area of their jobs or work environment. Using a mix of survey responses and emails, sentiment analysis discovers areas that might need intervention by a HR (Human Resources) manager.

For example, sentiment analysis can help you understand the impact of a rollout of a new software system or benefit plan. When you have the data, you can use it to measure the overall impact.

Scenario Analysis

Managers write messages for team members periodically for the rollout of a new software application. Employees provide feedback through regular surveys. The information is recorded and organized. The final report is published though an outbound **application program interface (API) export.** The HR or equivalent team within the organization can then review the insights (and take action on them) from the newly AI-structured data without reliance on anecdotes and hunches. When the landscape of what is driving dissatisfaction is made visible through sentiment analytics, it becomes easier to work on the specific issue at hand. For example, maybe the negative sentiment was a result of a relocation or move, a management change, or a modification in the benefit plan. It's also possible that missteps in leadership can be sighted and corrected.

Business consists of many interconnections. Sentiment analysis is an exciting development that can help your company diagnose areas for improvement and understand how your workforce is tracking. The value of this activity is clear - by understanding the general mood of a population of employees, a business can better serve its team members and meet their needs. By taking a modern approach to employee feedback using real-time machine learning, the management team can take action to improve employee engagement, having an obvious impact on morale and retention. And management can now analyze employee survey ratings to make sure that the inevitable changes and transitions to new processes are conducted smoothly.

DESIGNING A COMPELLING EMPLOYEE EXPERIENCE

The organizations that invest most heavily in EX are found:

- **11.5x** as often in Glassdoor's Best Places to Work
- **4.4x** as often in LinkedIn's list of North America's Most In-Demand Employers
- **2.1x** as often on the Forbes list of the World's Most Innovative Companies
- **2x** as often in the American Customer Satisfaction Index

Source: Jacob Morgan

The employee experience is influenced by three factors:

- The physical environment in which an employee works.
- The support and tools an employer provide.
- The interest an employer takes in the well-being and success of employees.

Here's an example:

A retail store stated their employees were the "heart of the business." The retail area was clean and well-stocked. Aisles were wide and well-marked with bright signage. Even the parking lot sparkled — there was rarely any litter seen in customer parking areas. Customers were impressed. Employee space was an entirely different matter. Stock rooms were cluttered and dark. Staff locker rooms were poorly lighted and poorly maintained. The break room was bleak, with old, uncomfortable furniture, and trash bins overflowed. Even the vending machines were inadequately stocked, and only with junk food.

The message was clear — the company cares about customers, but not very much about employees.

> *"You can't be the best place to buy if you're not the best place to work"*
> -Fred Reichheld

If you believe that employees are your most valuable asset, you will create a healthy work atmosphere, and provide them with the tools and support to do their jobs effectively.

Creating a compelling employee experience (EX) is the essential to building greater levels of enthusiasm, engagement, and commitment within your company. EX is the overall level of satisfaction enjoyed by employees on a daily basis. It includes everything you can think of that could affect how your employees feel about their work. EX is influenced by a number of factors. These include user interface of desktop and phone apps; the physical workspace; the design and range of learning and development opportunities; and workload and flexibility. According to Deloitte, the five most important factors that influence EX are meaningful work, supportive management, work environment, growth opportunities, and trust in leadership. And feeding into much of this is a related factor, your corporate culture. You want to promote a culture that engenders a caring, collaborative, team-based, family-like work environment. An atmosphere like this will naturally create shared memories across the organization as time and positive interactions slowly grow a community that works together seamlessly to grow the business.

Employee experience should be cemented in strategy. **Promoting a people-first culture optimizes business results.** If you build a great culture by emphasizing the employee experience, this will lead to employee advocacy. Your current employees will eagerly share your positive culture which will attract new talent organically. Many companies focus mainly on external customers but treat employees — their internal customers — poorly. Charity begins at home.

CHAPTER EIGHT

IT'S TIME TO PUT BACK THE HUMAN IN HUMAN RESOURCES

If you ask most HR (Human resources) leaders and professionals why they got into HR, they are most likely to reply that they wanted to work with people, build teams, nurture talent, and learn people management. Then why is it that the HR function is resented and cast in such a negative light these days? **Why do employees believe that the foremost role that HR plays is protecting the organization against the employees?** If we dig a little deeper, we will find that we have stopped treating employees like humans and started viewing them as resources. Humanity, which is one half of the domain, has been missing for some time now. As a result, we've reached a situation wherein employees in most organizations are fearful of being unwell or caring for elderly parents or honoring personal commitments; they assume that putting work and the organization before everything else is HR's ideal of employee behavior.

ARE YOU DRIFTING?

Have you ever gone to the beach with your family? Left your slippers and belongings on the shore and went into the water. After a couple of minutes, looked up and asked, "What are these people doing in our space?" Only to realize it's us that had moved. We didn't notice or even feel we were drifting. Drifting happens all the time and without awareness. It's good to have a landmark (constant) to evaluate your position. Accountability keeps us in check. We don't drift off course overnight. Drift is characterized by a slow deterioration of standards and operating principles and is often accompanied with rationalization. It can be the result of the pressures of competition and the desire to get to and stay at the top. Leaders tend to justify deviations. the end justifies the means.

THINK BACK TO YOUR YOUNGER YEARS WHEN YOU STARTED ON YOUR LEADERSHIP JOURNEY:

- Has there ever been a time in your life, when you were more excited about your vision?
- Has there ever been a time that you were more committed to that vision than you are right now?
- Has there ever been a time when you felt a deeper sense of fulfilment about your daily work?

We have a culture that's drifting, and many leaders routinely drift from their purpose, and some never return to their original mission. Drifting may lead you into the middle of the ocean, at a destination you did not intend. The problem is that the onset of drifting is subtle, and requires that you continuously focus. We do not arrive at our desired destination in life and business by accident. Without having our purpose deeply anchored, drifting happens to all. No leader is exempt from the danger of drifting away from their personal leadership philosophy. There are many currents in the leadership journey. The number one factor that causes drifting is losing touch with the people we serve. **Then there is time. Time changes us all.**

Drift often happens in small and subtle ways. Left unchecked, it eventually becomes significant. We may start out not realizing anything is amiss or wrong. One little thing occurs, and we justify it. Something else happens again. Subtly boundaries and good judgment may get lost for a while until or unless there is some awakening, either from within or coming from the outside. We need to be consistently reflecting and evaluating where we are drifting, and if we realize we are, we need to find a way to get back on track before it's too late.

Much of our jobs as HR professionals involves dealing with people, listening to their problems, issues and complaints and trying to

resolve them. As a manager of people, you need empathy to ensure you understand where the people you're dealing with are coming from before you make any judgement. It could be that they just need a listening ear. Or they might be airing their grievances looking for help. Whatever the case, it is the HR manager's responsibility to listen to the employees and ensure they got their message across clearly. We need to have a people-centered approach. This will take reimagining and tweaking the HR function to be more humane, flexible, and open-minded.

An HR VP (vice president) once told me that I needed to stop standing up for employees, all because I was trying to put through two extra days an employee needed for bereavement. This employee had been finding it hard to cope with the sudden loss of her husband, and she didn't have any more vacation days left.

HR stands for human resources, as in, treating humans like they are a valuable resource and not an expendable one. The real job of HR is to make the organization an amazing place to work. Thus, HR needs to rebrand itself and infuse a healthy dose of humanity into their roles. We need to consciously make transactions more humane and drive recruitment, learning, culture, and leadership through the lens of humanity.

How do we do this?

It starts with looking at all the touch points at which employees or potential employees interact with your business to ensure contact is made in a humane manner.

RECRUITMENT

In almost every industry, the best talent is in short supply, and it will only get worse. In PwC's 22nd Annual Global CEO Survey, 79% of chief executives around the world said that a lack of key skills threatens their business growth.

In today's highly competitive technological landscape, getting the right people has never been more important. As we increasingly rely on data and predictive analytics for recruiting and performance management, we are in danger of losing the true essence of human resources. There is a massive explosion of HR technology now, and the biggest area of disruption is in recruitment.

When the entire narrative in the business world focuses almost exclusively on the bottom-line, everything else takes a backseat. It is no surprise that most organizations are struggling to elicit trust from their workforce because they are committing the grave error of treating their employees as replaceable units. The ramifications of using algorithms, keywords, and tech tools in every process, big or small, are severe. There is an evident shift in the mindset of the workforce wherein HR is no longer working in their best interests.

To stay afloat in today's unpredictable and ever-changing business environment, organizations are adopting more agile policies and processes. So, it's crucial that organizations find agile and collaborative talent to match. This enables them to build a culture which fosters innovation and success.

Smart technology will increasingly replace even complex roles; however, it will be some time before it can outperform humans in emotional intelligence, empathy, problem solving, creativity, critical thinking, negotiation, collaboration, and conflict resolution. Many people think to be technologically-advanced, we need to completely remove the human factor. But that is not the case. We must never lose sight of the fact that humans are the essential link in this new age of automation and artificial intelligence (AI).

What is MISSING in the Recruiting/ Hiring Process?

A HEART!

Many recruiters treat jobseekers like they're at a shopping mall. It's not just applicants but people you are dealing with. Since we are still working with human beings and not robots, we need to add a human touch to connect with people. I am happy to see how AI technology is supporting the HR function because as HR practitioners, we spend far too much time living in spreadsheets. However, there is a growing risk that firms will become over-reliant on technology. Several new Applicant Tracking Systems (ATS) now use AI to evaluate CVs and resumes. ATS can be incredibly helpful for HR recruitment as it significantly reduces the manual workload and cuts down both administrative and personnel-related costs. However, algorithms cannot sense passion, loyalty, and drive. Computerized screening process can't access human's capabilities, experience, character, hard work, and skill.

We need to bring back the human element. Nothing can replace the human-to-human approach. Anyone can write a perfect resume with all of the "key words" that will ensure passage through the electronic process. It appears the recruiting process has become lazy. HR, recruiters, and staffing agencies rely heavily on "buzzwords" and algorithms. They either can't or don't care about reading between the lines or getting to know candidates.

When you rely on a system with just algorithms and keywords, there is room for manipulation. Many people know how to trigger the ATS the right way to get results, while the right candidate may well be eliminated. It is crucial to understand that technology is not foolproof. We need some level of human intervention in a tech-reliant system to maintain checks and balances. For instance, if an ATS system is left unchecked, the danger of abusing the system goes up. Candidates might simply paste the exact text from the job description to better their chances of being selected.

Additionally, we now have robots infused with AI doing the hiring in many companies. What will you end up hiring? Really good actors. Sometimes the best candidates are not good at interviews. Many talented people I know don't perform well in that situation. Similarly, if we rely entirely on technology to screen applicants, some candidates can manipulate the system by controlling their facial expressions, tone, or words. Instead of allowing robots to glean information about candidates from these attributes, shouldn't our focus be on whether someone has the skill set, right attitude, and ability to fit in with the team? Isn't this a better predictor of job success?

Too many qualified candidates are falling through the cracks because of our total reliance on computerized screening systems. The automation process excludes many great candidates. What you often get is someone perfect on paper. Looking good on paper and performing on the job are two different things. AI can be used to pre-select candidates for a role, but determining who will be the best fit ultimately comes down to a human-to-human interaction.

The automation process of applying for positions is supposed to be a help, not a replacement for human reasoning. And why are great candidates excluded? Oops, you're three credits short of a Bachelor of Science degree. Or we're not seeing the right buzz word in your application. It has become more of a specification matching process. It's all about having the right buzz words, the right key words – almost like a magic incantation. "Open sesame" and look! I've got the perfect candidate! It reminds me of a similar problem in our education system, which highlights the ones who studied for the test rather than studying to learn and apply the subject.

I understand wanting to be more efficient in the hiring process. But machines don't recruit people, people recruit people. Human judgement and intuition still need to play a role even as we are aided by new tools like AI and digital computing power. AI alone can't recognize the best employees, especially since the qualities we look for will continue to evolve. **Talent selection ultimately requires a human touch.** The task of recruiting and onboarding new employees will be affected by AI, and I believe in a positive way, but technology will not completely replace the need for humans to interview potential employees to determine character, culture fit, talent, and personality.

Using smart filters helps you shortlist qualified candidates faster, freeing up your time and energy for interviewing people and finding the best fit. If you want the best talent, there are no shortcuts; you will simply have to put in the work. We live in a world where we want everything quickly, and many of us lack the patience to engage in human interaction. Understanding the personality behind a resume is crucial in hiring the best talent for your team.

Automation and AI technology will have a significant impact on the gathering and analyzing of data — but making thoughtful interpretations, determining practical solutions, and delivering results through to completion - here the human element comes into play.

Going forward, organizations will need to attract and retain the right talent to cope with this looming technological transformation. Ditching human involvement in favor of efficiency in the recruiting process is a critical mistake. It is of paramount importance that those involved in recruitment bring back the "HUMAN" element in Human Resources.

Using automated systems eliminates more than some good candidates. The algorithms that are used don't leave room to consider skill sets that are aligned with a job posting.

Issues:

— AI has no clue about your attitude, how hard you work, how loyal you are.

— AI tends to hire people similar to those they have hired in the past. So for example, if they never hired over 50, the system is likely to perpetuate their bias. That's because **machine learning looks at who you did and did not hire and "learns" from your preferences**, mistakes and all. It looks for the types of people you hired before and excludes those types who were excluded in the past. In 2018, Amazon abandoned a recruitment tool that used artificial intelligence to grade job applicants after it emerged its new hiring system preferred male candidates over female candidates. The system learned to favor *men over women* after being trained on past CVs written mostly by male candidates.

Recruiters, hiring managers, and companies continue to be vigilant to ensure your process does not exclude qualified candidates. **Don't get me wrong. I am not saying we shouldn't use automated systems, but they need to be balanced with the human element. The total recruitment process must not be relegated to machines.**

THE RESUME IS VANISHING

For years, submitting a resume has been a prerequisite for applying for a job. But things are changing. My friend Richard sent me this: "I never bother with a resume. I make a YouTube video of me answering the criteria directly and then attach a second techie video showing off my skills. 100% success rate getting to the first interview. 75% success rate getting any job I apply for." I think this may be the future of interviewing, but it opens the flood gates of biases in the process since, if the interviewer has a preference for a particular race, gender, etc., certain individuals would be immediately eliminated.

Technology is already upending the traditional relationship between candidates and employers. Networking will take precedence. **The truth is many individuals are hired because of familiarity rather than actual merit, and 85% of jobs are filled via networking.** I can safely say that almost every job I ever had has been as a direct result of a referral. And in today's connected world, referrals are made without the need to exchange resumes or cover letters.

Build your personal brand. Your profiles on job sites like LinkedIn, Indeed, and Monster will be your resume. Many HR practitioners and recruiters already use LinkedIn to source candidates, and many jobseekers use their LinkedIn profile as their resume. A Resume Go study reports that resumes that include a link to a comprehensive LinkedIn profile have a 71% higher chance of getting an interview than a resume without a link or one with a link to a barebones profile. It's all about building relationships and networking, and a digital presence facilitates that connectedness.

INTERVIEW QUESTIONS NEED TO EVOLVE

The recruiting process is broken. The problem I see with recruiting today is that it tests the candidate's ability to apply and interview for jobs, rather than their ability to perform on the job. Are we automating a broken process? I believe the recruiting process needs a complete overhaul.

It's time to ditch the textbook questions. Canned questions beget canned responses. HR has to change the way they hold interviews with "standard" cliché questions and begin asking more human questions.

Replace "Why we should hire you?" Instead, explain why they should join your company.

Replace "What is your greatest weakness?" with "What skills do you need to develop most?"

Replace "Where do you see yourself in five years?' With "Tell me about your professional development and career goals and how those will align with our company's objectives."

Other questions you can ask:

- What transferable skills not listed on your resume can impact your job success?
- What do you expect out of your manager?
- How would you handle a non-performing colleague?
- What could you do to improve the organization and running of your past workplace environment?
- What do you like most in a working environment?
- What would be your ideal place to work?
- What makes you happy?

- What boosts your creativity?
- What are you passionate about?
- What else is important to you to make a decision to join us?

Do not try to hire people to work for you, hire people to work with — people you can learn from, whether from their enthusiasm, their vast experience, or their skillful X factor.

This is the age of an empowerment and collaboration where individual performance becomes less important. Ask candidates team-based questions. For e.g., "Describe the perfect work environment and level of interaction with coworkers in which you would experience the most success."

Don't ask demeaning or inappropriate questions, like "Are you married? Planning to have children?"

Jacklyn sent me this:

"I am always scared of how the recruiter's attitude will be more than the selection process. In 2014, I went for an interview for a sales position which turned out to be so embarrassing and humiliating. The interviewers started off by asking if I was married, I said yes. They asked if I had any kids yet, I said no. Next, they questioned if I was pregnant, if I can handle pregnancy and working, If I can promise not to get pregnant in the next 3 years etc. One even asked why I got married since I looked young. These questions lasted for about an hour. The only work-related question they asked during the interview was where I worked. Two weeks later, I got a call that I wasn't getting the job 'based on the concerns raised'. I cried. A person should never leave an interview doubting themselves or have low self-esteem. I felt all of that after leaving that interview."

There are so many such interview stories like this that will make you cringe. One interviewer had a plaque facing the candidate that read, "Yes, I am judging you". Unbelievable!

Furthermore, don't judge a candidate's skills based on how well they interviewed. Candidates who have a knack for interviewing and have mastered the STAR style (specific situation, task, action, and result) of interviewing typically get hired. However, many of them, in my experience, have not been a good fit. I've always been successful relying on my gut — never failed me yet. Every candidate that I felt was not a good fit but was hired anyway turned out to be a regrettable choice. I have the same track record with those I encountered after hiring - if I sensed something less than optimal, it turned out I was right. So I find real value in listening to your intuition.

I always thought of the set interview questions as a guideline. We know what we're looking for, so use these questions to search for specific skills. But, I've always found that it's best to focus on the person and their qualities, opposed to how close they are to the image we're looking for.

Sometimes you just have to go with your gut. Take a chance on someone. There is no perfect candidate. You can also ask a seasoned HR person to take over the reception desk from the usual receptionist. That senior HR person may gain some real insight into the behavior and attitude of the candidate talking with them and observing their body language. That may be helpful - just a thought, if someone wants to try.

Change the scenery so candidates can feel more relaxed. It doesn't have to be overly formal. **Improve the interview experience and hire the right candidates the first time.**

When HIRING, I often look for the "three H's" in candidates: Humble/Honest/Hungry. If they have the "three H's," training is easy. You can teach anyone anything as long as they are open, motivated, and sincere. Soft skills are the skills most often overlooked in hiring decisions, but they play a greater role in success on the job. I have hired persons who didn't look so great on paper. When I met them, though, I just knew they would fit well with the rest of the team and do a good job in the position. Focus on the real person. It's the person, not the resume, who performs the job.

Being on both sides of the interview process gives you a different perspective. I try to have a conversation with candidates to make them feel comfortable so I can get to know the real person. This gives you a better opportunity to evaluate their true personalities and ability to adapt to the culture. Most interviewers forget that the more comfortable that they make a candidate, the more information they will get. I have seen good candidates nervous during the interview. When I've noticed this, I make sure to put them at ease. I always try to tell our candidates that we're just having a conversation. I'm there to make sure that this is a good fit for both parties. Offer candidates water and let them know to feel free to excuse themselves, if they need to use the washroom at any point in time.

In a process that is already difficult, I wanted to put them at ease and have open communication. I found you get a better understanding of who they are and what they are looking for. We discuss their work history, their passion, their approach to work, problem-solving, working with others, team building, conflict resolution, etc. One tip that I've learnt is to talk a bit about their hobbies which somehow makes them more at ease.

There will be a day when interviews are more like a discussion — where the employer and the candidates get to know each other and the job requirements rather than just asking a series of cookie-cutter questions. Having a natural flow of conversation allows the candidate not only to feel more comfortable, but to come across more authentically which is key for me as a hiring manager.

A good interview should be a 2-way conversation, an open dialogue for both parties to explore whether the employment relationship is a good fit, not a one-sided grill session designed to only serve one. There should be two-way communication with mutual respect with the goal of getting the best fit candidate for the job. I grimace when I see managers that interview by a strict format and will not deviate from the list of questions.

It seems some employers are focused on dissecting the person being interviewed, running everyone through a robotic process, and not very interested in hiring someone who can get the job done. For example, this is how a major e-commerce company based in Seattle interviews in my experience - there is zero interest in you as a person, no personal angle - and they will spend up to 15 minutes dissecting a single answer to a question, for a "gotcha" moment. Instead of giving you any eye contact, they are busy vigorously typing out all of your answers on a laptop to compare with each other later. In one instance, I could tell two interviewers were messaging each other while I spoke, it was so uncomfortable. It felt solely like they were just after a prototype. An interview is more about exploring and understanding what the candidates knows rather than grilling him/her based on what he/she does not know.

You only have a 15-30 minutes window to determine a candidate's abilities and fit for a specific role. Irrelevant textbook questions with predetermined answers do not lead to selecting the best candidates. **Do you want someone who can give you scripted answers to irrelevant questions, or someone who can actually perform on the job**? Skip the theoretical or pointless questions, and focus on the job-related skills.

HR automation should focus on detecting skills and motivation as early as possible. Give strong preference to practical questions. Evaluate work samples from candidates' portfolios. Ask the candidate to write a little project plan, or a piece of computer code, or make a sales call to one of your employees. Give them a problem to solve or a task to complete. If they are a technical person, let them produce a diagram. Let them point out problems and alternatives with your set-up. You can also incorporate virtual reality (VR) technology to test candidates' job-related skills in the hiring process. For example, with VR you can now put candidates into a simulated environment to test their problem-solving skills.

Furthermore, a job interview should not just be a series of tests and hoops to jump through. A one size fits all approach doesn't work either.

Some managers use the interview as an interrogation session. That seems like a counteractive approach to finding quality employees. The style and behavior of the interviewer(s) can be a major turn off. For this reason, panel interviews are not always the best idea in every case. Although they are used at times to give the opportunity for multiple people to be in on the interview phase, if not conducted carefully, it can look and feel like an interrogation session. Quite often, the best candidates even get stressed during normal interviews and the "interrogation type" questions just make it worse. You are interviewing candidates to hire and not humiliate. It's sad that some interviewers have an attitude of superiority. Being an interviewer is not just a title, but it is a responsibility. You are deciding the career of an individual. When you grill people in an interview, it puts people in defense mode which doesn't go well for anyone.

Some individuals believe that aggression shows assertive authority and/or confidence... It actually shows none of the above. In this low unemployment market candidates have a choice. Grilling someone in an interview is a quick way to see them working for the competition. Instead, hiring managers need to emphasize what is great about working for their organization.

Sometimes my interviews turn to counselling sessions - teaching candidates how to better sell themselves. And it's always rewarding to see the light in their eyes. I once had a candidate whom I asked about remuneration and she said: "anything." I was so upset on her behalf and later counselled her never to leave her fate in the hands of an interviewer/employer.

Some of the better companies I've joined, led the interview with a company overview and role description first, before proceeding to the questions and I think this trumps the traditional methodology where they simply asking questions. **Remember, interviews are**

supposed to be 50/50. Candidates are also interviewing to know if they want to work for you. The companies that will set themselves apart give the candidates the chance to figure out if the position, company, and future is right for them.

AN INFLEXIBLE CHECKLIST

I was on a HIRING committee where the CEO didn't like any of the candidates interviewed. He said none of them met his criteria. We clashed on this, and I told him that there is no "perfect" employee. He ignored my suggestions, and the position remained vacant for four months. Long story short - he finally hired someone who had all the qualifications he wanted. This guy had quite an impressive resume. But sadly, he did not perform well. He was "perfect" on paper but did not have good people skills. Qualifications are important but so are soft skills. A perfect resume does not equate to success on the job. A candidate may not tick every box on your checklist, but that may be the one who can bring much-needed value to the organization.

I look for people who can answer questions I can't, or who will tell me what I need to hear, even if it's not necessarily what I want to hear. Every day I see the same jobs re-posted, some of them being left vacant for months. Yet there are so many talented individuals still searching for jobs.

This is why you can't find the right people. Personalities and life experiences don't fit into cookie cutter molds. The qualities you need are not on a resume. You really need to be looking for human qualities like EI (Emotional Intelligence), humility, passion. Only human interactions and vetting can pick up these traits.

Paul sent me this:

"It gets frustrating trying to get my resume through the electronic screening process. I know I can knock their socks off if I could just talk to a real person."

What I find interesting is how many companies claim they can't find qualified people, yet they continue to cling to recruiting processes and practices that clearly are not effective. In between is the applicant tracking system with a lot of buzz words, categories, and filters that don't work. Like many automated systems, they can do real damage (in this case, missing out on great candidates) before you even realize there's a problem.

It is nearly impossible to get someone to fulfill all your needs. Look for a person who has the "will" to become what you need; someone you can grow with in the workplace. Maybe a candidate didn't look the neatest or wasn't the most confident, but that does not mean that they are not qualified for the job. If you want the best talent, stop looking for perfection. It does not exist! We need to be intentional about matching the best person to the job based on skills and characteristics. Don't say every candidate must meet these 20 criteria or they're out. Focus on what value a person can bring. Look for passion and potential. Additionally, some hiring managers simply have unrealistic expectations about what is possible from a single candidate. I have read some job ads and thought "Who could possibly live up to these requirements? They seem to be looking for unicorns."

I once hired someone who had no experience in the position we were filling. This guy was in the midst of switching careers, but he had the skillset we were looking for. I believed his entrepreneurial experience would easily transfer to corporate. In the end, he was just what our organization needed. Sadly, today I see many qualified candidates being overlooked or eliminated because they are not working in the same position. I wish recruiters and hiring managers would be versed in identifying transferable skills, ingenuity, drive, and potential. Many people can't fit into the narrow parameters of a linear career history in a particular field. A candidate doesn't have to tick every box in your checklist to be the "best fit." A job can be learned. By being so narrowly focused and inflexible, many companies miss out on employees who are great team players, change agents, innovators, and progressive thinkers. There are so many individuals in this situation, and it's a complete waste of talent!

I am now seeing a trend requiring BAs or MBAs even for entry level positions. For the naysayers, just to clarify, I am not speaking about jobs where it comes down to life and death if someone does not have the qualifications.

James told me he had trained underwriters and salespeople and outsold most of those with a college degree. Yet he couldn't become a manager because he didn't have a degree. So, what if Bill Gates, Steve Jobs, Michael Dell, or Mark Zuckerberg, all of whom were college dropouts, had applied for a vacancy in your organization? Would their applications even be able to get through the computerized screening process? Employers are missing out on so much talent in the workforce. I have learned over the years that having a degree does not make you better at performing at a job. You sometimes find there are people far more qualified to fill a position who may not have a degree but have the experience. Experience is priceless. Having a certificate of skills and being able to apply those skills are two different things. Nowadays you can have a degree from any source. A person can have many letters after their name but that won't substitute for being a decent, hard-working individual.

We shouldn't be too quick to cross someone off who has experience but not the accompanying paper. Give them a chance to prove themselves. A resume can be impressive, filled with educational and professional accolades, but the person may lack the ability to get along with other employees. I can teach the job, but I can't teach you to be nice to your co-workers.

This is what you should be looking for in candidates:

- Attitude.
- Ability to perform the role/Skill
- Experience.

- Soft skills (communication, teamwork, leadership, creativity, critical thinking, EI, etc.)
- Adaptability
- Workplace culture fit.
- People who can teach you something.
- The person who can ultimately replace you.

Few things make the person in charge of hiring feel more threatened than an applicant who has more education, experience, or skill than the candidate's potential supervisor. Many people, when they need to hire a subordinate, go on the defensive. They feel the best tactic of ensuring job security is to hire someone less qualified or skilled than they are; in their minds, it makes them look smarter and more valuable.

EMPLOYMENT GAPS

"Brigette, my husband is 46 years old and has been a stay-at-home Dad for the past 3 years. He took a career break to take care of our children, He continues to try to get back into the work industry but has had no luck at all!" — Tracey

This guy took the time off to be a stay-at-home dad for his kids. His resume read "professional sabbatical to care for my family." I find it admirable that a parent takes some time off work to look after their children. There are two major prejudices that no one discusses (or want to discuss). One is the unemployment gap, and the other is absolute age discrimination (overqualified).

It is very narrow-minded to judge a person's qualifications on such criteria. Our society needs to change. A gap in employment history should not discount someone's abilities. Gaps are more common today for multiple reasons. Stay-at-home parent, going back to school, caring for an elderly parent or even job searching.

Taking a break from work is not taking a break from learning, growing, and gaining experience. This guy did professional certifications, small classes, and online training to keep up with the times. The stigma that still exists regarding employment gaps are "old school" (and not in a good way) and really should be done away with. We need to be more flexible and open-minded. We need a new progressive and positive program for HR recruiting.

Life happens and so do special circumstances. This was an excellent candidate who kept his skills up to date. Yet all they could see was the gap. People who take a long break from work tend to have a very good reason to do so. Instead of magnifying the gap, focus on the individual's skills and talents.

We are not robots. Shouldn't a gap in employment be expected at some point in our careers? **It's striking that, while we have watched the evolution of the office workplace over the years, the hiring practices remain outdated and flawed.**

The gap is most problematic for someone who either fears it or uses it as an excuse. It's not a problem for someone who's found the right recruiter or the right employer. It does not need to be "solved." It's a good screening tool though. No way would I judge anyone for taking time out for sabbaticals or family time. In fact, I would respect them more. Why? Because they are completely capable of making the most important life decisions and managing their lives by their values as humans. That takes strength, resilience, and self-discipline. This is everything you want in a person you want to work with shoulder to shoulder when the going gets tough.

A person taking some time off from their professional career should not be punished or disadvantaged when trying to re-enter the job market. I do not penalize people for the career gap. We need to applaud dedication to family and changing personal circumstance. Sometimes it may mean a slight step back while you catch up on your skills, but if you're in, I'm all for helping you get back into the workforce! Let's spread this movement. Ironic, isn't it, that one of the most important jobs you will ever do in your "career" (raising children), and it's seen as a negative rather than a positive.

This outlook needs to change, and that requires mature thinking and mature people at the recruiting level. All that should matter is if the candidate has the right skills and the right attitude to do the job.

Rather than searching for consistency in past work, you should look for resumes with a "reskilling profile" that shows off the ease with which a potential employee might go through a multi-stage life and career. Think of yourself and your employees as continuous works in progress. Given that top talent is likely to become more and more scarce as time goes on, this is a practical solution.

CHATBOTS

One idea is to incorporate chatbots in the recruitment process. In the recruitment process, for instance, they might form part of the candidate experience; as a candidate, I can get immediate answers to my questions, or I can be guided through the onboarding experience by a chatbot. This can also relate to some of the typical questions or tasks that employees have to complete at work. It could be getting information about the company pension policy or maybe booking a day's holiday/time off.

FEEDBACK

After a three-week period involving a phone interview, in-person interview, and a second-round interview, the candidate has not received any feedback. He is unable to reach the recruiter or HR Manager. Has common courtesy become extinct? *It appears that professional courtesy has fallen by the wayside in this job market.*

How many times do we tell candidates that "we will get back to you" but fail even to tell them if the position has been closed, let alone provide feedback on the interview? Once a candidate gives their time to be interviewed, they deserve feedback. We need to understand that people invest financially and emotionally in applying for a job and are always hopeful that they might be selected. They need a sense of closure, and even more importantly, they need to be treated with respect. We need to start treating our employees, present and potential, with care, respect, and humanity. This is intricately linked to the kind of culture we have at our organization. Today as experiences are shared on social media, your brand can be negatively affected by how you treat potential employees.

HIRE CHARACTER, TRAIN FOR SKILL

"My biggest mistake is probably weighing too much on someone's talent and not someone's personality. I think it matters whether someone has a good heart."
~Elon Musk

Qualifications matter, but if you don't have the right approach, attitude, and willingness to learn, it isn't much use. You can't teach life skills or common sense. A person is made up of experiences (work and personal), and it is those experiences as well as their personality that make them a high performer — not education alone.

Select individuals with a passion for performing and a strong work ethic. You can teach a skill, but you can't teach integrity. Competency must be coupled with character. You can always train skills, but you can't train character. Resumes don't perform jobs, people do. So hire people, not resumes! Look for the value they can bring. I'd rather have the right fit in person than the right fit on paper.

A degree does not override qualities like humility, authenticity, and integrity. If an employee lacks these traits, they can bring a corporation to its knees. Unethical employees cost companies billions of dollars each year in lost revenues, settlements, and other damages.

"To educate a man in mind and not in morals is to educate a menace to society."
~Theodore Roosevelt

A narcissistic team member can impact productivity on your team. Technical skills for a role are essential and easy to measure, but traits such as "team player" and emotional intelligence are better predictors of long-term success. Intelligence can get someone a job, but soft skills are required to perform well in the long run.

In today's world, we need to place higher value on these skills (humility, authenticity, integrity, etc.) because they are becoming extinct.

In our digital age, and with the metrics used to filter resumes, so many people with great work ethics, the right attitude, good heart, and good character don't even make it through the selection process. Too often our sole focus is on skills. There needs to be a healthy mix of both talent and character.

AGE DISCRIMINATION IS ON THE RISE.

"He is 'too old' for this job," the HR manager said to me after we interviewed John. She continued, "He will not fit into our culture." John had been laid off by his previous employer due to restructuring at the age of 53.

Ageism in the workplace is very real. It is the elephant in the room. I see uproars over every other "ism" (sexism, racism, etc.), but everyone turns a blind eye to ageism. It is being swept under the carpet. To the HR manager's disappointment, I did hire John. John brought a wealth of experience to the company and taught me a lot that I never learned from an MBA.

Matias emailed me this: "Unfortunately he's not alone. I'm 39 years old, and I was told in my face 3 times in the last 20 days that I was old (with other words) for a concierge and bartender position. Looks like experience is not very much appreciated."

We live in a youth-oriented society. The hype about "out with the old, in with the new" needs to stop. A person's age doesn't lessen their ability to work hard or to make a valuable contribution to the organization or society. When someone crosses 50, that doesn't mean they cannot function, that they should just retire and sit in a corner. Common myths: "They can't learn. They are not creative. They are not as productive as younger employees. Customers do not respond as well to older workers." These are all based on false premises and assumptions.

Anna sent me this email:

"I would get telephone interviews, which would go quite well. However, when I showed up to the face-to-face interview, it never went further as they would classify me as "overqualified." "Seasoned" is another word I was routinely hearing. I feel like my 30 years of experience has become a double-edged sword. So I stopped putting the year I graduated from college on my resume. I also left out years from my employment history and started dyeing my hair, and I finally got a job."

It's sad when someone must conform to this ideal to land a job.

It's easy to drop the years from the resume. It's more difficult to hide that required information (DOB) on an online job application. A large majority of people don't even get to that point. Keyword searches, ten second resume scans, and other high-volume candidate churning processes exclude many such candidates.

German researchers find older people tend to be more productive than younger employees. Research also confirms verbal communication and employee loyalty improves with age. Companies are looking for diversity to foster innovation and growth, but which one? Only gender or ethnicity? Why not age diversity? Older skilled workers add a level of diversity to a younger team that helps create well-rounded solutions. Institutional knowledge and maturity together make people 40 and over the perfect balance. Sadly, many of them are being made redundant in favor of restructuring, outsourcing, or grads entering the workforce. We need to do more to capitalize on the skills, talents and experience of the significant number of "senior" workers who are usually overlooked and undervalued.

In reality, ageism in the workplace is just an extension of the decreased "value" our society places on the meaningful and is more engrossed with the superficial. I remember one company letting go of their older workers, then complaining of low productivity and high turnover. It's sad when experience, resilience, wisdom, and principles, which are the pillars of a society, are seen as having little significance.

In previous generations, age was something to be admired and honored. However, in today's world it is looked upon with contempt. Only in certain high-level positions is being over 40 acceptable. We recognize it in management and politics where we trust those with decades of experience. Many individuals 40+ have to stay in whatever job they are doing once they reach that age because their opportunities are limited. This form of discrimination continues to make the workforce unhealthy for individuals and creates stagnation within our society as we are not open to change. We need to teach our younger generations to respect our seniors instead of discarding them. And that starts with us. This can only form part of the organizational culture when it's endorsed from the top.

A top CEO once said, "If you are over 30... successful companies should not employ you." This brought no outcry. Why? Because ageism is widely accepted and silently encouraged. Just look at the job ads; we don't see persons over 40 in those settings. The majority do not view it as discrimination. The Age Discrimination in Employment Act (ADEA) forbids age discrimination against people who are age 40 or older. Yes, there is legislation, but it is hard to prove. At the moment, it seems the Equal Employment Opportunity Commission (EEOC) has no interest in enforcing the law. Most employers require application via ATS systems, which does require dates. If they don't ask your age, they require employment dates for each position in your work history, and the date of college graduation. There are too many ways to break this law.

A person should not be afraid or feel embarrassed to state their age. With age comes wisdom, experience, knowledge, resilience... and the list goes on. Age and experience should be rewarded, not punished. It's time to stop discrimination on the grounds of a person's age. We need strong advocates to stand up to businesses who embrace ageism. We can no longer sit idly by and tolerate this type of discrimination. It has gone on for far too long. Age diversity is just as important as any other type of diversity and should be included in a company's diversity plan. The line "We are an equal opportunity employer" should have real meaning.

With the increased life expectancy and with many countries opting to push back the retirement age, ageism has become a critical issue.

Insurance company Hiscox released its 2019 Ageism in the Workplace Study which revealed some sobering statistics about the growing problem of age discrimination for American employers.

The number of age-related discrimination charges filed with employers and the EEOC by workers aged 65-plus doubled from 1990 to 2017.

- 44 percent of employees report that they or someone they know experienced age discrimination in the workplace.
- 21 percent report they faced age discrimination themselves.
- 36 percent feel their age has prevented them from getting a job since turning 40.
- 26 percent feel there is some risk they could lose their current job because of age.
- Only 40 percent who experienced age discrimination filed a charge or complaint.

Employers paid $810.4 million to settle age discrimination charges filed with the EEOC between 2010 and 2018 (excluding litigation).

These numbers are only going to get worse.

The baby boomer generation may be getting older, but they still flex a tremendous amount of economic (and voting) power. Only when we, as individuals and as a society, make it clear to employers that the legal, financial, social, and other costs of age discrimination will be much steeper than any benefit (perceived or actual) gained, will we begin to see an end to this type of discrimination.

Even if you think this does not concern you now, your decision to remain silent will come back to bite you. Inevitably, we all grow old.

WE NEED MORE WOMEN IN THE BOARD ROOM.

It's no secret that women still lag behind men in the workplace. The latest *"Women in the Workplace"* report by McKinsey & Company and LeanIn.org shows that only one in five executives in the C-suite is a woman. Although the figures are slowly rising, there is still a lack of women in the world's boardrooms; in particular, there's a lack of women of color, who remain underrepresented at all levels. Only 1 in 25 C-suite executives is a woman of color.

Organizations that don't hire women at the board level are missing out on huge benefits. Several studies have shown that having women on boards results in better investment decisions and in less aggressive risk-taking. Women are more likely to use co-operation, collaboration, and consensus building, and they are more likely to take into account the interests of multiple stakeholders. This results in a stronger financial performance.

You've probably heard the following statistic: **Men apply for a job when they meet only 60% of the qualifications, but women apply only if they meet 100% of them.**

There are several actions that can be taken to improve gender diversity:

- Conduct a diversity hiring audit on your current hiring process.

- Pick one metric to improve for your diversity hiring - for example, increasing the percentage of qualified female employees in leadership roles by 10% within 12 months.
- Avoid rotating candidates from within the same elitist groups.
- Train women for higher levels, which will give them confidence in their abilities.
- Set up mentorship programs for women.
- Encourage referrals from minority employees.
- Diversity attracts diversity. Make it clear that diversity and inclusion are a top priority for your company.
- Support groups dedicated to diversity.
- Integrate "blind hiring." This can help to reduce unconscious bias by removing names, schools, and even addresses from resumes.
- Focus your efforts earlier in the pipeline to make real progress. You can reach out and connect with on-campus, women-led groups such as the "Women in Computer Science" club.

I think as more women have come into the workforce at higher levels, they brought an awareness of things like work-life balance and the more social and relational factors. It's not just women who are better off when women have more opportunities - it's everybody!

THE NEED FOR SPEED IN HIRING IS INCREASING

In recruiting, time is absolutely of the essence. While it's important to be meticulous when vetting candidates, having a process that takes too long can cause you to lose your top choice in today's job market. Often times, a long and drawn-out process causes us to lose exceptional candidates in the age of tech. The most talented candidates have a choice(s) of where they want to apply their talents. Top talent can come and go in the blink of an eye. I found out the hard way how important it is to speed up the hiring process.

We were hiring a social media manager a while ago, and it took 60 days from application to offer for the chosen candidate. He took another position just a few days before we made the offer. Fortunately, we got the next round down to 14 days and found a great candidate. You can investigate ways to speed up your hiring process while still demanding high-quality candidates. Start by identifying unnecessary delays that seem to be common in each hiring effort.

How to speed up the recruitment process:

- **Write a very clear job description.** Choose your words carefully. Specify clearly the skills needed for the position without going overboard. While you may want to list every requirement, you envision for the ideal hire, including too many skills and qualifications could deter qualified candidates from applying. I have read some job ads and thought to myself, "Who could possibly live up to these expectations?" But if you're not clear enough, you're likely to end up with lots of non-qualified applicants just trying their luck. And it's a smart decision to add the salary range in your job description. A poorly written job description will lead to spending a lot of your time (and money) figuring out which candidates are qualified for the job.

- **Shorten your application process.** Top talent is in high demand, and most candidates will quit lengthy application processes. Applications that can be filled out in five minutes or less attract more applicants. Ask candidates to upload their resume and complete a few pertinent qualifying questions. Gen Z candidates expect and demand faster decision-making. The hiring process is also a time when the interviewee is evaluating the company. Some may view your slow hiring as a mirror of the speed of general decision-making at the organization.

- **Try tests**. If you give candidates an online test with job-related questions that takes 10-15 minutes, followed by the usual application process, you've already eliminated candidates who are too lazy to do the test and the rest of the application after that, who simply can't handle the test, or who already realize the job won't fit them. That will give a HR department fewer resumes to handle, and the resumes they get will be from candidates who are at least reasonable, who have already made an effort to complete a test of 15 minutes. You can use the test scores, along with their resumes, to see who you want to invite for an interview.

- **Structure interviews but be flexible.** It's very unprofessional when hiring managers come to the interviews unprepared. This may seem so simple, but it happens too often. Have questions prepared, and read the job seeker's resume prior to the commencement of the interview.

- **Reduce the number of interviews -third and fourth interviews are absolute time wasters.** If you put in the effort in the pre-screening phase, you should have a very good overview of candidates' capabilities by the interviews. So, you don't really need to be doing that third and fourth interview.

- **Promote your job ad on social media.** Many of the best candidates are those who aren't necessarily looking for a job but might be interested if they see an attractive offer. In order to get more high-quality applicants, post your job ad on Facebook, LinkedIn, Twitter, Instagram, etc. Use engaging job ad visuals and catchy headlines to get people to share and promote your job ad. Build an employer brand that attracts relevant people and makes them want to be a part of your company. Additionally, make sure that your job ad is easy to navigate via mobile phone and tablet.

- **Utilize technology.** A great way to speed up the hiring process is to utilize technology. Emails, text messaging, and video interviews are all great ways to help speed up the hiring process. When you are more flexible in your channels of communication, you will get quicker responses from candidates. For example, perhaps a candidate is unable to take your phone call but is quite capable of quickly returning a text message.

- **Flexible interviews.** Also, when your candidate or client has limitations in attending an interview because of distance, you can schedule a live video interview. Make it simpler and faster to get those interviews scheduled and the process moving forward.

- **Ask your employees for referrals**. Who better to source hardworking, skilled staff who will fit into your culture than your current employees? Nobody is going to recommend someone they think would do a bad job since this would reflect poorly on them. Including employees in these decisions will make them feel like a valued part of your company and create vested interest.

- **Use the services of a recruitment agency.** Recruitment agencies aren't for everyone, but for many companies, they can be effective. They have experience and resources to speed up the entire process and find the best people. It also costs you less in the long run.

- **Invest in interview training for your hiring teams.** This will help your HR team evaluate candidates better, which improves the quality of your hires.

It makes no sense to hold a job position open for the perfect candidate who only lives in your head (and will never exist in the real world). Let me be clear. I am not saying to rush the recruitment process. Don't cut down on the time it takes to do reference and background checks. Hiring the wrong person will waste more time and money in the long run. But if you want to have agile employees and organizations, you need to have agile hiring practices to attract the high-quality talent that your organization needs to survive and thrive. Employing high-performing people is a crucial factor in any company's success.

ONBOARDING
TIMES ARE CHANGING: THE ONBOARDING PR~
NEEDS TO EVOLVE

According to SHRM, 69% of employees are more likely to st~ a company for three or more years if they had a positive onboarding experience.

Onboarding should begin immediately upon the candidate's acceptance of the job. One of the most often overlooked steps is pre-boarding. Before your new employees step foot into your office, try to generate excitement and build a relationship with them. You can start to acclimate the new hires to the organizational culture and values. Engage with them, and let them know to feel free to contact you if they have any concerns or questions. You can also get the hiring manager and teammates to email new hires, expressing their excitement to have them join.

A study by Bersin by Deloitte's industry states:

- 4% of new hires leave a job after a disastrous first day.
- 22% of turnover occurs within the first 45 days.
- These cost the company at least 3X the former employee's salary.

When you have a new employee, you need to ensure their transition is as smooth as possible by making it easy for them to understand all they can about what you do, how you do it, and how they fit into the big picture. Often new employees have to wait weeks to get access to systems. I have heard horror stories from employees having to wait at least 6 weeks for a laptop whilst others had no workspace and were stationed in the canteen. Stream the onboarding process to ensure new users can begin contributing from day one.

oarding programs should be customized for various job roles. **Automate the experience.** Automation eliminates the necessity for classroom or instructor-led sessions and creates a positive impression and experience, especially for digital natives.

During the first week, in the initial meeting, managers should focus on clarifying expectations, responsibilities, standards of evaluation, and reporting relationships. Goals should be clear, specific, and challenging. Use the onboarding process as a chance to provide guidance about when and how to use relevant support channels.

Give your new employees an interactive and fun first day on the job, but keep it realistic in line with your culture. You don't want to create this hype; when employees settle down, they'll feel disappointed and, possibly, mislead. You can also decorate their desk with balloons or even take them out to lunch. But this must not be a one-off thing. It would end up like a marriage that goes downhill right after the honeymoon because of unmet expectations. I have seen this too many times. Appreciation must be rooted in your culture to ensure a consistent experience. Throughout their tenure you should always make employees feel appreciated.

It doesn't take a big budget to keep the fires burning. People love surprises. Sometimes I will come in early in the office before my staff, and leave chocolates or even fruits on their desks, and they get so happy and excited. I love their facial expressions as they ask one another, "Is this for me?" "Aww... how nice!"

Although, I am an adult now, I love that the elderly church members still bring little treats (fruits, cake, sweetbread, banana bread, nuts) for me. They take their time and do this. They spoil me and I love it. It feels absolutely wonderful to know that people are thinking of you and they genuinely care about you. Most of the time when I am traveling, I have slices of banana bread made by them, in my handbag and suitcase to munch on. It gives me great comfort because I know it's baked with love. The seemingly little things you do can go a long way in making people feel special, valued and appreciated.

An onboarding gift box for new employees filled with goodies and company schwag is wonderful, but go further to make sure their first impression is a memorable one. Successful onboarding doesn't require an overcomplicated playbook. Create a warm welcome, give them an agenda for their first day, an employee handbook, and map out the office layout to ease their stress and fears. Moreover, link them with an **onboarding "buddy,"** someone they can rely on, and make time for questions. As you guide your new hire through the first week of training, encourage them to write down any questions or concerns.

There must always be frequent check-ins made by their manager.

Questions to ask the new employee:

- How are you doing?
- Is the job and company what you expected?
- What are you enjoying most about your role?
- Has training been helpful?
- What would you add or change?
- Do you feel like you have gotten to know your coworkers well?
- What is working/what is not working?
- What can I do to make your transition easier?

Ask them to be honest since you want to make sure they have the best experience and will do what you can to ensure it. (And it's good to have feedback about the onboarding experience so you can make it a better experience for those who follow.)

When was the last time you upgraded your onboarding process? Great onboarding leads to a reduction in transition time, increased employee engagement, and increased retention. If you invest the time and energy to refine your process, you'll be able to create an experience that will benefit your company for years to come.

RETENTION
THE NEW APPROACH TO PERFORMANCE MANAGEMENT

At one company where I worked, you could work until 7:00 p.m. No one would say a word. And no, they didn't pay any kind of overtime. However, when it was time for annual performance reviews, they could list every mistake an employee had made. It was a morale killer.

A survey by the Society for Human Resource Management, a professional organization, reported that 95% of employees say they are dissatisfied with their employers' appraisal process. Traditional annual reviews typically focus on one employee feedback event, the end of year performance review. That model is increasingly being replaced by more regular reviews. Many firms are opting for frequent conversations, informal check-ins, and regular meetings between managers and employees. It's about time. Annual reviews are backward-looking, and they don't help people perform better. They're conducted too infrequently, allowing situations to deteriorate between reviews. Regular conversations about performance, development, and goal setting help to improve employees' performance and engagement. More than 90% of employees would prefer their manager to address mistakes and learning opportunities in real time, according to a study from Wakefield Research.

Companies such as Deloitte are way ahead of the game. Deloitte replaced its review process with performance snapshots which are often conducted after a project is completed. Snapshots enable managers to engage in productive dialogue and give real-time feedback. In this context, recognition can be given, challenges can be identified, and if needed, coaching can be arranged. General Electric also scrapped its formal annual reviews and replaced those evaluations with touchpoint discussions. Instead of performance scores or rankings, it has an app to help employees and managers share feedback for continuous improvement.

Sadly, as I travel the globe, I still see many organizations holding on to annual reviews. I am guessing they don't want to increase creativity, collaboration, and innovation.

Early one December morning, the CEO called me into his office, very upset. He handed me a couple of files and said, "All your employees can't possibly meet or exceed performance in their appraisals. There must be two or three who fail." When an employee meets or exceeds expectations, they get a bonus, and he told me the department didn't have the budget to pay this. He instructed me to fail at least two employees. I explained to him that my team has been working hard the whole year, and if an employee was not up to par., I would coach them and work closely with them to improve their performance. He said he didn't care because all the other managers have employees that failed, and I needed to follow their example. I refused. He punished me by giving me a fail (Needs Improvement) in my performance rating. It's sad that some employers have no intention of rewarding employees for their hard work; instead of setting employees up to succeed, many managers set them up to fail.

Once an employee puts in the effort and gets the results, we should not shortchange them. Goal setting and compensation systems should be created to foster the culture and the behaviors you want everyone to express. Just as annual reviews are becoming a thing of the past, a onetime end-of-year reward system should be a thing of the past too. **This is the "instant" generation. Don't wait too long to reward employees.** It doesn't have to cost much. You can now send digital gifts instantly. Be creative, and keep looking for every opportunity to recognize and reward your team.

YOU GET THE TALENT THAT YOU PAY FOR!

Four years ago, CEO Dan Price slashed his own salary of almost $1 million to raise those of his employees, bringing the minimum salary of every employee to $70,000. Now he's opening an office in a new city and promising another salary increase.

In 2015, he was heralded as one of the most generous employers. Two weeks after he made the initial announcement, the company was flooded with 4,500 resumes and new customer inquiries jumped from 30 a month to 2,000 a month. Price's belief is that by investing in his employees, the company will grow faster. Sadly, most employers don't get this. If you want to increase loyalty, engagement, and productivity, start by paying people what they are worth.

Today, many companies will not hire the candidates who are considered "overqualified." However, ignoring the "overqualified" because you think they are too expensive, and you can hire two employees for the price of one, will cost you in the long run. **You can't Google experience.**

Most people don't expect ridiculous salaries or raises. They just want to be paid what they are worth. It's a shame how we have designated employees as "liabilities" while machines and buildings are assets. We invest in assets; we limit liabilities.

At the University of Pennsylvania, researchers discovered that businesses that spent 10% of their revenue on capital improvements saw a 3.9% productivity increase. But get this — when that same 10% was invested in employees, productivity went up 8.5%.

> *"The minute you settle for less than you deserve,*
> *you get even less than you settled for."*
> ~Maureen Dowd

Additionally, I see many job seekers and employees, whether interviewing for a job or negotiating for a raise, undersell themselves. Learn to stand up for yourself. Learn to say no. Don't be afraid to ask for the salary you deserve. It's about the skills, experience, and value you bring to the table. **Know your worth and don't be afraid to ask for it.**

We need to understand the motivators of people. This is only the first step as you have to stay engaged and connected with them as they evolve and change over time. I have a friend who worked at a startup company and loved the free snacks, soft drinks, and games in the break room. Five years later, she had her first child, and now has another on the way. Now what she really wants is a better paycheck via more career growth, and benefits like remote working options. What drives people at any one time is never a fixed state. **The tangibles that motivate people can change yearly depending on their stage in life.** My tapping in strategy is for the long haul and is never a one and done methodology. I have seen employees change what motivates them multiple times in a decade. That is why I am always checking in with each employee.

DATA-DRIVEN CULTURE, FEEDBACK AND EMPLOYEE ENGAGEMENT

The future of work is digitalized. Engagement in an AI age can increasingly be accomplished using digital means. The tools employees use should be simple, modern, and easily to integrate with other solutions. Many companies are implementing a variety of digital tools for top management to capture and respond to topics of interest from all employees. These include a live chat application, a company-wide social intranet, and even an app that regularly surveys employees about their current work experiences. "Continuous Conversations" are a part of a new strategy and skill of all stakeholders in an organization.

At the most basic level, we all want to feel valued and appreciated, to feel like we belong. This can be ensured by putting people in positions where they can use their skills and abilities to their highest capacity. Engage with employees to ask them for feedback and suggestions; when you encourage "open feedback," make sure you aren't merely giving it lip-service. It is critical that we nurture emotionally intelligent managers who do not hold grudges, breed resentment, or view employee feedback as personal attacks. **Empower employees to be collaborative and creative so that they can perform at their best.** Train and coach employees to excel in skills that machines cannot mimic — negotiation, creativity, critical thinking, collaboration — and provide them the tools they need to excel in their roles. Identify all the touchpoints where you interact with employees and work towards improving them.

In many organizations, surveys and feedback forms do not lead to significant changes; this makes employees disenchanted and disgruntled, making them feel as if they aren't being heard. Here, we can use technology to ensure ongoing and continuous feedback instead of relying on end-of-year reviews to ensure long-term planning.

I once sat in a 360-degree review meeting for our manager. He couldn't believe the low scores he got. So, he would go through each question and asked everyone if we really understood what it meant. It was mental torture because no one wanted to speak up, in case he could identify who said what. I just felt like he was trying to undermine our intelligence. The scores he received were exactly what we thought of his leadership style overall, but he refused to accept it.

If you see a pattern in the feedback for a certain manager, the question is, how do you act? Do you brush off the concerns or make sure that the manager undergoes training?

It is essential to remember that when we are implementing technology, it must be to make people better off. We shouldn't get caught in the trap of using technology to monitor or track employees by compromising their privacy as this will undermine employee morale. The objective of all workplace technology must be to increase employee satisfaction and help people work better.

RESPECTING EMPLOYEES AND THEIR EXPERIENCES

This is where emotional intelligence and social awareness come into play. Are we aware of the people around us and the things that are dear to them? Are we aware of the things that bother them? Or are we too focused on numbers? This is one of the leading reasons why workplace engagement levels are plummeting across the world;

most employees assume that management do
and that all they need to do to get by is work th

TRAINING AND DEVELOPMENT

Personalization

Our learning tools were designed in the 1990s. We have the type of learning experience that we were having 30 years ago in our consumer lives. Gone are the days of telling someone to sit in a corner office with a big manual and call that training. The way we consume content has changed. If we take a look at the world of consumer technology, we see more personalization. The algorithms behind the scenes are creating a more personalized experience, and that's the piece that really stands out when we think about the impact of AI on HR.

When we think about platforms like Netflix, we think about a personalized experience based on everything that you're doing on their platform - from the types of shows you like to the different ways that you're clicking on the screen (for instance, pressing pause). The algorithms behind the scenes are creating a more personalized experience. The shift in our experience in our consumer lives is changing the expectations of the workforce. We are using these types of technologies in our non-work lives, and then we come to work and have a very different experience.

In days gone by, you could roll out one-size-fits-all training programs and expect to see results. Not the case anymore. The landscape of the workplace is changing at a rapid rate. Companies are moving away from the one size fits all mindset, and **we are seeing more personalization and incorporation of digital technology in the workforce**, to improve training and increase employee engagement levels.

This same experience in the world of consumer technology can now be applied to the learning environment. We can move away from the way that we've delivered HR programs in the past based on one size

can encourage employees to use our platforms and to
data just like they do in their consumer lives. The system
ultimately learns about them and helps improve and
personalize their experience.

**We need to look at how we can incorporate technologies such as VR
(Virtual Reality), chatbots, and other smart technology in designing
our learning programs**, if we want to keep employees happy and
engaged.

CAREER PATHING

It's no secret that millennials and GenZ employees want more than
just adequate compensation. They require a personalized plan for
their individual career path, without which they are prone to look for
greener pastures outside their organization. Your employees want to
learn and improve themselves. They want their lives to progress.
And if you are not able to provide these, they will leave. Your
employment brand is determined by whether they can learn and
grow in your company. The truth is these generations have different
expectations. It's important that you map out a clear track for
advancement. Allow them to set their sight on the big prize,
formulate stretch goals, and empower them to manage their career
path.

By assisting your workers in formulating their career-pathing goals,
you not only help fill internal vacancies but also uncover valuable
insights into their skills and learning gaps. As a result, the employee
is continually engaged across their tenure in the company, in the
light of which they can see new avenues and a brighter future.

I was talking to the CEO of one company who, up until four or five
years ago, was one of the most highly regarded companies in the
Caribbean. He realized that their reputation scores were dropping
precipitously. If you're not a place that millennials want to go
because you're not doing anything new or different, that's going to
show up in your brand metrics.

Research conducted by Gallup found the majority of millennials (55%) feel like they are not engaged at work. Millennials expect more from their jobs in terms of the technological tools, general working conditions, work life balance, flexibility, and opportunities for growth and development.

It's important that businesses create an engaging, positive workplace starting with the onboarding experience. This starts with having the technology that offers incoming employees a positive experience. Without a strong HR tech strategy, it will be hard for employers to stay competitive in attracting and retaining the best talent.

HERE ARE SOME THINGS THAT LEADERS CAN DO TO ENABLE EMPLOYEES' FULL POTENTIAL:

- **Elevate** — Put them in positions where they can utilize their skills and strengths. Give them projects that will help them grow and develop their leadership skills.
- **Engage** — Encourage them to share their ideas, suggestions, and feedback.
- **Empower** — Grant them autonomy to make decisions.
- **Recognize** — Appreciate their efforts and contributions. Recommend them for opportunities.
- **Expand**— Set goals that are realistic but expand their performance threshold.
- **Equip** — Provide them with the proper training and tools.
- **Energize**— Inspire and encourage them to develop the capabilities you see in them.
- **Support** — Mentor and coach them.

EXITING EMPLOYEES - OFFBOARDING

In this age of disruption, many companies resort to reducing the headcount as the first response to adversity.

Reactionary management is not strategic leadership. Layoffs are a short-term solution that ultimately harm a company's long-term value. Companies handling bad times in a strategic collaborative way with their team will bolster how they retain and attract top talent. Why not work together to find solutions to keep loyal employees on hand—going to a 3-day work week, cutting salary by x%, management taking a salary reduction, etc. **How you treat your employees will determine the fate of your company.** Research shows that organizations that layoff employees experience a:

- 20% decline in job performance from the remaining employees.
- 36% decline in organizational commitment.
- 41% decline in job satisfaction.
- 31% increase in voluntary turnover the next year.

Meanwhile, innovation declines. If your crisis management strategy is just to throw people overboard when the going gets tough, you will be in for a rude awakening. **Cost cutting by cutting your main pipeline may not be such a smart idea**. You would be losing intellectual resources and at a bigger risk of not maintaining a competitive advantage. Employees are the branches of a tree that makes a company grow. They are your best brand ambassadors. Customers are also paying attention to how companies and brands are treating their employees in difficult times.

Just as employees join your business, the time will come when they leave your company, for whatever reason. Layoffs are inevitable. Make the effort to ensure the employee experience of entering your organization is positive, and that they also leave with a smile on their face. Make employees feel valued till the last day. I believe the offboarding part is as important as onboarding. If you are going to treat them with value on the way in, treat them with the same value on the way out. First impressions and last impressions can have a big impact on how employees view and feel about your organization.

John told me one morning he came to work and was told he no longer had a job. Security was waiting to escort him out the door after 25 years working in this company. He said he was at the verge of suicide as he still had two kids in college and a mortgage to pay, and his wife was unemployed. He said he wished they could have given him one kind word or more time, but nobody showed any concern for how he was coping.

What could this company have done differently in the lead up to this? They could have been preparing their employees early on for change. Communicate openly and honestly. Let them know their jobs are not permanent and change is coming. Nobody likes change, but at least they could be prepared for it. Additionally, incorporate lunch time learning for employees to update their skills and keep themselves relevant. Offer counselling to employees who would be affected. The company could have also provided services such as interviewing skills and resume writing, which is what departing employees need, or even, as in John's case, financial planning services. Moreover, show them empathy and let them know it hurts you to see them go. Tell them you are there to help, whatever they need. For instance, if they ever want a recommendation, tell them not to hesitate to contact you.

I find that most managers are not well-trained in dealing with leaving employees. They feel it's personal and react poorly. Some think that a resignation is a betrayal. They make it about themselves. They see it as a transactional issue and forget another person, with their own drives and pressures, is involved.

Too often when an employee resigns, and it seems the company has no use for them, they are treated poorly. The Golden Rule is not outdated. It still applies today. "Treat others as you would like to be treated." We need to be kind and compassionate. Kindness and compassion don't cost anything.

You can pretty much tell the values of a company by how they treat:

1. Jobseekers.
2. Those leaving.

Leaving is never an easy decision for anyone. When I resigned from my job. I had the letter of resignation prepared, but I deliberated for quite a while as to whether I should really hand it in. Change is hard.

We should always encourage and support others. Don't make employees feel like it's the worst decision they ever made and that they're going to regret it. We should always be à motivator no matter the circumstances. Few employers understand the value of keeping a good relationship when the employment ends. Genuine appreciation and encouragement go a long way toward making sure your leaving employees final experience with you serves as a good memory.

Martha sent me this:

"I was laid off from my job of 20 years. TWENTY YEARS and the entire process took less than 5 minutes. No one thanked me for my contributions. I was not treated with respect, by virtue of the fact that I was stripped of my computer, keys, phone, etc., with no opportunity to get any personal documents from the computer/phone, etc., and no one wished me the best, let alone offered any type of support. 20 years gone in a matter of minutes, and all I got was some very sad/uncomfortable looks. Layoffs are hard, I get it, but when someone has dedicated 20 years of their life to an industry (social services at that), employer and people, you don't just hand them a letter explaining the layoff and get them out as quickly as possible. Hearing positive words would have been a game changer."

> *"I've learned that people will forget what you said,*
> *people will forget what you did, but people will*
> *never forget how you made them feel."*
> ~Maya Angelou

I know in some companies it's policy that someone leaving will have to leave immediately if they're going to a competitor, or if they're in a position to do damage because of the nature of their work and access to sensitive data. However, we should always treat everyone with respect and dignity. Managers can sometimes demean employees by their tone and choice of words.

One of my employees resigned. She left to start her own business. I was disappointed to see her go, but I let her know how happy I was for her. This is what I told her:

"Thank you for all your wonderful contributions. I hate to see you go, but I am so excited for you, and would like to congratulate you on this new chapter. I am so grateful to you for all the difference you have made. You will do very well. All the best, and perhaps one day, I will get the privilege to work together again with you. You will be truly missed. Please don't hesitate to contact me if I can support you throughout this transition. I wish you every success."

From the time an employee resigns, some bosses immediately start treating them like traitors and can't wait to march them out the door. That's like blaming someone for their own inadequacies. This should not be the case. Your ex-employees are your ambassadors for life. Don't give them the cold shoulder. Treat them well.

When an employee resigns:

1. Show them appreciation for all their good work.
2. Wish them the best.
3. Keep treating them with respect.
4. Let them know you are here, if they need anything.
5. Be genuinely happy for them. Employees do not owe you their whole lives or their dreams.

I do wish this was standard practice. Perhaps someday it will be.

As a leader, give your employees wings to fly. We should celebrate others and continue to support them. Life is unpredictable. After all you never know if one day, you may be working with or for them - or maybe you just keep a friend for life.

If we take our role seriously as business owners/managers/leaders, we should be encouraging our employees to grow as people every single day. That is very likely to lead them to seek new horizons beyond what we can provide for them. I've had two amazing employees leave my organization, not because they didn't like it here, but because they grew personally and professionally here and wanted to take the next step forward. That should be received as a compliment to our culture, training, and leadership, not the opposite! Had I not had amazing leadership in my previous roles, I wouldn't be where I am today, and I take pride in knowing that other people say the same thing about me! It's a privilege to see others grow and flourish under your leadership.

Someone once told me that when an employee leaves because they've reached their full potential in your organization and need to grow further elsewhere, you've done your job. It's called growth this is what I see it as. In this regard, when your children leave home, do you tell them? "Oh, you don't love me!" You were happy for them. They just grew up. They must go and find their true purpose. There is a season for everything in life.

Too often when employees start to leave their companies, HR makes sure to schedule exit interviews to find out what is going on. **I have conducted many exit interviews, and I have found they're pretty close to useless most of the time**.

Here's why:

1. The individual emotionally let go a long time ago.
2. The reason for leaving is not always salary.
3. Exit interviews are not always accurate.
4. Employees view them as a waste of time.
5. Many people like to leave on a good note, so they don't tell the real reason why.

It's like trying to figure out what went wrong after being served with divorce papers. I think time and energy would be much better spent focusing on creating a culture of transparency, continuous check-ins, open communication, and most importantly, training managers on how to lead people, etc. The truth is, if you are aware of issues as they happen and consistently take the necessary steps to rectify them — then you may just find yourself not needing to conduct exit interviews at all.

Treating employees well on their way out also helps leaders and HR with branding purposes and building great culture. Companies fail to realize that departing employees have the potential to be their best brand ambassadors and company advocates. They are as important on their way out as the employees coming in. If someone moves forward on a good note, the employee is more likely to refer people from their network. They'll also be sharing their experiences and their satisfaction with the company. Others will hear about whether (or not) the company is really a great place to work.

We need a set standard for off boarding employees since it varies across all organizations. It's subject to a manager's discretion which is never a good thing.

THE NEED TO FOCUS ON THE "HUMAN" IN HR

The vulture and the little girl, also known as "The Struggling Girl", is a famous photograph taken by Kevin Carter in 1993. It is a photograph of a frail starving Sudanese girl, who had collapsed on the ground with a vulture lurking on the ground nearby. The child was attempting to reach a United Nations feeding center about a half mile away. This photo later won Kevin the Pulitzer prize for an "exceptional" caption. He said he was careful not to disturb the bird and waited about 20 minutes to get the best possible image. He took a few more photos before chasing the bird away. The photograph was sold to The New York Times where it appeared for the first time on March 26, 1993.

Hundreds of people contacted the newspaper to ask the fate of the girl. But Kevin did not know. Carter came under criticism for this shot. He was bombarded with questions about why he did not help the girl, and only used her to take a photograph. The St. Petersburg Times in Florida wrote: "The man adjusting his lens to take just the right frame of her suffering, might just as well be a predator, another vulture on the scene". This guilt contributed to his depression and eventually Kevin ended his own life.

The photographer was so focused on getting the best shot that he forgot his humanity.

As human resource practitioners, have we become so focused on getting the best talent we forget we are dealing with people?

In a recruiting world where speed and numbers sometimes seem to be all that we care about, I want to remind us of a central truth: there are real human beings behind each phone call, each email, each on-line application.

More than ever we need to be infusing humanity in the workplace. I'm waiting and hoping for the leading-edge companies to drop the HR title completely and go back to the **"Personnel Department"** and also require the department to treat everyone as people not resources!

We need to stop calling employees "resources." People are colleagues and team members — not dehumanized resources and commodities. We need to treat employees as human beings and not just statistics or numbers on a graph. A person comes to work to do a job, but if that's all that matters, that human being is being seen as just another gear in the machine. People are living, breathing, and feeling creatures who want to be valued. Small gestures of care and support go a long way in building loyalty, and organizations can foster a loyal workforce by being more mindful and thoughtful of how we treat our employees.

CHAPTER NINE

A MULTIGENERATIONAL WORKFORC
MACHINE COLLABORATION

Good talent is scarce. How do we attract and re_____ent? It's understanding your current and future workforce. There are four generations in the workplace. The reality is that the workplace is now full of people aged 18 to 60, with entirely different expectations of their careers, of authority, and of technology. As competition for talent continues to get more competitive, companies are going to have to develop new methods to attract and retain top-level talent. Understanding each audience helps us craft the right message on the right channels.

By 2025, millennials (Generation Y - those born between about 1981 and 1996) are forecast to comprise 75% of the global workforce. Depending on where you're marking the birth years of millennials (the eldest are in their mid-30s already), it's fair to suggest decisions in business have been made by this generation for several years already. For example, Finland's recently appointed Prime Minister, Sanna Marin, at 34 years belongs to the millennial demographic. Millennials usually prioritize family over work and are most likely to switch jobs. Gallup found that 60% of millennials say they are open to a different job opportunity. They are willing to act on better opportunities. Many of the changes you made to recruit, train, and retain millennials will work for Gen Z as well.

There are similarities between all the generations, since we are dealing with people. Everyone wants:

- Flexibility
- Autonomy
- Work-Life Balance

Just when we thought we had figured out the millennials (also known as Generation Y), a new generation is here - Generation Z (Gen Z). Gen Z, also known as iGen (or centennials, born 1997-2012), are now just starting to enter the workplace.

I like that the focus has been on millennials, but it's time to move on. Generation Z is a huge group with spending power of over $143 billion in the United States alone. The entrepreneurial Gen Z's are already influencing and running successful start-ups and will reach decision-making roles earlier than millennials. Hence my stance that while it's good to acknowledge millennials - their pace of progress will appear pedestrian compared to Gen Z, when we reflect back in 10 years' time. Their whole mindset is different from anything we have seen before. Smart companies are beginning to shift focus and use customer intelligence on Gen Z to their advantage. Gen Z's are clearly our future leaders. Not focusing on them at this stage is a grave mistake.

Gen Z Distinctions – These traits can also apply to millennials but for Gen Z, you will have to intensify your strategy. As someone stated, Gen Z are "Millennials on steroids."

1. Technology Savvy

In the case of Gen Z, growing up with access to the internet has significantly impacted their view of the world and how they want to work. Technology has been their middle name. **They expect more innovation.** A recent survey of 12,000 Gen Z teens conducted by Dell Technologies revealed that 91% say the technology offered by an employer would influence their job choice if faced with similar employment offers. They expect digital tools to be deeply integrated into your business. You will need to keep monitoring the development of smart technologies and digital tools and where applicable, incorporate them into your workplace.

Whether accessing social networks or company websites, Gen Z is most likely doing it on their mobile devices. According to Global Web Index's 2019 report on Gen Z, this age group greatly prefers the on-the-go convenience of their mobile devices over PCs and even laptops. Additionally, they are not afraid to shop online unlike previous generations. Ensure your website is optimized for mobile. If it is slow or buggy, this can turn them away. Your app or website should also allow these jobseekers to accept offers, self-schedule interviews, or complete referral tasks online. Keep upgrading your website to make sure it is engaging, interactive, and user friendly.

2. Social Media Presence

You will need to develop your employer brand through social media. **The key is selling the benefits of working with you. It's a marketing effort.** Have an active social presence. When you want to find out more about someone, you either Google them and/or check their social media posts. In that regard, to attract these digital natives, you will need to showcase more of your culture. Demonstrate online how your organization is an awesome place to work. Although these generations socialize differently, using their phones instead of getting together in person, they still yearn for the human connection. **Use existing employees to market your company.** You can also use your current employees as a recruiting tool by sharing their positive testimonials. Get current employees to participate by joining in on the conversation. Share pictures and videos of staff having fun, supporting each other, and working together. Post snippets about good things happening to and for the workforce in your organization. **Make your office place more humane.** Two things go viral on social media quickly – acts of kindness and negative circumstances. You always want to showcase instances where employees are displaying empathy, kindness, and compassion. If an employee is on extended sick leave, share on social media what you and the team did to cheer the individual up or help them get care (e.g., driving them to the doctor). This is what tugs at human hearts and draws people in.

You should consider diversifying the social media channels you use. For social media, members of Gen Z gravitate toward Instagram, Snapchat, and YouTube, according to a survey by Business Insider. TikTok has now taken the world by storm. Do you have a TikTok account? TikTok, the short video creation and sharing app, has now hit the mainstream. More than 41% of TikTok users are between 16 and 24 years old. If your company doesn't already have Instagram, Snapchat or TikTok accounts, it's time to sign up.

3. Social Causes

Money is important, but it's not the only thing they want. Gen Z are more passionate and outspoken about social causes. They want companies to give back to society with their profits and are more willing to make a purchase if your company supports some type of cause. Going forward, they wouldn't want to buy products which do not have a social impact on society.

"This generation often puts aside its differences and rallies around causes that will benefit the greater good," research by Facebook explains. "Gen Z expects brands to do the same—to live their own values and to offer value. In fact, 68% of Gen Zers expect brands to contribute to society."

While Gen Zers feel personally responsible to make a difference and 76% believe we will have made headway on important issues in five years' time, 90% also believe companies must drive action on social and environmental issues, according to the 2019 Porter Novelli/Cone Gen Z Purpose Study.

Lots of things are going to change from a branding perspective. **Brands are slowly realizing they can no longer get away with non-existent environmental and ethical commitments.** Companies making products will have to reinvent how they make and source products that also benefit the environment, the local ecology, health, and human well-being. (You don't have to save the world, but they want to know you're doing something to make things better). One of my previous employers organized team meetings to seek ideas to redefine the company ethos. As usual, all of us wrote our thoughts on post-it notes that went to the team-leader whose job was to read them out and put them on the whiteboard. I wrote, "Giving back to the community" on one of my post-its. It was scoffed at and never made its way to the whiteboard.

As leaders, we should genuinely care about our planet. We shouldn't just be concerned about our environment because of Gen Z or any other group, but because it's the right thing to do. Climate change is very real, and it's hitting everyone hard. I can't forget the pictures of the dehydrated and badly burned koalas being comforted and fed bottled water by fire fighters during the Australian fires.

Everybody does not agree on climate change and global warming. However, the potential future effects of global climate change include more frequent wildfires, heat waves, longer periods of drought, stronger hurricanes, severe flooding, tropical storms, and earthquakes. Human-induced emissions that trap heat in the atmosphere contribute to these dangerous conditions. Additionally, many chemicals for home and commercial use have been instrumental in depleting the Earth's ozone layer that shields the Earth from the sun's ultraviolet rays.

The devastation will only get worse as glaciers continue to shrink and ice on rivers and lakes melts at a faster rate. **The intensity of disasters will only increase; the likes of which we have never seen before.** Therefore, leaders need to step up to the plate. Climate change affects human health and well-being by threatening crops, water supplies, infrastructure, and livelihoods.

Many large companies have significant plans to cut carbon emissions, but given the scale of the crisis, these efforts are inadequate. Companies must lobby for the policies that will lead to a low carbon future, and go a step further by forming partnerships with those on the same page, subsequently cutting ties to climate deniers. **Businesses can also use their buying power, customer base, stakeholders, and supply chain to catalyze change across business and society.** In recent years, corporations have increased the pressure on their suppliers to operate based on ecological sustainability. General Mills, Kellogg, and Hewlett Packard Enterprise have all set science-based carbon goals for their suppliers. Corporations also need to rethink their business models and how they conduct business. Mark Schneider, CEO of Nestlé, spoke recently about investing in plant-based proteins, which will reduce the carbon footprint.

Employees are now pressuring their companies to do more for our climate. Google employees have asked their executives to cut ties to climate deniers, and Amazon employees signed an open letter to CEO Jeff Bezos demanding a plan to get to zero emissions. Their efforts paid off, as Jeff Bezos recently announced the company's plans to be carbon neutral by 2040 and to buy 100,000 electric vehicles.

Extreme weather and climate-related natural disasters disrupt businesses, communities, and natural habitats. Global climate change is already affecting the bottom line. Therefore, it would be in your best interest to take a stand against this now.

Consequently, I think the entire mindset of these new generations is founded in a deep belief that sacrifice is best reserved for the pursuit of our own purpose including those larger purposes to which we connect. Furthermore, new generations have the benefit of exposure to a broader range of human examples than previous generations. They can see the machinations, pitfalls, patterns of happiness and success and failure of a thousand lives being lived just by clicking around the internet and observing the tweets of personalities and the person next door. Enlightened is a word that comes to mind; nevertheless, that enlightenment will need some time to mellow into wisdom.

A Warning About Generalizations

I've provided a number of generalizations here that I find valuable in understanding and, ultimately, serving Gen Z. But I want to add a caveat to these generalizations. In the end, it's people we are dealing with. We all want to feel valued and appreciated. **It's just the approach, devices and systems used to attract and retain the incoming generations might be different.** However, all your marketing efforts to attract and retain these employees will fail, if you don't develop the human connection. Build relationships, support your employees and show people how much you appreciate and care about them.

LEADING THIS FUTURE WORKFORCE

Leading this future workforce will take vulnerability, humility, empathy, authenticity, and flexibility. In a world of artificial relationships, with so much dishonesty and manipulation on display, they are searching for something real. They want leaders who truly value people and will create a sustainable future. Only caring about the "here and now" will not work anymore. They are very outspoken and will not stand for or accept poor leadership.

If we want to succeed, we need to know our audience - what they care about and what makes them tick! Be ahead of the curve. Gen Z is already here. They are independent and creative but are dependent on technology. Gen Z craves feedback and guidance. They often need frequent praise and reassurance. Mentoring and coaching is a must. They are less focused on traditional career milestones such as graduating from a four-year college; instead they are focusing on certifications. They have little patience for working set hours in an office and would rather have flexibility. They are entrepreneurial. According to a field study from the Online Schools Center, 41% of Gen Z's are planning to start their own business.

If you want a thriving business, you must adapt to your future target audience. Early adaptation is vital for a business to thrive. If businesses only focus on where the market is today, then they miss the boat when the market is someplace else tomorrow. And in the age of digital-social media, not adapting to new tech and communications can be the kiss of death. A smart audience development strategy is about forecasting tomorrow's market and adapting to it - and that is simply good business strategy.

HUMANS + ROBOTS AS THE NEW BLENDED WORKFORCE

More and more processes are being automated. An interdisciplinary research team from the Universities of Göttingen, Duisburg-Essen, and Trier has observed that cooperation between humans and machines can work much better than just human or just robot teams alone. The results were published in the *International Journal of Advanced Manufacturing Technologies*. The results were that the mixed team of humans and robots were able to beat the other teams; this coordination of processes was most efficient and caused the fewest accidents. The researchers concluded that companies should pay more attention to their employees in the technical implementation of automation.

As robotics technology continues to advance, the human-robot relationship will be become even more closely integrated. More attention needs to be directed at developing cooperation between humans and robots. The narrative that independent machines can do all the work with no help from humans is misleading. When it comes to tasks with repetitive motions or where heavy lifting is required, robots perform well, but they experience difficulties when handling flexible materials. In many corporate and business situations, decisions will continue to be driven by people.

Knowing how to work side by side with robots will be an important skill set moving forward. In the recruiting process, we would have to include questions such as:

- If your boss was a robot, would that be a difficult for you?
- Would you feel comfortable working alongside robots?
- If your teammates were all robots, could you handle working in such an environment?

It's important to ask these questions. However, humans should not be forced to adapt to their nonhuman counterparts. Rather, developers should design technology to serve as good team players alongside people.

The augmented workforce is already a reality. Bots are fast becoming common features in every organization. Humans and bots will need to coexist. Gartner, Inc., predicts that by 2021, "25% of digital workers *will use a virtual employee assistant* (VEA) on a *daily* basis." Beyond Gartner's forecast, 58% of organizations said they plan to invest in virtual assistant technology within the next two years. It's crucial that we nurture human-bot collaboration now, to pave the way for AI acceptance since chatbots and automated workflows will become the norm in every business environment.

A number of issues may arise when implementing Robotic Process Automation (RPA) in the workplace. The inclusion of automation in our workforce causes concern about job security for many people. Technology is disrupting entire industries (and types of work) — which in turn may economically disenfranchise certain segments of the population. While certain roles will become obsolete, many new roles will be created. **Automating tedious tasks will improve the quality of processes and free up people for more innovative, deeper thinking and strategic work.** We must therefore promote a culture of continuous learning.

More importantly, we need to enforce stringent safety procedures, especially in human and robot work areas, since one error or wrong movement by a machine can spell the end of a human life. As robots and automation become mainstream, safety will remain a paramount concern to make sure that workers are not put at any additional risk.

CHAPTER TEN

SOCIAL MEDIA BRANDING AND STRATEGY

A brand is the way a company is perceived by those who experience it. It's not just your logo or mission statement. It is the essence of your business. In the era of Google, it's clear that anyone can be a brand. Everything we post online is representative of who we are and what we do. Social media is the here and now. The old ways of controlled corporate talking points and designated spokespersons are outdated in this social media age. Acknowledging its presence and impact is so critical to any business strategy. **On social media, it's important to sell your brand, not just your services.** Start by asking yourself this question: what comes first, your product/services or your customers? Without customers, what can you do? Branding is important for anyone who wants to experience long-term success. In our current market, social media reigns supreme. What is a brand? Brand is commodity. Brand is authority on the market. Brand is an internal promise to deliver externally.

The business world is going digital and virtual, so we have to be creative. A lot of people will be left behind because they refuse to learn, unlearn, and relearn. The world has changed – people want to see people, and they want to buy from somebody they know.

My mentor once told me, "Business deals are made between people; now go out and have as many conversations with people as you can." Personal branding goes hand in hand with building relationships with your prospective client base. The foundation of those relationships reflects the brand.

Employees are the biggest brand advocates for a company, but sadly, most organizations don't realize this. Your company is nothing without the team of people that do the work. Always remember that they are the treasures that make it happen.

Employees are your company's most important brand champions. Your biggest raving fans should be your employees. You win from the inside out; this is a staple in most facets of life. You can't expect your employees to connect with a mission they don't believe in. If your employees are not excited about your brand, then your company cannot be fully aligned with your customers' needs.

Your company brand strategy should include the organization's mission, vision, and core values. You should ensure that this is well-defined and communicated, and shared with everyone in your organization. Your core values are an expression of your brand, your brand personality, an extension of your purpose – the guide with which you will operate to fulfill your mission and the framework with which you pursue your goals. **Core values provide a strong sense of identity and give you a thread of continuity that weaves worthy moments into your stories.**

If a company is not set up internally to deliver on its external brand promise, your marketing efforts will fail. Today, many businesses still believe that "brand" it's an external promise. **Your brand is an internal promise of your company's culture, mission, and vision.** A company's success is always built from the inside out. There is no brand whose success is not determined by a proper set of agreed-upon values. And such values must be intimately lived by the companies' human "assets," not just a list of buzzwords copied and pasted on a nice slide. There's no sustainable external success without an internal, genuine, strong, and long-term, human-capital-oriented culture.

Many businesses are leveraging their most valuable assets, their own employees, to help them market their brands. Encourage employees to post content that will represent your company well and drive traffic to your site. This can save a lot of money on ads. Social media is about being "social." The people who really make sincere connections are the ones who are able build an emotional bond with their followers. Having employees sharing their own version of social media posts brings life and loyalty to a business that is otherwise just another company page. People will trust your employees far more than they trust your CEO or marketing team. Employees are your most credible spokespeople. Employee advocacy is a cost-effective, scalable alternative to influencer marketing.

Teach your employees to become brand ambassadors – not by selling, but by creating mindful connections. Your company culture, mission, vision, and values will create an organic culture where your employees will want to post about your company – of course, with guidelines. **Companies need to shift from selling and promotion, to employee evangelism by training and enabling employees to be social brand champions.** Many employees already share their brands activities. However, if this is done more professionally, the outcome is that the brand will grow organically. The term "brand ambassador" is already a shift in mindset. It will empower employees and make them more responsible towards the company's brand, especially if training is involved so that they share and respectfully defend their brand in social media.

The best marketing strategy is authenticity. People share content that helps communicate their desired identity. Authenticity is a key to building a long-lasting brand. Personal branding amplifies authenticity and builds professional success. It also shines a light and makes you a positive voice, which defines you from the noise.

People buy from people they know and trust. People don't buy from brands. Businesses can no longer afford to be faceless entities. Focusing on the branding part without considering the personal side is not an effective strategy. Humanize your brand. Nothing replaces the personal human touch, and that is what defines the user experience, not a team or some technology to put in place of real humanity. Your employees know the company better than anyone else, and empowering them is key. When your brand has humanistic qualities, it gains wider acceptance than just a mere materialistic achievement. In the current world, it is essential to "humanize" yourself as much as possible to establish strong and sustainable professional relationships. Above all and despite our digital profiles, what makes us unique and different is to be human beings.

Your social networks profiles are extensions of who you are. Focus on starting conversations, not advertising your products and services. Many people recommend the 80/20 rule; 80% of your content should be engaging, with only 20% of it being self-promoting. This is where brand storytelling comes in. Brand storytelling weaves together the facts and emotions to captivate your audience. Instead of only giving your customers reasons why they should buy your product, start sharing the story behind your brand, why it exists, and why it matters. Consider the emotion you want to evoke in your audience every time they interact with your business. **Always keep your posts positive.** People are quick to unlike a business if posts are negative or controversial.

Brand storytelling starts with telling a story.

A company that sells cars may focus on the features and benefits, but if it tells a story behind how it connects people together, this is somehow more compelling and captivating. Your brand's story needs to involve your customers and community, to make them feel like they are connected to your brand.

If your company helps the community. Share it. If your company has a great culture. Make it known. Share stories about your community, your employees, and your products. Use a hashtag that involves your customers and feature or acknowledge your customers' stories about your brand. Give a call to action. Invite your customers to retweet, tag someone or share a memory.

Airbnb is a great example of compelling brand storytelling. Airbnb's creative use of storytelling and intricate understanding of their customer has made it one of the most iconic brands of today. Airbnb created a memorable storytelling moment on the anniversary of the fall of the Berlin Wall with a wonderful and cool animation titled, "Wall and Chain." It tied immediately into the, 'be anywhere' theme the company has worked hard to create. It's about family, connection and being a global citizen. Anyone who watches their animation videos, will be hit by the simplicity of the ideas and the emotions it triggers. Make your brand story (ethos, message) part of something bigger. Compelling stories forge a meaningful relationship that goes far beyond products and services.

Emotions move people. Emotions influence customers purchasing habits more than logic. For your brand to be etched in the hearts and minds of customers, it needs to become so much more than your product and service. Ask yourself; What sort of value are you offering your customers every time they engage with your content? What feeling do you want them to walk away with after interacting with you? What do you want to be known for? Use storytelling to create a deep emotional connection. Once your audience likes and trust you, they will more likely buy from you. Brand storytelling will ultimately maximize your business's visibility, profit, and impact.

The goal with branding is to ultimately create a unique, recognizable identity through your own voice and style that you can use to establish and maintain a positive professional reputation. Instead of patting yourself on the back by posting statistics, endorsements, etc., focus on making your brand memorable, and real. Wrap your message into a story that simplifies information, provokes an emotional response and wondrously transports people to a place they want to be.

We should strive to be of value, and success will automatically follow. Building connection for your people to take the organization's vision and make it theirs requires leaders to not only know the vision, but role model the values. Many leaders prioritize their own vision, and it creates a disconnect for their people, so they are not clear on the expected behaviors that bring the vision to life for the customer/consumer.

All too often, it seems that stated company goals, mission statements, vision statements, etc., are not reflected in their actual operations. For your employees to adopt the vision of organizations requires real leaders who know the values that support this vision. You must create an excellent relationship climate, one of respect and trust, because trust is the foundation of building fruitful relationships.

Creating brand ambassadors requires conversation about values and intent. Values guide our behavior, providing us with a personal code of conduct. Core values shape not just who you are, but also the culture and character of your company. Connecting their personal passions with the organization's priorities is the secret sauce. Companies need to train their employees for that. There is a company right now on LinkedIn that has their 50k employees as brand ambassadors. Imagine the impact they are creating!

The leaders in one company I worked for talked about brand and marketplace constantly, but they never did anything positive to encourage their employees to "believe" in the brand. Unless your branding is bought into by your team — unless your mission and purpose resonate with the people who create your reputation — Customer Experience (CX) will fall flat / be artificial at best. **Remember your brand is your reputation, and that is the sum total of actions carried out by your people.** Thus, unless they buy in, whatever they carry out will be inauthentic. When you get that true buy-in (which can come through fair process/input from your people), CX becomes everyone's responsibility naturally.

True branding is a part of what a company does to succeed. But even a company who succeeds can't do it alone. Your team only can win for you. It's foolish to believe otherwise. A championship trophy is won neither by the coach nor by the captain, but by the team. Products are just things without people. Your team is the life of your product and company. People are the reason you have a business. Every single person within an organization plays such an important part. Branding has to be owned by whole organization.

The entire organization has to be on board from the top down, and that includes inviting input from the leaders down to the employees. But none of that is possible without the core belief, which would be the reason why the company is serving the public in the first place. When you identify your core values, it's easier to share your story in a way that shows you care about your customers. This should feel completely natural, and it should resonate fully with your audience. Money is always the motive in any successful business, but it shouldn't be the only thing that drives it. **For a company to really succeed, it needs to put people first.** Employees are the most valuable equipment in any business, and yet many times, a printer gets more attention. It's going to be hard to run the business if you don't take care of the people that work for you. The moment you start valuing your people is the moment your company will take off.

Companies and cultures are made up of uniquely talented individuals. Companies cannot show values, and companies cannot create culture. People make the vision, mission, credo, and value statements, and people choose to either bring them to life or prioritize their own agendas over the agreed-upon values. The brand's ability to influence does not come so much from strong marketing initiatives as from strong respect for its values. I believe that the current environment is getting better at holding leaders at all levels accountable, and the internet is allowing us to share examples of bad leaders and call them out for being bullies. Companies will have no choice but to remove them if the people who do the work rise together and push back against bad leadership. Never underestimate the value and the power that the entire team brings to the table. **Be supportive, be open-minded, but also be brave and have the difficult conversations with those who are responsible for shaping a toxic culture.** Know your values and stand by them.

It is always a good idea to encourage your employees or customers to talk about your business through their social media accounts, but it's even better if a brand has a system in place which motivates them to do so. Employees must be rewarded for championing the brand through their daily actions. Indeed, the gains from the efforts of the employees can be shared accordingly.

SOCIAL MEDIA BRANDING CAN BE A DOUBLE-EDGED SWORD.

Therefore, special care and attention must be given to devising a thorough social media strategy. Proper training should be given to your employees who are brand advocates to ensure emotional intelligence and decorum is used on social media sites.

Many respected individuals in leadership positions have been fired, or asked to resign from their jobs, because of ill-timed tweets and social media posts. Everybody thinks they can handle social media, but most cannot. **It really baffles me that so many people use social media to express their feelings on every issue.** Don't tweet when you are upset. Thinking about consequences is something most people do not consider these days. They cannot "see" the big picture or don't care. You would think the act of typing, as opposed to speaking in person, would give people the opportunity to momentarily reflect on whether or not what they are about to say would be something they are okay being associated with for the rest of their lives before hitting the "post" button. Yet this is not the case.

Let's take Tesla as an example. Tesla's primary platform of branding and promotion is Elon Musk's Twitter account. Tesla is an expert when it comes to social media branding. Think about it. Have you ever seen a Tesla speeding on a meandering mountain road in a television commercial? Or heard a radio advertisement telling you to "get a Tesla today"?

However, in 2018, Elon Musk agreed to step down as Tesla chairman and pay a fine of $20 million after reaching a deal with US regulators over tweets he posted about taking the firm private. Under the deal, he will remain as Tesla CEO but had to step down as chairman for three years. Was the tweet a joke? Was he serious? There are consequences to our actions, and we must never tweet in the heat of the moment or say things that are false, hateful, malicious, or derogatory.

SOCIAL MEDIA POLICY

A social media policy simply outlines how an organization and its employees should conduct themselves online. This policy provides guidance for employee use of social media.

According to Pew Research Center, 74% of adults use social media. **However, 73% of companies don't have an official social media policy.**

Some companies only develop a company social media policy in response to a major PR disaster. Social disasters are more common than you might think. For example, think about the backlash that Dove received in 2018 for their commercial featuring a black woman in a brown shirt taking her shirt off and turning into a white woman with a light shirt. The outcry against the commercial was swift. A spokeswoman for Dove said that the commercial "was intended to convey that Dove Body Wash is for every woman and be a celebration of diversity, but we got it wrong and, as a result, offended many people." Because Dove was quick on their feet, they mitigated some of the long-term damage that commercial could have caused. A well-crafted company social media policy can help you effectively address undesirable situations before it does too much damage.

Always have a second pair of eyes to scan through content before someone posts something from your official account. **Have a diverse social media and marketing team**. Homogeneous teams are not always sensitive to diversity issues. Many posts causing public outcry seemed to be innocent when posted.

SOCIAL MEDIA POSTING GUIDELINES FOR BUSINESS

1. Use of Official Accounts

Clarify who can speak for your company on social media. Authorize which staff members will be running accounts and the procedures for accessing and posting to those accounts. Make sure the policy includes guidelines and standards for posted content.

2. Prohibited behavior

Your company social media policy should prohibit posts including:

- Bullying.
- Inflammatory comments or obscenity.
- Inappropriate jokes.
- Offensive images.
- Discriminatory remarks.
- Content that infringes on people's privacy rights.
- Plagiarized content.
- Fake news/false information.
- Defamatory or hateful content.

Employees who choose to be brand ambassadors cannot switch between posting derogatory content and company experiences. People will associate the negative images with your business. So those employees who engage in arguments, controversial discussions, and gossip should refrain from posting about your company altogether.

3. Handling Conflicts

Conflicts about your business on social media can escalate quickly especially when emotions are involved. Employees may want to jump into a discussion to defend the company, but this never ends well. Tell employees to notify you or the relevant personnel or department of any potential online conflicts. In this way, the situation can be handled appropriately to prevent it from getting out of control.

4. Confidentiality and Privacy

Do not disclose the company's confidential information, or personal information of anyone at the company including stakeholders, in online postings or publications. Employees should also be restricted from publicly discussing unannounced company performance, business plans or acquisitions. Sharing these types of information, could result in harm to the Company and legal proceedings against you or the company.

5. Disclaimers

Employees have a right to their own opinions. However, your company social media policy should state that employees are not allowed to speak on behalf of the company unless authorized. For instance, Adidas encourages employees to identify themselves and "make clear that you are speaking for yourself and not the Adidas Group."

You can't spell out every single area to avoid. It would be a never-ending list. The most important thing to remind your employees is that whatever they say on social media, they're representing the company. Encourage employees to use good judgement when posting public content. If social media is used in a proper way, it can really help in your business growth.

SOCIAL MEDIA CUSTOMER SERVICE STRATEGY

Do you have a **social media customer service** strategy in place? Do you use Twitter to stay connected with your customers? If not, the time has come to integrate Twitter into your customer service strategy.

Some companies are struggling with leveraging social media as an opportunity to provide exceptional customer service. They use social media sites but ignore customers comments, complaints, questions, and suggestions. If you don't listen to your customers on social media, they will have a bad impression of you and your business. But if you pay attention to what they say and respond well to their problems and needs, they will embrace your brand. Social media is a powerful tool to offer customer support while strengthening connections at the same time.

Brands that use Twitter to respond to customer complaints and service questions gain product loyalty by making customers feel valued and heard.

Customers are reaching out on Twitter because it's quick, easy, and they feel comfortable communicating via this social network. Gone are the days when people would call a company and complain. Be prepared to respond to them in a helpful and timely manner.

A study conducted by Simply Measured showed that 99% of brands are on Twitter, and 30% of them have a dedicated customer service handle. The average response time was 5.1 hours, with 10% of companies answering within an hour, and 93% of companies answering within 48 hours.

Consider writing a list of FAQs for your team to reference when they get similar questions and queries on Twitter. But make sure your customer service tweets are personalized, to show customers you value them and are interested in solving their concerns. Automated or pasted responses are a big turn-off. Handle negativity with grace and sincerity.

Personalized responses will make your customers feel good and make your brand human. Use emojis, images, and GIFs to show empathy and make the exchange fun (when applicable). It's okay to make people laugh. Don't be afraid to show emotion. You can also re-tweet your fans' posts and offer discounts to customers who are celebrating birthdays or some major milestone.

Some companies are way ahead of the game when it comes to social media customer strategy. JetBlue is known to **be extremely responsive to customers** mentioning their brand. Nike Support is also a prime example of customer service done well. They constantly **respond to followers on Twitter,** whether it's about their apparel or other products.

What is appropriate for a large organization such as Nike isn't necessarily right for a small business. I think some of the bigger companies like Nike need to have separate twitter accounts for support because they have so many different products that it can get overwhelming. For most businesses, I would recommend keeping it all in one Twitter account. By having a single Twitter handle devoted to responding to all customer-service related issues, you make the lives of your customers much easier.

Some companies are good at providing customer service on Twitter, while others drop the ball. Of course, before you start down this road, you need to ensure that you are able to stick with it. Otherwise you will only create your own PR (public relations) disaster. If you're going to provide customer service on Twitter, you'd better show up and check your account. Don't ignore your customers, and don't wait to answer them. Saying "I don't know" doesn't cut it. A quick response that isn't helpful is just as bad as no response at all. I think it's very beneficial to let a customer know you're working on an issue and have seen their tweet rather than saying nothing.

Twitter is an instant response medium, and customers expect extremely quick responses. To make your customer service strategy more effective, you might want to **consider having a plan in place for crises** when the volume of engagement is higher than the norm. You might also want to consider the specific times of the day or night you need to be available. People expect quick responses. However, dedicating a team for Twitter may not be feasible for smaller companies. A great example of how this can be managed is to tweet daily to introduce who is on duty that day and the time they will be online answering queries.

Social media management teams should have standards in place so they can give the customer the best answer initially and quickly. Make sure you have the right people, those who are social media literate and knowledgeable about your product/service – and trust them to do their job. The challenge in larger organizations can be a lack of empowering such staff, which is guaranteed to cause delays and further customer frustration.

Furthermore, some customer service issues simply cannot be handled via social media, so knowing when to take it to Direct Messaging (DM) is a must. It's also very hard to give technical support online because it can be so elaborate, or because personal information must be shared that shouldn't be made public. Ask the customer to DM you, and take the complaint out of public view. This can help with damage control. You can also give a personal email address at the company for the person handling the complaint too, so that the customer feels they have personal contact with the company rather than just talking to a nameless inbox. Where you can, manage expectations on response times as well.

Tammy sent this email:

"I run a Twitter account for a large city corporation, and it shocks me the kinds of things people will think to ask us on social media! Everything from downed trees to graffiti complaints to road construction. But I think that especially with city government, they figure they'll get a faster answer from Twitter than from trying to call a department. And generally, they're right!"

So be prepared for anything, but always be respectful and courteous in your responses even if you think the concerns voiced by customers are absurd or irrelevant.

I think using social media for customer service is smart and has to happen in a world of digitalization. People are going to use social media against you (because invariably, broadcasting complaints via social media is seen as the quickest route to a response), so you need to be on top of it and respond quickly to questions and criticism. If you don't, then it will hurt your brand in the long run. Responding quickly and with useful advice is a very important strategy for any successful company.

CHAPTER ELEVEN

BUILDING A SUCCESSFUL, SCALABLE RESKILLING PROGRAM AT YOUR COMPANY

It can sometimes feel like the world is moving faster than ever before. It seems that every week brings with it a new technology or method of working. As technology and the digital landscape change, some jobs are going to become obsolete while others are going to unexpectedly become crucial. As the future workplace integrates new digital products and services, it will require new processes, systems, and roles to support the digital landscape. Your organization needs to be prepared for these changes.

Generally, businesses would notice changes coming and recruit qualified staff if skills were needed different from those the company already retained. However, this is no longer possible. Progress is happening so quickly that this approach would mean rehiring too frequently. As AI and smart technology take over many repetitive or basic cognitive tasks, the jobs that remain will include both technical skills and the softer skills, such as personal interaction, creativity, and judgment. **The rising demand for these skills means that companies need to develop talent from within.** This approach helps organizations gain new competencies while maintaining in-house operational knowledge, experience, and awareness of company culture.

The rise of automation, robotics, and artificial intelligence is prompting some of the biggest companies — including Amazon, Walmart, and AT&T — to take action. They have developed extensive plans to retrain large segments of their staff. The "future of work" is already here.

A recent report from the McKinsey Global Institute, for one, predicted that by 2030, 375 million people, or roughly 14% of the global workforce, may need to switch occupational categories. Additionally, according to the World Economic Forum, 1.4 million U.S. jobs will be disrupted by technology and other factors between now and 2026. Consequently, more than half (54%) of all employees will require significant reskilling or upskilling by 2022. We'll see hybrid jobs, where workers use skills in combinations rarely demonstrated today.

These are the top 10 hottest jobs of 2019 according to data from jobs software company PayScale:

1. Construction foreman
2. Full-stack software engineer
3. Director of marketing
4. Machine operator
5. Personal shopper
6. Lead UX designer
7. Director of community engagement
8. Maternity nurse (RN)
9. Wealth advisor
10. Email marketing specialist

Last year, 6 out of the top 10 fastest growing jobs within PayScale's employee survey data were all in technology, but this year the results included a much more diverse set of job titles popping up in the data across a broad spectrum of industries.

Some of the same jobs and skills that were in demand in 2019 will continue to see growth into 2020, PayScale research showed. Job areas in tech, such as artificial intelligence, cloud computing, big data, cybersecurity, virtual/augmented reality, and digital marketing will continue to be in demand. PayScale research also found that jobs in the finance, energy, health care, retail, construction, and real estate industries will also be hot in 2020 and beyond.

As organizations face demands for new skills and entirely new occupations arise in the job market, employers will have to overcome these challenges to keep the company competitive. Businesses that have not adopted a digital strategy may find themselves incapable of competing in the evolved market. Now is the time to anticipate and create the experiences that align skills with business needs and goals.

Companies proactively anticipating the future of work dynamics and implementing these strategies are drastically improving their opportunities to improve both the employee and the customer experience, increase speed of innovation, and increase productivity.

A "2019 Deloitte Global Human Capital Trends" report surveyed nearly 10,000 respondents in 119 countries to get their insights into the changing world of work. The Deloitte research suggests that "most organizations look at alternative work arrangements as a transactional solution, not as a strategically important source of talent." The findings also state, "To be able to take full advantage of technology, organizations must redesign jobs to focus on finding the human dimension of work. This will create new roles that we call 'super jobs': jobs that combine parts of different traditional jobs into integrated roles that leverage the significant productivity and efficiency gains that can arise when people work with technology."

WHAT CAN BUSINESSES DO TO STAY AFLOAT IN THIS ERA OF RAPID DISRUPTION?

Change is the constant that today's companies must prepare for, and the skills and jobs that are valuable today may not be the same in a few years' time. One necessary approach is to focus on upskilling and reskilling employees. It's treating your personnel as flexible rather than solely seeing everyone in set roles. This allows you to transform your workforce without consistently having to increase your rate of hire, allowing you to better meet the challenges of modern-day business.

Employers will have to teach employees the new skills that tomorrow's market will demand. It's a process called "reskilling." If you have talented employees, but their area of expertise is becoming less relevant, you can focus on retraining them so you can put their talent to use elsewhere. For instance, retailers will need fewer cashiers and stock workers as automated check-out and robotic inventory scanners are implemented. But some of the workers who have held these roles are already being trained to interact with customers and answer questions, thus improving customer service.

Another area companies should focus on is upskilling. Unlike reskilling, this involves training employees but keeping them in the same positions, rather than changing their jobs. For instance, if automation overtakes certain job duties, upskilling involves training those individuals in new work. You want to select loyal employees with the most potential and offer them the training they need to succeed in this new AI economy.

Reskilling and upskilling will require more than just a new set of instructions. It will require a mindset shift. Learning a new skill requires change. And change creates discomfort, which is aversive. Significant change can also produce significant fear. The discomfort and difficulties of change further push people back into their old habits and mindsets, making new skills even harder to learn. By helping employees build new mindsets, you will be in a far better position to accelerate the reskilling process. You will need to increase information flow.

Practice open and honest two-way communication. Keep employees informed. Don't let them have to hear of upcoming changes through the grapevine. Communicating frequently and openly prevents false speculations from morphing into generally accepted truth and reassures employees that they can count on you for important information. Communicate not just the "how" but the "why." Recognize that the emotional responses to change are normal.

Emotions are a necessary part of the change and transition process. This will require emotional intelligence. Show empathy.

The biggest issue with training is that many companies view it as a one-time event. But learning is much bigger than that. It is an ongoing experience. Learning needs to be continuous. And it's a journey that needs to be carefully planned, documented, scaled — and personalized. The goal is to meet employees where they are and ensure they get where they need to go, rather than just passively engaging with the training program.

As London Business School professor Lynda Gratton points out, the future of work is changing, and careers have become "more fluid, flexible and multi-staged." As a business person, you will need to change the lenses through which you view new hires.

You can develop cross-functional teams in your business by assigning employees secondary roles that are completely different from their primary ones. Have each person on the team rotate as a team leader in addition to performing his or her primary function. For example, someone whose role is software development could learn leadership skills long before he or she might have contemplated applying for the chief technology officer position within the company.

"Your organization is moved by the skills that you have," says Matthew Sigelman, CEO of Burning Glass Technologies, a firm that monitors skills in the workforce in real time. "The evolution of individuals in a company ultimately translates to the evolution of a company."

THE EMPLOYEE OF TOMORROW WILL NEED THESE THREE SETS OF SKILLS:

Technology skills — You don't need to be a data scientist, but you must have basic data literacy to applying artificial intelligence to real-world problems. Consider the use of AI to augment disease diagnosis. In addition to knowing how to use the technology, employees would need domain knowledge as they would have to understand what to look for in health records.

Business skills — including general management, project management and planning, financial management, marketing and sales, strategic thinking, research and analytical skills, and time management skills. Business skills, whether acquired in a formal setting, a training room or even the school of life, are important at whatever level you work within an organization.

Human or soft skills—including communication, empathy, emotional intelligence, critical thinking, adaptability, problem-solving, negotiation, collaboration, leadership, networking, creativity, and innovation. These have become even more essential in a digital organization.

IT STARTS AT THE TOP.

Start by analyzing the workforce to identify skills gaps. This will help you to determine what gaps (staffing and skills) exist between current and projected workforce needs. The goal is to identify gaps so you can help individuals focus on specific areas to reskill or upskill. Assess the skills and capabilities of your current personnel against the capabilities you'll want in the future. By comparing existing skills and competencies with the skills you want people to have, you can make an informed decision about the type of training each individual or team needs and provide it. It is important to know the desired outcomes of the reskilling and upskilling initiative. Outline how the results will be measured or quantified.

Explore adjacencies — jobs that may seem different but share related skills. For example, a skills assessment at a software company revealed that the less-in-demand graphic designer role shared many of the same competencies as the highly-needed digital marketer role.

Then host a planning meeting with key leaders to develop the reskilling and upskilling objectives and strategies. This will require a thorough analysis of how your industry is changing. "Who are our real competitors? What has changed in the marketplace?" Sometimes you don't know who your next competitor might be, so the focus has to be on meeting a potential future market challenge or customer need, rather than just reskilling in reaction to what your competitors are doing. Once you have a clear destination in mind, draft processes and procedures to drive corporate planning for conducting reskilling and upskilling. Determine the number of positions which need more staff. Determine the process for retraining staff (course work, on the job-training, rotational assignments, mentoring). Then work with immediate supervisors / managers to develop reskilling and upskilling performance goals and employee performance plans.

Companies will need dedicated leadership to sustain this effort. For large organizations, this may involve adding a new role to the leadership org chart: A Chief Skills Officer (CSO) or a Chief Learning Officer (CLO). Just as the role of Chief Technology Officer (CTO) became common over the past two decades, the CSO or CLO role may become more common in the decade ahead as organizations need to retrain, redefine, and redeploy workers.

EXAMPLE OF RESKILLING AND UPSKILLING APPROACHES:

COACHING — **Coaching** bridges the gap between current and desired performance levels. Coaching is the continuous two-way feedback between the employee (coachee) and the coach with the intention to work on areas for improvement, help the employee work through challenges, and build the employee's strengths and skills to improve their performance. **It helps employees gain the confidence and direction they need to perform at a high level.** The coach needs to adjust the method of coaching according to the employee's learning style. A good coach will have good communication skills and show empathy and patience when working with the employee. Communication and preparation are important for coaching to be effective.

MENTORING —It is usually a formal or informal relationship between two people, a mentor and a mentee. It's a relationship where someone more experienced (mentor) puts time and energy into a less experienced person's (mentee) development. To make a good match, you need information that asks employees about their career objectives, communication styles, and what they are looking for in a mentor or mentee. Then pair them up according to their responses. It's a two-way street that benefits both mentor and mentee. For example, a digital native may be able to help veteran employees understand how to use social media while being mentored by them. The most compelling learning experiences results in relationship building whereby some members stay in touch informally, sometimes even for years.

JOB SHADOWING — Job shadowing provides valuable exposure by observing an experienced employee in daily activities for a defined period of time. By watching well-trained employees in action, the observer gains exposure to the nuances of a particular job and observes how concepts learned are applied in real-world situations. It allows one to gain a different perspective on their work by learning from others' experiences.

ON-THE-JOB TRAINING — This can include everything from traditional classroom or online courses to new ways of learning, such as intensive bootcamps, team learning, gamification, etc. It is a hands-on method of teaching the skills needed for employees to perform a specific job within the workplace. On-the-job training uses the existing workplace tools and knowledge to teach an employee how to effectively do their job. Therefore, no stand-ins exist that will require an employee to make the training transfer to the workplace. Training takes place as employees perform their actual work.

At one point, I was consulting for a company that was rolling out a new application. The trainer was demonstrating the steps involved from the front on her computer. Employees had to look at the projector screen to follow. It was very confusing as no one else had a computer to go through the actual steps. Don't assume you know how your employees learn. For instance, I learn by hands-on training. Don't just tell me — show me. I need to do the steps myself. Therefore, offer varied forms of learning for different individuals. Your workforce transformation plan must give employees the cognitive support they need to do their jobs with confidence and excellence.

ACCELERATE EVERYONE

To accelerate and sustain skill change in your company, you'll need to create new spaces and new experiences. Many companies are experimenting with incubator or accelerator programs. **Accelerators** advance the growth of an existing company. The focus is on scaling a business while **incubators** develop disruptive ideas with the hope of building out a new business model and company. They are more focused on innovation. In both these activities, individuals with diverse skills convene in multidisciplinary teams to break through siloed thinking. They apply their skills to real challenges the organization faces and create totally new solutions.

IMPLEMENTATION

The second step is the implementation phase which involves the identification of strategies to close gaps. Companies must decide on how to deliver training and one-on-one coaching in rotational stints. Online modules can incorporate multimedia, interactive content, and newer approaches such as virtual reality that can create immersive experiences.

Companies may need dedicated physical spaces that are conducive to learning. Amazon, for instance, is setting up classrooms in some of its fulfillment centers so that warehouse workers can attend certification programs qualifying them for roles as data technicians.

Start small. One company I worked with spent millions on an ill-advised reskilling app and tried to put 3,000 employees through it at once. It didn't end well as the program had to be abandoned. They tried to teach too much too soon, and this set back their reskilling efforts. Start small, whether you work for a five-person company or a global conglomerate. Introducing a limited pilot program allows you to try things out while making adjustments along the way, before everyone's eyes are on you. Chaos creates distrust. This will help to get greater employee buy-in when you are ready to launch the full program.

Moreover, promote transparency so your employees understand where they are now compared to the future skills they'll need to master. Communicate clear goals, progress, and strategies on a regular basis to ensure constant and ongoing improvement in reskilling the workforce. Communication with employees is essential to clear performance expectations and results.

We tend to favor the short term over the long term. That is the reality that we face as humans. This may lead us to focus on performance goals while neglecting learning goals. As we look for ways to reskill and upskill the workforce, we need to focus not only on learning goals as well as performance. Framing work around learning goals increases motivation. And when employees are motivated by learning goals, they will not only acquire more skills that will be useful in the future, they'll increase their skills and abilities in their current performance.

EVALUATION PROGRESS

The third step is evaluating progress. Evaluation is an important step. It begins at the design phase and continues beyond implementation. Create a real-time system that helps monitor progress over time. Determine the necessary performance milestones and measures to track progress toward the completion of goals. This will require you to take corrective action as needed. Capture data and results of reskilling and upskilling and use it to drive future planning and decisions. **To measure the success of your efforts, don't just focus on business metrics, but look into employee**

sentiment metrics. What is the voluntary turnover rate? How do people feel about the changes?

Form Partnerships

You can't do it alone. You really need people who are going to be with you every step of the way. Reskilling workers and preparing the workforce for the future will require help from external sources. Businesses may need to turn to outside partners with educational expertise or capability-building programs. Online providers such as Coursera and Udacity are working with companies to develop customized training programs. Another option is partnering with government entities, policy makers, and academic institutions. Arizona State University, the University of Florida, and Georgia Tech are just a few universities that are working with companies to offer online courses and degree programs. **Develop apprenticeship and internship opportunities to build capabilities and to create a talent pipeline for future workers**; 18% of CEOs globally say they expect to grow their company's workforce through such programs.

Training

Training budgets are often the first things to get slashed during an economic downturn. The most successful companies know that's the wrong direction. Their people need to acquire **more** skills and training to be able to give crucial feedback, serve customers better, and drive the company forward. If you expect employees to give their best, give them the tools and support they need.

Training is the key to success in every position. As Richard Branson stated, "Train people well enough so they can leave. Treat them well enough so they don't want to." Sadly, many companies are guilty of doing neither — TRAINING nor TREATING employees well. Proper training is a great motivator for your employees. It empowers them, and it's shows you trust them. You need to train properly without shortcomings and with proper follow-up to ensure the individual can comprehend the tasks assigned.

Choose Compassion

A 2015 study by Case Western Reserve psychology professor Richard Boyatzis and his colleagues found that coaching with compassion was more effective than coaching for compliance. That's because coaching for compliance generates stress. Asking people to conform with externally-set goals (and under a watchful eye) increases the subsequent stress. Coaching with compassion, on the other hand, pushes people to see the big picture and increases motivation. This approach can help people relax when thinking about their future state and look with optimism at what is to come. Managerial trust is so fundamental to employee engagement and retention. We only get better in any organization when there is open feedback, discussion, and a willingness to learn from mistakes. Employees should never fear feedback, correcting mistakes, or sharing of one's ideas. Such environments are sterile to positive change and creativity, and those companies will be left behind.

Upskilling and reskilling are only part of the solution. It's true we will need to adopt a continuous learning mindset and proactively engage in reskilling if we want our employees' skills to remain relevant in the future. **But we also need to rethink the jobs: redesign the workflow, merge some roles, add positions, and eliminate some.** We also need to be more creative in finding and onboarding people. Finally, we must fill our enterprise with opportunities for continual learning and development.

SECTION THREE:

THE FUTURE WORKPLACE

CHAPTER TWELVE

CREATING A CULTURE OF INNOVATION

It's said there are two rules that should be accepted working under a boss. Rule No. 1 is the boss is always right. Rule No. 2 states that if the boss is wrong, refer to Rule No. 1. The fact is a manager may not be always right. Most people feel the need to be right all the time. I've seen strong companies fail at the hands of a boss who was unwilling to accept others' skills and ideas. When leaders accept that their role is not about having all the answers, a few things happen. They start to ask more questions, they don't take constructive criticism personally, and they see things from a broader perspective.

As a leader, one of the most crucial skills is *having the ability to admit you might not know the answer to every question.* It's okay to say, "I don't know," or "I would need more information before I can make that decision." It is also important to delegate decision making with comments such as, "Let me know what you think. I trust your judgement."

> *"Try never to be the smartest person in the room.*
> *And if you are, I suggest you invite smarter people*
> *or find a different room."*
> ~Michael Dell

Let's take a look at Blackberry, Kodak, and Nokia to illustrate some companies whose leaders thought they were the smartest in the room.

BlackBerry: At its peak, Research In Motion (Blackberry) owned over 50% of the U.S. and 20% of the global smartphone market. Former Co-CEOs Jim Balsillie and Mike Lazaridis were on top of the smartphone world, but sadly, they promoted a culture of closed communication and were unwilling to listen to ideas from below them. In a board meeting, Mike Lazaridis, the BlackBerry co-founder and former chief executive, pointed to a BlackBerry. "I get this," he said. "It's clearly differentiated." Then he pointed to a touchscreen phone. "I don't get this." To turn away from a product that has always done well with corporate customers and focus on selling yet another all-touch smartphone in a market crowded with them was a huge mistake, Lazaridis warned his fellow directors. Some of them agreed. Success had come almost naturally **to** BlackBerry until Apple released the first iPhone and upended their long-held strategy of appealing primarily to email-addicted professionals. This spelled the demise of blackberry.

Kodak: They knew about digital cameras early on. One of their own engineers actually developed the first digital camera — but they kept it quiet. And upper management wouldn't listen to the market research department, who sounded the alarm that the company had only a decade to transition to digital. According to Steve Sasson, the Kodak engineer who invented the first digital camera in 1975, people within the company reacted to his invention by saying, "That's cute — but don't tell anyone about it." Sasson was unable to convince anyone in Kodak of the potential of his invention. Soon Sony and others put inexpensive digital cameras on the market, and Kodak's moment was lost. In 2012, Kodak filed for Chapter 11 bankruptcy. In 1999, CEO George Fisher told the New York Times that Kodak had "regarded digital photography as the enemy, an evil juggernaut that would kill the chemical-based film and paper business that fueled Kodak's sales and profits for decades."

Nokia: In the late 1990s and early 2000s, Nokia was the global leader in mobile phones. Profits were sky-high. The shareholders were happy. However, Nokia didn't grasp the whole concept of software. They defined their business too narrowly as their focus was fixed on hardware. And they got stuck there. Nokia became overly satisfied with their success, and they forgot about the customer. They failed to foster a culture of innovation. They focused on building a better mousetrap when it was time to ditch the mousetrap. They didn't realize *tweaking existing products can only work for so long.* Customers want and expect more.

All of these three companies fell from industry leadership. Why? Their leaders operated in a bubble. Their top executives were all of similar age and backgrounds, and this contributed to their reduced ability to make sense of the changing business environment. The result was inevitable blind spots. **They refused to listen to creative and passionate disruptors.** They were overconfident and became complacent with their leadership position in the marketplace. They engaged in group think and ceased to innovate.

The lessons of these companies are a sad reality that too many companies realize after it is too late. Life is full of constant changes, challenges, and adaptations. The phrase "adapt or die" means we either grow and change or we remain stagnant and perish. It's not the strongest or the most intellectual who survives, but those most able to adapt. And that's even more applicable to technology, as changes in this industry are constant, and trends move at staggering speed. In the late 1990s, Infosys had a program called "Voice of Youth" designed to bring the insights of the under-30 crowd to the attention of the 50-something executive team. **If we don't allow diverse people of all ages and skillsets the opportunity to maximize the value of our team, the probability for success will be diminished.** Diversity can help you stay relevant as you follow the tide and new trends. Blackberry went into denial when the iPhone appeared. They thought it was a fad and they could withstand it. Innovation makes you or breaks you and is indeed the only practical source of your competitive advantage. The biggest threat to success is success itself. Success breeds complacency, and complacency breeds failure. It is difficult to simulate hunger when you are already full. They got into a comfort zone and contentment set in. There is an old saying: "Don't fall in love with your product." That is the hidden threat for so many companies.

If these companies had focused on customer needs and created updated products anticipating those needs, they would still be enjoying market leadership. Instead of selling what the company is producing, it is much better to look forward to the future needs of the customers.

It's important to listen to customers' feedback. This prevents your team from operating in a vacuum and requires managers and employees to talk to unhappy customers and suppliers to understand, address, and resolve their concerns. As the marketing rule of thumb states: "For every person who takes a moment to complain to a business, there are at least ten more customers who are just as angry but don't take the time to voice their objections."

GROUPTHINK

Sometimes, cohesive teams can also be the root of your company's ruin. Tight-knit teams with a strong spirit of cooperation and cohesion can also generate a feeling of invulnerability and a tendency to reject suggestions and recommendations that contradict popular points. And some teams can promote team spirit or enhance the strongest personalities' power and control through peer pressure, guilting or shunning anybody who disagrees. The problem for the successful group (as for the successful company) is one of complacency. The overriding pursuit of consensus above all other priorities develops as a tendency to conform and adhere to the group. The team's success and cohesion become their worst enemy. **Groupthink occurs when members of a group yield to consensus or to the most vocal members and fail to consider all the potential options and consequences.** *Groupthink* is a term first used in 1972 by social psychologist Irving L. Janis and is often tied to poor decisions that arise out of teams or groups. A study by Ryerson University published in the *European Management Journal* finds that despite past beliefs that "group cohesion" can only help a team's performance, it can also have a downside: groupthink. Sean Wise, professor of entrepreneurship at Ryerson, conducted a study of more than 180 teams at a national travel agency. Wise concluded that while social connections boosted a team's performance at first, too much cohesion eventually led to diminished performance. "Too much of a good thing can backfire over time... overly friendly teams lapse into groupthink, inhibiting their pursuit of new ideas and strategies."

Teams are more likely to slip into groupthink, especially when they are successful.

Embrace Diversity: when everyone approves and has the same background or experience, you have fertile ground for groupthink. Opinions will go unchallenged, ideas will go unquestioned, and eventually you will find yourself with a team of passive, change-averse employees who do not care to innovate or identify problems because they are quite comfortable with the status quo. Those who see defects in the way the group operates or who envision potential improvements may be politely ignored or even treated with hostility. Teams that go down this path can fail when their environment changes and they can't or won't adapt. Make sure there is room for diverse views. Create a culture that fosters creative conflict where employees are encouraged to critically analyze situations, thus ensuring a full understanding of all decisions, consequences, and options. Conflict within teams can be good. Conflict handled well can produce constructive ideas. In fact, it is arguably the hallmark of a great team. Set boundaries which are flexible enough to give permission for people to run hard and fast and make decisions that are outside the norm. **Opposing opinions, suggestions, and feedback are to be welcomed.** Assign a "devil's advocate" to ensure all sides of a topic are discussed. Inquiring into views that may not have been articulated can allow better team performance. By asking the team, "What else do we need to consider here?" effective leaders build team trust by encouraging a diversity of opinion. Always ask for and encourage mixed viewpoints. Finally, it may be time to rotate team members who regularly work with and are comfortable with each other if groupthink has become uncontrollable.

Support innovation and invest in learning.

Leaders must lead and inspire change. You can't foster innovation by challenging people to think outside the box and then ignore their ideas and suggestions. Promote taking calculated risks and learning from those mistakes. Our teams will only follow suit when they see their leaders embracing a culture of risk-taking. Such a culture unlocks the potential of your team.

Creative thinking involves risk. Members should be adept at brainstorming ideas and willing to transform routine processes to make them more efficient. Remove the roadblocks that hold back the people you serve, and they will take you further than you imagine. Give your team avenues and time to share ideas and think about their projects offsite. Listen to their problems and facilitate solutions. When problems arise, encourage team members to be solution focused rather than problem focused. Problems should be analyzed for what they can contribute to the collective learning process. **Focus on solving problems and not pinpointing individuals.** When a problem occurs, try to get to the source of it to solve it; the worst thing you can do is start finger pointing. This will unravel the bonds that have already been formed and dampen any interest in forming new ones. Constructive criticism is intended to help the team and its members to increase their efficacy. This allows for coaching and mentoring. Mentor and guide them. Provide support for them to understand and correct their mistakes. Inspire forward thinking; encourage team members to consider how a suggested solution to a problem serves the organization's goals and how it will impact those goals. The organizational structure and infrastructure should be developed to enable the achievement of a vision through the agreed-upon strategies. Your team needs to be organized in a way that allows its creativity to flow. Many organizational structures are outdated or bureaucratic. Too often, the methods for implementing great ideas are far too complex.

To be able to use the full potential of innovation, psychological safety within teams and organizations is essential. Psychological safety is the shared belief that it is safe within the team for interpersonal risk-taking. There is a direct relation between a psychological safe climate and performance of the team. (Edmondson 1999)

An environment has to be created that enables intentional success, and everyone needs to do their part to achieve the desired results. Give them the space to innovate, to be able to make mistakes and start over. In 1989, Steve Jobs had already pointed out the importance of the right team during an interview for Fortune Magazine: "Innovation has nothing to do with how many research and development (R&D) dollars you have. When Apple came up with the Mac, IBM was spending at least 100 times more on R&D. It's not about money. It's about the people you have, how you're led, and how much you get it."

Thinking out-of-the box is what you need from the team members. People are motivated to work for an organization where their professional and personal aspirations can be fulfilled. Give them the scope of the project and autonomy to execute tasks. **The acceptance of trial and error opens the door to ingenuity** which leads to innovation and growth. Create an environment where failure or saying, "I don't know" is not seen as a weakness. The ability to be honest and open will strengthen your team's cohesiveness. Empower your employees. Allow them to explore and experiment. A leader who can provide the right amount of room for experimentation can awaken the power of creativity. When your team feels a sense of freedom, they will come up with some great ideas. If they fail, ask them to incorporate the lessons learned from failures to keep moving forward.

In building a strong team and company culture, change will be inevitable. Changes can center on systems, processes, or equipment that need upgrading. Be transparent when going through change. Let your team know the impact it will have on the organization and on them on a personal level. Furthermore, invest in learning. Provide team members with the opportunity to learn and grow, and to undertake work they find meaningful and rewarding. **Understand that the team's growth is your growth and the organizations' growth**. Nurturing a culture of innovative thinkers takes advantage of the shared knowledge and experience of everyone in the company. It also helps to bring natural leaders to the forefront whose skills can then be better utilized within the business. Support professional development through appropriate conferences, training workshops, and seminars. This will help your people develop their abilities while enabling them to make a greater contribution to the company. They will become more valuable to you, the team, and the organization.

GOOD LEADERS DON'T TRY TO BE THE SMARTEST PERSON IN THE ROOM.

As much as people appreciate smart people for their ability to teach and to help, no one likes a know-it-all. So, listen more than you speak. Leaders who show some vulnerability are more authentic and approachable to their team. Employees will want to provide feedback and share ideas because they know it will not fall on deaf (or judgmental) ears. In the end, you have a more engaged and productive team when you have a team that feels valued.

Working for a boss who needs to be always right can be very frustrating and demotivating. Such bosses don't give employees opportunities to grow and develop, and they often resort to micromanaging. **The role of any leader within a corporate framework is to build up the team and to encourage growth.**

With advances in technology and unprecedented levels of change, leaders will need to hire people who are smarter than they are and draw on the diversity and expertise of everyone in the room. This can be the difference between success and failure. Ultimately, **your aim as a leader is to drive growth and innovation by surrounding yourself with a diverse team with skills that complement yours.** This takes humility and wisdom. My goal is to hire people who are smarter than I am and give them the freedom to do the work; in the end, they'll make me look good and make my job easier. Select the right people, provide them with the proper tools, and get out of their way.

The sad thing about today's corporate world is the internal politics that some people are willing to play in order to get ahead. It is dreadful to work under a manager who is more worried about throwing their weight around than building relationships. Instead of pulling others up, many managers choose to push people down. **Your most valuable asset is your people**. And how you treat them is literally the difference between *success and failure*. Micromanaging, blaming, and holding people back will only lead to a culture of distrust, high turnover, low morale, and reduced creativity.

The corporate world is plagued with managers but lack leaders. Bad bosses use fear and intimidation while leaders rely on influence and inspiration. Over the course of my career, I only had one manager who was truly a leader. He made quite an impact on me and deeply influenced my leadership style. It is a rare individual who excels in both managing and leading. Great leaders don't surround themselves with "yes employees" or need their ego to be constantly stroked. They consistently seek opportunities to inspire and motivate others. They invest in people. Such managers push employees to grow and develop in order to reach their full potential.

Developing leadership skills is a lifetime project. It's too easy, as a manager, to feel like you have to be the one who knows everything. Great leaders recognize that they need to keep learning. "You are only as strong as your weakest link." Build a strong team, and surround yourself with smart, passionate, and highly competent people. The greater your success, the more you need to stay in touch with fresh and diverse opinions and perspectives, and welcome honest feedback. Additionally, *treat everyone with respect* at all times whether they are employees, customers, suppliers, or partners. *Be humble.* Real humility encourages subordinates to share their suggestions and recommendations with you in an atmosphere of safety.

Leaders who cultivate other leaders multiply their own success. Some managers think that developing potential leaders could threaten their authority or position. But failing to optimize the talent of others is setting yourself, and the company, up for failure. It's not about you. The ego must go. It's about identifying and appreciating the differences each team member brings to the table and putting it to full use. Your success is a result of your team. Play to your team's strengths, and everyone wins!

Leadership is not about position or power. **Being the leader means that you have been placed in a position to serve others.** It is about how we treat people, how we make decisions, and the example we set. It's about looking for every opportunity to appreciate and inspire others. Leadership is not a right but a privilege. You are privileged to be in a position where you can direct, shape, and positively influence the lives of others.

Many managers get enthralled with the control and authority which comes with positional power. Rather than making people better off, they leave a trail of destruction in their path. It's disheartening working for a manager who is more concerned about pushing his/her weight around, instead of building relationships.

"No matter how educated, talented, rich, or cool you believe you are, how you treat others tells all. Integrity is everything!"

A manager's job is to provide guidance and support. It's facilitating a healthy environment where employees can perform at their best. Micromanaging is the opposite of empowerment, and it creates toxic work environments. It chokes the growth of the employee and the organization, and it fosters mediocrity.

When you empower employees, you promote vested interest in the company. An empowered workforce is more engaged.

BE HUMBLE

The stories are all too common: After years of hard work, many leaders let success go to their head. They gain satisfaction from people stroking their ego. Little do they know; humility is an incredibly powerful choice. It is a critical success factor. "With pride comes disgrace, but with humility comes wisdom." (Proverbs 11:2). Scientific inquiry into the power and effectiveness of humility has shown that it offers a significant "competitive advantage" to leaders. Leaders are more powerful when they're humble.

Humble leaders show vulnerability which makes them more approachable. Such leaders don't point fingers or divert blame and are willing to listen to differing opinions. If you don't listen or won't admit you're wrong, you can't grow. If you don't grow, your business won't grow. And success requires continuous growth.

Humble leaders are great listeners. Listening shows you care. Humility and emotional intelligence go hand in hand.

Humility is a sign of strength, not weakness. **When you can shift your focus from taking to giving, from hoarding the credit to recognizing the contributions of others, it shows inner strength.** We know success doesn't happen in a vacuum. It is a team effort. Learn to appreciate and value the people around you.

"Pride makes us artificial and humility makes us real" -Thomas Merton. Humility, if consistently pursued and prudently polished over time, is a *powerful force for good, that helps us to reach and sustain success.*

In reality, who in their right mind would rather be the one serving rather than being served? Is it not the whole point of life to get ahead, to become influential, someone who is waited on and attended to by others? Many people associate humility with being weak or ineffective, and most don't admire others for being humble. Humility seems very much lost in our self-centered culture, and narcissistic, ego-driven leaders have become the norm.

The average Fortune 500 CEO makes $10-$15 million per year, is surrounded by immense executive perks, and has hundreds of employees under their control. However, despite their lavish perks and pay, the average Fortune 500 CEO lasts less than five years. In a *Harvard Business Review* article, author Jim Collins postulated a higher level of leader characterized by humility and a fierce resolve.

He stated that "The *X-Factor* of great leadership is not personality; it's *humility*."

Humility is the gateway for other traits, such as empathy, authenticity, and integrity. Humble leaders are great listeners and welcome feedback. When we look at some of the world's greatest leaders whose influence seems to have strengthened in their absence, humility is one common trait they embodied.

According to a study from the University of Washington Foster School of Business, humble people tend to make *the most* effective leaders and are more likely to be high performers in both individual and team settings, according to associate professor, Michael Johnson. "Our study suggests that a 'quieter' leadership approach -- listening, being transparent, aware of your limitations, and appreciating co-workers' strengths and contributions, is an effective way to engage employees," Johnson, and fellow researchers, Bradley Owens, and Terence Mitchell, write in the study.

Jewish Rabbi Nilton Bonder explained it beautifully when he said, **"Many people believe that humility is the opposite of pride when, in fact, it is a point of equilibrium**. The opposite of pride is actually a lack of self-esteem. A humble person is totally different from a person who cannot recognize and appreciate himself as part of this world's marvels."

"*Humility* is a strange thing; the minute you think you've got it, you've lost it" —Sir Edward Hulse. *One story goes*, a small city wanted to identify and reward its meekest resident. A survey was taken which ultimately identified the person. In a ceremony attended by all the dignitaries, the meekest person was presented with a medal on which were engraved the words, "The Meekest Man in Town." However, the next day, they had to take the medal away from him because he kept wearing it and showing it off!

Alexander, Julius Caesar, Napoleon, and Genghis Khan, amongst others, all saw leadership in terms of power and authority over others.

"Sense shines with a double lustre when it is set in humility.
An able and yet humble man is a jewel worth a kingdom."
~William Penn

The X-Factor of Great Leadership

To be a great developer of people, you must embody humility because taking people to the height of their potential may mean they will eventually pass you by. **Leading with humility means focusing on others and practicing servant leadership.** True leaders always aim to serve rather than be served.

Are You Humble?

1. Is your vocabulary mainly comprised of "I" rather than of "we" and "us?" Do you put the interests of the team before your own? Humble leaders *consistently seek opportunities to help and to serve others*. Humility arises out of strength, not weakness. To be humble, one needs confidence and self-restraint. Humility is the ceasing to fight for your own agenda, but rather for that of the multitude. The humble leader is not occupied with self. The humble person is one who has learned to control self, which takes true strength. Many leaders mistake controlling, dominating, or other harsh behaviors for strength. Humility takes strength and is the opposite of pride and arrogance; it is the mastery of self-leadership. This is not to suggest that humble leaders are soft or unwilling to make tough decisions. They do make tough decisions, but for the greater good of their organizations. Humility develops from an inner sense of self-worth. Humble leaders are grounded by the principles by which they lead. Ultimately, they know that to lead is to serve others: their customers, employees, stakeholders, communities, etc. It requires acts of courage, such as taking personal risks so that others may benefit.

"True humility is not thinking less of yourself;
it is thinking of yourself less."
~C.S. Lewis

2. Are you boastful? Do you take all the credit for success? Humility promotes self-reflection and self-awareness, as you are able to honestly assess your own strengths and weaknesses. Being honest about the skills you possess and the value you can bring to clients and a company is the best way to avoid getting in over your head. Humility helps to keep us grounded and appreciative of what we have, and it helps us to see that there is a greater need than our own self-referencing desires. Humble leaders do not take advantage of their positional power. In the long run, fulfillment doesn't come from power, but through service. Leaders obtain influence not via position, but by building relationships with others through consistent empathy and integrity. They are not defined by their achievements (good or bad) and can easily separate who they are from what they do. When their accomplishments attract praise, they are quick to acknowledge the contribution of others and easily give them credit. Additionally, they don't shift the blame when they fail. **Proud leaders seem to have all the right answers; humble leaders seem to have all the right questions.** Humility means being open to the fact that I don't know everything, and that I can learn something from everyone.

3. How do you handle criticism or opposition? Are you open to other people's perspectives? How do you speak about others, including competitors? Narcissistic leaders take things personally and may speak without careful consideration. Humble leaders are able to accept expert input that may or may not agree with their own thoughts, and make good decisions based on all of the inputs, not just those that confirm their own bias. They are able to abandon their pet plans in favor of superior alternatives. Humble people recognize boundaries and respect others. Everyone takes notice of how praise and blame are handed out. Make sure your feedback doesn't demean anyone. Humility promotes an environment that values empathy. Listen while receiving feedback and have respect for others. Humility is manifested in how we relate to others. It is revealed in words, attitudes, and actions. *Humble leaders reward in public and discipline in private.*

4. How do make people feel when they are around you? Insignificant, great, empowered? If you can strip away the surface of pride, you show a human side. Humble leaders are not afraid to show their vulnerability, which makes them more human and approachable. Leaders are difficult to be around if they *always* have to be the smartest person in the room. That's important because people want to work with, and work for, leaders they like. People should be straightforward with you; they should not be afraid of you. Draw people by your humility, *not by your position and power.* Humble leaders look at others as equals, not as subordinates. Humble people allow others to assert themselves because they are already assertive. Humility reminds us that it's not about us, and it reminds us to focus on what really matters. Such leaders are polite, and not arrogant or egotistical. They don't allow their position of authority to make them feel that they're better than anyone else. We gravitate to such leaders because they make everyone they come in contact with, feel valued no matter their level, from the janitor to the Chairman of the Board. In difficult times, people rely on humble leaders even more to get them through crises.

5. Do you admit when you are wrong? Humility doesn't mean a lack of confidence. It is being confident enough to admit that you were wrong. Leaders are continuous learners, always willing to learn new things. If you can't admit you're wrong, you can't grow. Leaders must be willing to say when they are wrong and admit their mistakes. Humble leaders are great listeners and usually possess high emotional intelligence. *They are not afraid to show their vulnerability, which makes them more human and easier to relate to.* An apology is the sign of a strong leader. Great leaders are aware of their own imperfections, so they forgive others' mistakes. It's demotivating working for a manager who does not stand up for their team. If you make a mistake, that kind of manager quickly turns into judge, jury, and executioner. It's hard to feel passion for a job when you experience this sort of treatment. Great leaders need to care about and respect those around them no matter their level; they should possess the ability to offer forgiveness to those that have offended them. They also need to be able to see themselves for who they are and be willing to make the necessary changes.

6. Do you take yourself too seriously? Are your employees having fun at *work*? Are you having fun at work? Sometimes work can get so serious everyone forgets to lighten up and laugh a bit. **People appreciate leaders who not only work hard, but who are also fun to be around.** Humor is one of the secrets of great leadership. It can open your mind and widen your perspective. Humble leaders are strong but light-hearted. This helps promote an upbeat atmosphere. They can laugh at themselves and can see the funny side of situations, which helps to put everyone at ease. Humor is a great way to win over and influence a team. It minimizes status distinctions between leaders and followers, and it encourages interaction. That is less true of an arrogant leader, who is more likely to make fun of others. The humble leader, however, will often use self-critical humor, which is a great leveller, for minimizing status differences. The attributes of self-critical humor should include having an honest and humble view of one's self and an appreciation and respect for others. And when humility is combined with self-respect, the self-critical aspect is never taken too far. Good leaders know how to laugh at themselves in a way that unites rather than divides. Leaders who use humor well allow people to feel comfortable around them. It is humanizing and puts others at ease. And those leaders tend to be much more approachable than the person who never laughs, or who laughs at you.

Humor can act as a catalyst to influence and inspire others. It helps foster an upbeat atmosphere that encourages interaction, engagement, brainstorming, and creative thinking, all of which leads to greater productivity. Laughter brings to light the real person behind the professional façade, thereby building trust. Humor works as a bridge to build bonds.

Organizationally, research shows cultures that incorporate humor are more resilient. Humor is serious business. Recent Gallup data reveals that people laugh significantly more on weekends than on weekdays. Further, this data suggests that as people get older, they stop smiling and laughing as frequently. It's time we tried to bring workplace humor back into the workplace and in our lives. When appropriately used (not offensive, discriminatory, or insulting), a sense of humor can create lasting positive memories. Laugh and smile more. The results will be evident in the bottom line.

7. Do you embrace succession planning? Humble leaders share their knowledge and enjoy watching their followers grow and develop. Business scholar James Collins and his research team conducted a five-year historical analysis of companies that had made a sustained transition from good to great. Succession planning was a problem. Collins writes, **"In over three quarters of the comparison companies, we found that executives set their successors up for failure, chose weak successors, or both."**

> *"We rise by lifting others."*
> ~Robert Ingersoll

Humility is an essential quality for authentic leaders. People trust them because they know they are genuine and honest. Lacking those qualities in leaders leads to distrust and fear. When we teach people to be afraid, they are being held captive. Narcissist leaders want complete control of everything and they often lead by fear. Such leaders control others by ambiguity; they keep others guessing by not disclosing information or revealing the truth.

Humility is a virtue, but on the other hand, can you have *too much* of it? *Some argue that too much humility can be a bad thing.* The 12th century philosopher Maimonides believed that the "middle way" was the best way to live. Humility must not be confused with shyness or allowing others to trample all over us. Developing humility is a process leading to a higher consciousness. While humility can help you become a more effective leader, it also serves as an antidote to protect us from the poisonous effects of an unrestrained ego; it dispels harmful pride, and it negates the self-absorption of narcissism. Arrogance will betray an immaturity to power. The ego loves praise, clouds our judgement, and blinds us with a false sense of invincibility, leading to poor decisions and a breakdown of relationships. Humility, on the other hand, allows us to set our egos aside. When consistently pursued and prudently polished over time, it is a powerful force for good that helps to sustain success and draws people to us. If we have a root of humility firmly planted within us, it's not something we can turn off or on. It's the natural overflow of a pure, sincere heart.

CREATING A CULTURE OF INNOVATION

AI opens a new set of performance opportunities. Companies are finding new sources of value from data assets to deliver new capabilities and services to customers. Leaders need to think holistically and continually be seeking out new opportunities. Innovative collaborations, such as data collaborations, are elevating customer experiences and helping companies stay relevant in a rapidly transforming digital landscape.

- **Be Adaptable**

Adaptability means being ready to innovate and respond to opportunities and threats as they appear. It's being open to new ideas, changing an opinion or course of action when the situation warrants, and being able to effectively communicate that revised opinion to relevant stakeholders. In an AI age, changing one's mind, which can often be regarded as a sign of weakness, should be perceived as a strength when it improves decision making.

- **Make Diversity a Priority**

Data science is complex and relies on the interplay of people and processes. Leaders should encourage diversity not only in the creators but in data sets and methods for more accurate and balanced insights. Diverse teams produce better solutions to complex problems. Diversity can prevent the algorithmic biases that can ruin products and damage brands.

- **Invest in Understanding the Technology**

Organizations will adopt new technologies in increasingly shorter cycles. Leaders will have to make their organizations agile enough to respond quickly to trends and disruptions. Take a proactive approach, and educate yourself on the latest applicable AI and digital tools available in the marketplace. Stay on top of the revolution to harness its power to guide your organization towards success.

- **Communicate a Clear and Compelling Vision**

The greatest leaders of our time could articulate a vision so clearly that it seemed real and attainable. Martin Luther King Jr.'s "I Have A Dream" speech is a perfect example of this. In the AI age, characterized by rapid disruption, a clear vision is even more important because there is less clarity among employees about where we should go, what we should do, and why. We need to communicate the why, how, and what — why AI is important to the company's goals, how it can augment their work, and what every employee's role will be. Leaders with a clear vision have meaningful answers to these questions and communicate them in an effective way. By consistently and clearly communicating their vision, and engaging employees in the conversation, leaders can improve employee engagement and inspire greater productivity.

- **Develop Emotional Intelligence (EQ)**

Technology companies are working hard to develop "emotional artificial intelligence." However, machines cannot recognize human emotions beyond the surface level. They lack the emotional intelligence that only humans currently possess. EQ plays a big part in the development of wisdom. Knowing how to react and what to say, and what not to say in some situations, can make all the difference. EQ can be developed. You can take workshops, learn to respond and not react, practice listening, or just consistently practice putting yourself in other people's shoes. Developing your EQ skills will help you to identify, assess, and manage your emotions in a way that creates a positive impact. You are handicapped in relating to others to the degree that you don't understand your own emotions.

Leaders must evolve their thinking and try new things if they are to survive and grow.

Unlocking the innovative potential of your people comes down to a mix of management approaches, strategy, shared values, and resources.

There was a time when business leaders thought the biggest decision in their "digital strategy" was whether to build a website or an app first. The responsibility rested with the information technology team or the marketing mavens, and the goal was to convert new customers or create new tools. With today's accelerated pace in business, coupled with the mounting uncertainty in our economic climate, the business leader now has a very important role in digital transformations. (And it's not just approving the budget for it!). Today's leaders must be more than numbers, and they need to have an innovation mindset.

Smart leaders know they have to maintain a competitive edge within their industries in order to achieve and sustain success. But innovative ideas that lead to success don't just happen – it takes a deliberate approach to encourage innovation from your staff. So how does a leader encourage innovation in the workplace?

Albert Einstein had it right when he said: "We cannot solve our problems by using the same kind of thinking we used when we created them."

Innovation is the backbone of every successful organization. The need for constant innovation is a given in today's business environment. While a new product or concept can propel a company to the top of the market, in this era of steep competition, that advantage is often short-lived. Innovation is not a one-off but an ongoing event. it's the continual incremental innovations made by employees that give a company the sustained growth it needs. 63%

of companies are hiring chief innovation officers (CIOs), yet many still struggle to create a truly innovative culture across the board. It starts at the top.

Leaders create the environment that fosters sustained innovation. The commitment to establishing the psychological safety and support that employees need to innovate starts at the top.

10 STRATEGIES FOR SUSTAINED INNOVATION

1. Hire for culture.

Hire team members who understand your vision and align with your culture. This doesn't mean only hiring people who always agree with you. Too many managers are so obsessed with getting the job done that they sacrifice culture. Sometimes we tend to let a high performer's competency eclipse their lack of civility and people skills. But such top performers are destructive to other colleagues and create a toxic culture in your company. When the bosses ignore or indulge a jerk, it can be tremendously destructive of employee morale. **"What you allow, you promote."** You want people who are passionate about their work, believe in your products, and are willing to work as a team. You want people at your company who will truly care. Look for imagination and creativity when recruiting new employees. Adding people that want to improve your product will be the most beneficial for your company. Additionally, encourage diversity. Put together a team of different backgrounds, ages, and competencies. Encourage different perspectives. Having a group with a diverse set of ideas and problem-solving approaches helps unleash creativity.

2. Build creative time into the schedule. Set aside time for innovation.

You can't force creativity, but the right environment will put your team in the right mindset to find imaginative solutions. In a survey by Robert Half, 35% of chief financial officers said the greatest roadblock to organizational breakthroughs is a lack of innovative ideas. Executives polled also cited excessive bureaucracy (24%) and being bogged down with daily tasks or putting out fires (20%) as other major barriers. Innovation needs time, and with so much on their plate, many employees feel they have none to spare. When people feel overworked, their last priority is trying to be creative; they just want to complete their assigned tasks. **People are as innovative as you allow them to be**. The hustle and bustle of our daily office life can break concentration: emails, phones, meetings - the distractions are endless. Set aside time for innovation and create inclusive development space. Employees must know it's something management is committed to and wholeheartedly supports. Make sure you have processes and events to capture ideas. Some companies have hackathon sessions, innovation days; others have a weekly brainstorming session where out-of-the-box concepts are explored. It's allotting time for staff time to work on projects and develop and test new ideas.

The inventor of the Post-It Note came up with the idea during work time that was allotted for employees to pursue their own ideas and creations. Since 1948, 3M has given employees "15 percent time" for this purpose. Google, for example, allocates a notional 20% of time for their workers to develop their own ideas for the company and work on personal, intrapreneurial projects. Companies need to be willing to experiment and to look outside their teams, outside the company, and outside the industry for ideas that have worked elsewhere.

3. Develop a tolerance for risk and failure.

Innovation is a risk. If employees are constantly worried that they might lose their jobs, they will be risk adverse. Innovation is more about trying, failing and succeeding. We won't hit 100% of the shots we take. Accept failure and make it the norm. **Encourage risk-taking and experimentation** — don't punish employees who try new ideas that fail. Failures must be seen as important steps in the learning process. Tolerating a certain degree of failure is a necessary part of growth. Be careful about how you react when things go wrong, because employees will take note and will hold back on making suggestions if they're worried about negative consequences.

Innovation can only thrive in an environment of trust. People shouldn't be afraid to challenge the status quo. Managers need to trust their employees. Goals must be communicated clearly and employees need to have a flexible framework in which to operate. If a manager has a big ego and is always dismissing ideas, employees won't come up with new ideas again. That's why market leaders like Netflix and Amazon never shy away from acknowledging their past failures. Employees who trust their bosses are more likely to take calculated risks that have potential value for the company. Managers must be open minded, have a high level of emotional intelligence, and be humble.

> *"If the size of your failures isn't growing, you're not going to be inventing at a size that can actually move the needle."*
> ~Jeff Bezos

4. Reduce bureaucracy.

Management structures tend to create barriers to small-scale enhancements. A strict hierarchy stunts growth and innovation. An innovative culture must simultaneously be met with a structure to support it. **Bureaucracy slows down action and is a serious barrier to innovation.** While hierarchical ladder structures were a good fit for industrial age corporations, success in the digital age requires collaboration, flexibility, and agility. As organizations adopt more agile policies and processes to speed up decision making and adapt to change, this can only be effective by simultaneously creating flatter structures.

Many companies are implementing a flat management approach, allowing employees to break down silos and barriers between work areas. Others have adopted a combined approach of centralized, top-down management styles and decentralized, bottom-up management styles. The best thing is to make it known to employees that they won't be boxed in by rigid rules; they can focus on building the next game-changing feature. Consider which internal processes or systems might be stifling innovation. Look for ways to streamline the process so people can see their good ideas in action quickly. Different teams across different business units using different tools for different purposes doesn't result in collaboration. Real collaboration requires employees to work together as cross-functional teams.

Toyota's Production System has constant improvement as part of front-line employees' job descriptions. The company gives quality management and innovation authority to these workers. They can make adjustments in their work. If the innovation works, it's incorporated into operations. In most cases, the company rewards the team that came up with the improvement.

5. Instill a sense of ownership.

Give employees a reason to care. They shouldn't just think of innovation as something only senior management thinks about. Not every innovation has to come from the top down. **Innovation is the lifeblood of every organization and should be a part of everyone's job description.** An ownership mentality creates a powerful incentive for creative thinking. Frequent outside-the-box problem-opportunity identification can reinvigorate the workplace. When employees see how their individual efforts affect company performance, they tend to be actively engaged. Employees who are involved early on in plans and given the initiative to take action will be motivated to see them through to completion. Southwest Airlines gave pilots the autonomy to design a plan to reduce fuel consumption. Who better to come up with this than the people who actually fly the planes? Pilots eagerly participated because they understood the impact this had on the bottom-line and ultimately, on their own futures.

As I mentioned in an earlier chapter, I once had a boss who invited feedback and then punished me for offering it. It was just lip service. I quickly learned loyalists and sycophants were appreciated, while realists were punished. They built a culture of "yes employees." I knew I had so much to offer, yet I couldn't. Six months later, my boss was fired. He made a mistake on a proposal that cost the company its biggest client. This could have been easily avoided if he had just asked for honest input.

6. Inspire people to voice their opinions.

Cognitive diversity in the workplace is vital. Looking at ways of completing tasks can keep a workplace vibrant and more open to new ideas. "80% of ideas are in the heads of front-line people." — Alan G. Robinson This means less than 20% of business innovation is generated from members of the C-Suite. Front-line workers are doing the work. They see many problems and opportunities that you don't. When given the chance, they'll come with a solution to business problems. If you are willing to take the advice of employees and listen to their suggestions on how to improve operations, there will be a noticeable increase of new ideas.

7. Get your customers involved.

If you don't, you will just be innovating for the sake of it. Embrace co-creation and open innovation opportunities. Your loyal customers are the most likely people to have great ideas for new products and services. Starbucks ran its "My Starbucks Idea" portal from 2007 to 2017, encouraging customers and fans to share their ideas and suggestions for making the company's beloved products even better. They gave fans a reason to participate in the exercise, and if their ideas were a success, they would be eligible for monetary compensation. Starbucks enabled users to vote and comment on ideas they liked. If the idea gathered enough traction, or if the Starbucks administrators thought it was great, it could then be adopted by the company. This resulted in top-selling Starbucks products like hazelnut macchiatos and pumpkin spice lattes, and gave Starbucks a new way to market their products to their most valuable customer segment. It also helped them to build a valuable community of superfans for market research purposes.

LEGO is another great example here. The block toy company was facing a tough financial situation in the early 2000s but responded to these challenges by going on an innovation binge. The company began incorporating input from groups of young children in the design process. Through a mixture of innovation, co-creation, and customer collaboration, LEGO gradually reclaimed its status as a market leader.

Spending the time and effort upfront to co-create with teams, and customers - is a key success factor to determine what digital capabilities should be leveraged to support business objectives. The most successful companies are customer centric. **Customer-centricity is not only about developing stellar products and services; it also means providing a great experience throughout the customer journey.**

The main focus of your digital transformation efforts must be your customers; the transformation must solve their "dissatisfaction" and create a positive experience with your company. The other integral point to measure the success of a digital transformation with customers is to have clear metrics of adoption and reduction of the use of traditional methods (e.g., number of orders completed online vs phone or personally). Today, new technologies place few limits, so one's view of the desired outcome will determine the degree of impact. Customers are the best judges of how effective your transformation is, and they decide if they continue purchasing your products and services. Digital transformation puts the consumer at the center of everything the organization does.

Always seek to exceed customer expectations every step of the way.

"**Netflix** did not kill blockbuster. Ridiculous late fees did.

Uber did not kill taxi business. Limited access and fare control did.

Airbnb did not kill the hotel industry. Limited availability and pricing options did.

Apple did not kill the music industry. They did it to themselves by forcing people to buy full-length albums.

Amazon did not kill other retailers. Poor customer service and experience did.

Technology by itself is not the real disruptor. Being **non-customer centric** is the biggest threat to any business." - Alberto Brea

8. Implement ideas.

Companies must demonstrate an appetite for new ways of doing things. Don't just tell employees their ideas are always valued — show them. If you ask employees for ideas and do nothing, no one will take you seriously. It takes putting their suggestions into action. Vodafone runs a "1,000 Small Things" initiative whereby employees are asked to make one small improvement within their daily job. The company follows through with the input from employees. You also must eliminate projects and processes that don't work. This is what Peter Drucker calls "creative abandonment."

9. Reward innovation.

Make sure recognition and rewards are consistent. The best way to keep employees working toward success is to reward their efforts. Appropriate incentives can play a significant role in encouraging staff to think creatively. Goal setting and compensation systems should be created to foster the culture and behaviors you want everyone to express. Employees thrive when they know their work is valued and they feel appreciated. There are numerous ways to compensate excellence. Timely recognition and acknowledgements of a person's behavior, effort, and accomplishment is often sufficient motivation for the person to support the organization's goals and values beyond expectations. Companies should look to reward motivated employees who put in the extra effort and deliver results. If they don't, those valuable employees will soon be somebody else's valuable employees. It feels good to do a great job. It feels even better when it is noticed by the boss. Internal motivators are wonderful, but praise by someone who is respected always helps.

Recognition for a job well done doesn't always have to be about big bonuses or financial rewards. It can be in time off, paid leave, freebies, or flexible working hours. Promote the value of collaboration and encourage a team-first atmosphere. Companies that successfully foster a culture of innovation focus on positive reinforcement to establish the culture they want. Westin Hotels rewards employees regularly for their best ideas by providing an all-expenses-paid vacation. Companies should come up with meaningful ways to thank employees for their contributions and efforts supporting the innovation process.

10. Promote a culture of innovation and continuous learning.

The Leesman Index, which examines the effect workplaces have on employees, found that the highest performing workplaces create environments that capitalize on existing knowledge within the organization and facilitate internal knowledge transfers. Lead by example. Document your triumphs and failures for incoming employees. Promote **openness and knowledge sharing** between individuals and teams. Incorporate continual improvement as one of the foundational values upon which your company operates. This attitude should be pervasive throughout the business. Ignore titles and let everyone share their ideas. Be specific about the ideas you want to address. For example, ask for ways to improve a specific work process or ways to reduce the cost of a specific service. Ask for anonymous feedback to make it easier for introverts to contribute as well. Create a digital suggestion box. Employees are most innovative when they are engaged in their process. There are lots of ways you can encourage your employees to broaden their skills. It's a win-win situation, too, since they benefit from new opportunities for advancement and you benefit from having innovative employees which translates into improved products and services.

Encourage Personal Development

Ensure your employees have access to courses, training, and tools to learn and cultivate their skills. **Create an office library.** I bring great books that I have read into the office and add them to our library. I also encourage my employees to do the same. Over the years, we've built up a library of 100+ life-improving books that everyone is encouraged to take out and learn from. It's also important that employees have enough time to commit to their learning and development so they can be the best they can be.

Tesla has a reputation for being unconventional. Tesla's employee handbook, titled "The Anti-Handbook Handbook," document sets a high bar for employees. It reveals how it expects employees to push boundaries and help the company succeed.

"Your #1 job — everyone's #1 job — is making this company a success," the document says. "If you see opportunities to improve the way we do things, speak up even if these are outside your area of responsibility. You have a personal stake in Tesla's success so make suggestions and share your ideas. Your good ideas mean nothing if you keep them to yourself." Working to improve Tesla should take precedence over the conventions of office politics, the document also says. "You can talk to anyone without anyone else's permission. Moreover, you should consider yourself obligated to do so until the right thing happens." The main idea is that a Tesla employee is expected to do everything in their power to maximize their performance, even if that means reaching out directly to CEO Elon Musk. -Tesla Anti-Handbook Handbook by Insider Inc. on Scribd. Talking to the CEO in most companies is discouraged, in fact you can get fired for skipping the chain of command. Elon Musk is certainly not a conventional CEO.

As someone with a background in HR, I have to say this is one of the best employee handbooks I have ever seen. I may not agree with everything, but in terms of driving a culture of engagement, creativity and innovation — this is how you do it. Just look at the comparison — FORD shares: $8.25. TESLA shares: $805.00.

A culture of innovation takes time to build. It works best when leadership sets the example. An environment of regular recognition and positive reinforcement helps employees take risks, see failure as a learning experience, and become more invested in the process of continuous innovation.

CHAPTER THIRTEEN

REIMAGINING WORK: BUILDING THE WORKPLACE OF THE FUTURE

It was six months into my new job. I received an email that I was needed in the conference room immediately. I went into this meeting and was ambushed by three other managers. All three of them have a problem with my leadership style. One of them tells me, in a condescending tone, "Brigette, we know you are new here, and you need to understand management is not on the same level with staff. You need to make this distinction clear; you give them too much freedom."

I was shocked. I realized in that moment that I didn't have a future there because this type of culture was endorsed from the top. It's sad that in many organizations, managers think that to be effective, they need to micromanage employees. My team was delivering excellent results, but their focus was on control. Yet this same company would bring in external consultants to figure out why turnover was high and to boost engagement.

Trust is the foundation of any successful relationship, whether professional or personal, and when it's broken, it is extremely hard to repair. When employees feel they can't trust their boss, they feel unsafe, like no one has their back. They end up spending more energy on survival than performance – more effort to keep their jobs than do their jobs.

The corporate world is cluttered with such micromanagers. Sadly, many organizations prefer these managers because they seem to be on top of and in control of everything. In the short term, they may produce results, but in the long run, they leave a trail of destruction in their path. Nobody can perform at their best being constantly monitored and scrutinized.

MICROMANAGEMENT MAINLY STEMS FROM THESE FOUR REASONS:

1. Manager's own sense of insecurity and inability to trust people.
2. Insufficient training or unclear objectives for employee to effectively perform tasks.
3. An environment that doesn't allow any room for failures and learning from them.
4. Poor selection of employees in the first place.

"Some people truly need to be micromanaged." I hear this all the time. It's sad that some individuals are justifying micromanagement. Micromanagement works great, if you're operating a daycare — and then, only if you stick to micromanaging the children. Train, mentor, and coach employees, and give them clear objectives. If a company needs to micromanage employees, they need to check their selection process. Furthermore, did the employee receive sufficient training and proper tools? Were the objectives clear? Get to the root cause of the problem and fix it. Hire the right people. Play on their strengths and set them up to succeed. The worst thing you can do as a manager is to be a stumbling block to your employees. Authenticity, respect, and being a people builder gets noticed and respected by employees.

Employees want meaningful work, and they want autonomy in how they work. I allow my employees flexibility in lunch time, breaks, sick days, family leave, further education, etc. I don't believe in micromanaging. It puts undue stress on employees. **I train, coach, and mentor, but I don't have the time to micromanage.** If you hired individuals for a job, it means you believe they are capable of doing the job. Then trust them to get the job done. You don't need to be constantly monitoring their every movement.

Empower people, provide clear roles and responsibilities, define expectations, and hold people accountable. You'll have happier and more productive employees who will care about the business. The typical "bad boss" spends their time directing and supervising employees rather than empowering them. I believe in supporting my team. And because I support them, I can benefit from the feedback they give me which helps me grow as a leader and as a person. Coaching is key, as we all need guardrails. Micromanaging is a thing of the past. Most leaders can't distinguish between leadership and dictatorship. My favorite leader Jesus said, "My sheep hear my voice and follow me."

FIVE DAMAGING EFFECTS OF MICROMANAGEMENT

1. **Decreased Productivity** — When a manager is constantly looking over their employees' shoulders, it can lead to a lot of second-guessing and paranoia, and ultimately leads to (at best) dependent employees. Additionally, such managers spend a lot of time giving input and tweaking employee workflows, which can drastically slow down employee response time.

2. **Reduced Innovation** — When employees feel like their ideas are invalid or live in constant fear of criticism, it's eventually going to take a toll on creativity. In cultures where risk-taking is punished, employees will not dare to take the initiative. Why think outside the box when your manager is only going to shoot down your ideas and tell you to do it his/her way?

3. **Lower Morale** — Employees want the feeling of autonomy. If employees cannot make decisions at all without their managers input, they will feel suffocated. Employees that are constantly made to feel they can't do anything right may try harder for a while but will eventually stop trying at all. The effects of this will be evident in falling employee engagement levels.

4. **High Staff Turnover** — Most people don't take well to being micromanaged. When talented employees are micromanaged, most of them eventually respond in one way; they quit. No one likes to

come to work every day and feel they are walking into a penitentiary, with their every movement being monitored. "Please Micromanage Me" said no employee ever. I have never seen a happy staff under micromanagement.

5. **Loss of Trust** — Micromanagement will eventually lead to a massive breakdown of trust. It demotivates and demoralizes employees. Your staff will no longer see you as a manager, but an oppressor whose only job is to make their working experience miserable.

Micromanagement is a complete waste of everybody's time. It sucks the life out of employees, fosters anxiety, and creates a high-stress work environment.

Your role as a manager is to motivate your team and provide guidance and support. Build up the employee, and you build up the company. It's facilitating a healthy environment where employees can perform at their best. Always be quick to recognize, appreciate, and reward employees' efforts. Micromanagement breeds resentment and disloyalty. A high level of trust between managers and employees defines the best workplaces and drives overall company performance.

In my opinion, a good manager only has two main priorities:

1. Remove all unnecessary obstacles from your subordinates' path so that they have a greater chance for success.
2. Make available as much support (time, resources, effort) as possible to increase your subordinates' chances for success.

Every other priority should support these first two or else they are just distracting the manager (and subsequently the team) from what is important.

Micromanaging is the opposite of empowerment, and it creates toxic work environments. It chokes the growth of the employee and the organization and fosters mediocrity. **When you empower employees,**

you promote their vested interest in the company. The best ideas and advancements are a result of empowering your team.

How can you empower others? Understand their strengths, and support and utilize these strengths. An empowered workforce is more engaged. Engaged employees drive higher customer satisfaction and boost the bottom line. A Gallup study concluded that companies with higher-than-average employee engagement also had 27% higher profits, 50% higher sales, and 50% higher customer loyalty.

Organizations are employing new digital channels, such as automated self-service, chatbots, and support kiosks; these channels empower users to resolve their own issues. Automated password reset functions, for example, allow for immediate resolution, which in turn leads to improved productivity. Empowered employees are more confident, more willing to go the extra mile for employers, and more willing do whatever it takes to care for customers. All in all, keeping great talent really can mean the difference between a business succeeding or failing. In this volatile global marketplace, happy loyal employees are your biggest competitive advantage.

I have come across many companies that have invested a big chunk of their budgets on new and innovative technologies to run the organization in the most creative ways. Too many of them fail because the leaders can't bring themselves to change their mindsets. They are convinced that micromanagement (to the extent of managing break times, work-from-home options, etc.) is absolutely necessary when, in fact, it's actually counterproductive.

BUILDING THE WORKFORCE OF THE FUTURE

The pace of technological change is exponential. In many workplaces today, AI and other smart technologies assist employees in their daily work. As organizations continue to focus on this technology, they are overlooking the most important part of the equation — the human side of the disruption. Disruption isn't solely about how you manage the technology; it's how you lead the people in your organization. Technology is a tool that empowers change, but people make it happen.

In an AI age characterized by disruption and ambiguous change, we need to rethink how we lead people. It's no secret that technology is transforming the workplace, and unfortunately, employee morale is only getting worse. To engage your customers, you'll need first to engage your employees.

Employees want to feel like they belong, are heard and appreciated. Ping pong tables and sweet treats are not enough. Engagement doesn't have to be a challenge. Today, it can be accomplished by using digital tools. It's all about building a culture of feedback and continuous conversations.

As someone who travels a lot, I have had to get a little creative when it comes to engaging employees. I try to include two virtual coffee breaks a week into our schedule - one in the morning and the other in the evening on different days. Team members can take a break and chat with one another via video call. Video calls provide a small glimpse into a remote employee's life, while taking it up a notch (to including video home tours if employees feel comfortable doing this) allows employees to share more of their personality and day-to-day life with their coworkers. Employees are encouraged to spend some time weekly taking these calls, with the goal of creating a more family-oriented work environment for all involved. We have discovered, among other things, that some colleagues have vegetable gardens and others are talented designers and builders. I love giving employees virtual tours of my garden and especially of the fruits in season. Shared practices like these can make our culture strong. What's more, they can help employees discover connections with each other that can spark more conversations in the future.

Additionally, every three months, my team meets up for a themed virtual party. In advance of the party, we send everyone a gift card to get food, drinks, or other materials according to the theme. This costs about $300 - $500 per party, but the small gesture of thanks really resonates with employees. The past themes have included pizza parties, national holidays and even movie themed parties. Our last party was last month in December, and the theme of course was Christmas. It was so much fun. I make the effort to try to show our employees I appreciate them and their hard work. Recognizing them as individuals goes a long way in driving motivation. Thankfully, video conferencing makes it possible for this happen.

Virtual hangouts and parties are ideal for remote workforces, as it ensures no remote employee is left out. While there are plenty of video tools out there, you can try spending a little money on rewards such as gift cards. This adds a wonderful touch, making the celebration feel even more meaningful. **Whether you're hosting events or instant messaging employees, even the smallest gestures can leave employees feeling appreciated and valued.** This helps them feel more connected to their work, and to the company.

It's important not to just use technology in a transactional way. **Have fun. It doesn't need to be overly formal.** Technology enables opportunities for fun, from discussing mutual hobbies to sharing GIFs, which can help create a cohesive, caring, and supportive culture. Employees will look forward to these activities. It's important to build playful elements into meetings. One approach I use is telling employees that they have to share a lightbulb moment, share something they liked, or just appreciate other team members at the end of a meeting. This can help build more connections between distant team members who wouldn't otherwise chat.

Instant messaging and virtual meetings are vital to me. **I make time to engage in one-on-one conversations with my employees. The emphasis is not only on how to make their jobs easier, but also to connect with them on a deeper level.** I ask them about their work progress, career goals, and just what's going on in their lives in general. I also let them know how much I value their efforts and contributions. Virtual bonding is core to our company culture of building relationships.

THE FUTURE IS HERE

Many of you are probably familiar with *"Star Trek."* Captain Kirk and his crew regularly use a 3D hologram projector in the Starship Enterprise to virtually transport someone from where they are or to simulate a virtual world. Although the use of hologram technology is still in its infancy, holographic presence is one of the technologies identified as an upcoming trend for meetings and presentations. Seminars and calls can be attended by more people than would have been possible with a physical meeting, and participants can be more engaged than they would otherwise be via a video link. (And nobody gets stuck in the back of the room where they have to squint at the blackboard.) Holographic technology allows for a near real-time communication experience.

Microsoft has been working with Spatial, a mixed-reality content company, to build workplace collaboration applications that happen in virtual space. Spatial cofounder Anand Agarawala gave a demo of a virtual meeting where attendees wearing HoloLens collaborated on the design of a robot hologram. Attendees not present were represented by holographic avatars. Since HoloLens tracks hand movement, someone could pick up a virtual document and throw it over to another participant in virtual space. You could even adjust the positioning and size of the robot with your hands. Spatial also uses the HoloLens 2's eye tracking to reflect user eye movements in their avatars in virtual space. The eye tracking let avatars convey subtle levels of user emotion.

Holographs allows you to produce, revise, or edit documents that are plastered mid-air — no silly red, black, and blue marker pens! The development of augmented and virtual reality has been steadily increasing, which in turn encourages the adoption of holographic tele presence technology. It is just a matter of time before it becomes a mainstream communication system.

Death of emails — According to the Workfront 2018 State of Work report, U.S. workers spend about 40% of their workday on primary tasks. Why is that? They are tied up with email and wasteful meetings. As more companies begin to rely on digital tools like mixed reality instead of email and meetings, teams will have better alignment of work to strategy, so the right things get done at the right time.

The workplace of the future promotes agility and empowers employees to communicate and collaborate in ways that will boost morale and positively impact the bottom line. It will be a network of teams and based on trust. With a click of a button, I can see what my employees are working on at any point in time, and this allows me and other team members to jump in and offer solutions or recommendations. Problems are solved faster when the aim is to capitalize on the teams' collective intelligence.

If I am working on a major project in one country and I join a meeting with my team members, rather than talk about the work I've done, I can simply show them because now we can resume the project from a tablet in the meeting. Technology allows us to manage our documents and collaborate seamlessly in one place.

In this digital marketplace, we need to be ready to innovate and respond to opportunities and threats as they appear without being bogged down by hierarchy. If an employee has an idea, he/she doesn't have to navigate through upper management to get the idea to the key person making the decision. Our structure relies on cooperation and communication that focuses on achieving shared goals.

My employees don't need to be in the office every day, and some of them reside in different countries. These strategies have helped my team socialize more, even though they span six countries. Allowing employees to work from anywhere using technology doesn't have to slow down productivity. It's 2020 not 1920. Digital tools allow us to collaborate across time and space effectively. **Results should be measured instead of hours spent behind a physical desk.**

The most successful leaders unleash the creative power of their employees by granting autonomy and supporting behaviors such as disruptive thinking and risk-taking. **Great leadership isn't about control. It's about empowering people.** It's okay if an employee doesn't get from point A to point Z using the same methods as I do. Everybody works at a different pace. I had to accept my way may not always be the best way to complete a task. My purpose is creating an environment where employees feel safe and comfortable to express themselves.

The world is constantly evolving. The workplace, on the other hand, is lagging behind in these modern times. Businesses continue to utilize the same business routine which has been applied for the last 100 years: Monday to Friday, 9-to-5, cubicle farms, 30-minute lunch, a yearly performance appraisal - and the list goes on. Not much has changed besides the investment in new computer equipment and technology. Moving forward, businesses will need to compete for talent by modifying their work practices, which may include adopting a flexible work schedule or instituting a more virtual environment.

My new employee asked to work from home. Then she started to tell me the reason.

I told her, "No need to apologize and I don't need to know the details."

I do not pay for seat warmers.

Come to the office? Fine.

9 to 5? Fine.

Work from home? Fine.

Work from the garage while they fix your car? Fine.

I don't need to know you will be late because of a doctor's appointment, or you are leaving early to attend a personal matter.

Everybody works at a different pace. You choose how to get your work done.

It's sad how we have infantilized the workplace so much that employees feel the need to apologize for having personal lives.

I am not a clock watcher. I trust you to get your job done.

Keep clients happy. I am happy.

THE FUTURE LIES IN FLEXIBLE WORK PATTERNS.

I have moved to a task/goal-based schedule for my team, and it has been revolutionary for morale and efficiency. I tell them, "Here's what we as a team need to accomplish, here are our milestones, and here are the expectations. Now when you work to reach that goal is up to you. As long as deliverables are submitted on time and to expectations with strong and fluid communication along the way, we are good to go." Our culture relies on a strong sense of individual accountability which in-turn empowers our employees to outperform.

I learned then that if you focus on presence, you get presence. If you focus on results, you get results. And if you focus on the best qualities of people, you get good performers. So focus on best qualities of people; they will get you results, and you will not even need to worry about presence and where they work.

The freedom to work when and where they choose is a huge incentive for today's workforce. We need to start letting go of the traditional 9-5 work week. Not everyone is an early bird. Embrace your employees' natural rhythm and watch productivity soar. Tomorrow's workplace will be more than just an array of employees and jobs; it is being transformed into an ecosystem—a "boundary-less" set of workers and work, not the typical jobs and employees within an organization today." — Dr. John Boudreau, university professor.

Employees are now choosing jobs based on the level of work flexibility they offer. Thirty-eight percent of hiring managers predict that their employees will work predominantly remotely in the next ten years," says Zoe Harte, Senior Vice President, Human Resources and Talent Innovation, Upwork. Unless private firms want to experience a labor shortage and remain uncompetitive, they will need to adapt and alter their course. And this is indeed a win-win for workers of all generations.

The World Economic Forum published a report in September 2019 identifying the best cities for work-life balance, and Helsinki, Finland ranked number one in the world. I was glad to be in Helsinki in January 2020 for an HR conference to learn from those managers present what made their city top the list. What really surprised me the most was the flexibility that they provide their employees. Flexible working has been embedded in Finland's working culture. This is largely due to the Working Hours Act, passed in 1996, which gives most staff the right to adjust their working day by starting or finishing up to three hours earlier or later. **It starts at the top.** Their newly appointed Prime Minister Sanna Marin mentioned the idea of a four-day work week in a panel discussion in August 2019, while she was the Minister of Transport. Although it is not on the agenda at the moment, it's great that as a leader, she is open-minded and believes in flexibility. Finland's government also announced a plan to provide equal paid parental leave for men and women. The new policy gives nearly 7 months of paid leave to each parent, for a total of almost 14 months of paid leave. Additionally, new legislation, which will come into effect in early 2020, will make the average 40-hour working week even more flexible. Employees will be able to decide when and where they work for at least half of their work hours.

Allowing remote work could be an effective way to communicate to present and future employees that your work culture is based on trust and employee empowerment.

If you want performance at scale:

- Select the right people;
- Provide them with the proper training, tools, and support;
- Give them room to get the job done.

Employees need to be given space to breathe, to think independently and bring out their innovative ideas. And this is possible only when they are trusted enough to do their jobs well.

Workplaces have been organized around hierarchical divisions of labor for centuries but now they're evolving to reflect the changing world of work. Work in future will be more mobile, project-based, collaborative and fluid. Teams are set to play a critical role in the organizations of the future. We will need the ability to create teams, get them performing effectively, and then disband them as priorities change. The hierarchical structures of the past are giving way to agile teams that can respond quickly to new challenges and innovate at speed. Research suggests that already only 38% of companies are organized by function, so we will see more and more cross-functional, multi-cultural, and virtual teams.

REMOTE TEAMS

Since 2016, the number of job posts on LinkedIn that mention work flexibility rose by over 78% according to the 2019 Global Talent Trends report. By 2025, an estimated 70% of the workforce will work remotely at least five days in a month. In the UK, freelancers alone make up around 40% of the entire self-employed population, contributing £109 billion to the UK economy every year. Deloitte reports that only 12% of the executives they contacted feel they understand the way people work together in networks. Connecting with, motivating, and holding a remote workforce accountable brings unique challenges for leaders. **65% of remote employees report that they have never had a team-building session.** Successful virtual team players all have a few things in common: good communication skills, high emotional intelligence, and an ability to work independently.

REMOTE WORK IS GROWING IN POPULARITY. HERE ARE A FEW TOP BENEFITS:

- Remote work increases productivity. In one survey by Flexjob, 66% of survey respondents said their productivity improved when not in an office, and 76% said there are fewer distractions outside of offices.

- Remote work saves employers and workers money. AT&T reported savings of $30 million a year in real estate alone from their telework initiative. Businesses can save as much as $11,000 per person per year by allowing them to work from home, according to Global Workplace Analytics. Employees also save money on commuting costs.

- Remote work is a motivating work perk. According to a study by Softchoice, 74% of North American office workers reported they would change jobs based on a work-from- home policy.

STRATEGIES FOR BUILDING TEAM EFFECTIVENESS IN REMOTE EMPLOYEES

- **Encourage communication.** Effective communication is very important within a virtual team. **Open and effective channels of communication are vital to success.** Continuous communication increases effectiveness, prevents misunderstandings and can reduce feelings of isolation. It also helps to build relationships and improve overall team spirit. Keep lines of communication open. Promote ongoing communication by video conferencing and simple check-ins — which will help increase employee satisfaction. Open a chat room and leave it perpetually open to boost team spirit. It will foster better working relationships within the team; they will not feel as if they are working separately but are truly a part of the organization.

- **Get face time.** Your remote team needs face time with managers and colleagues at regular intervals to ensure closer collaboration through fostering personal connections and getting feedback. Remote team members don't have a chance to rub elbows at the photocopy machine or lean over a cubicle for some idle chat. So don't cut the chit-chat. Your kick-off meetings should have an icebreaker at the start to engage team members. Try to spend a couple of minutes at the onset of each meeting discussing personal updates.

- **Empower your team.** For teams that rarely meet face to face, empowerment is critical for performance. Every team needs defined roles, a clear task strategy, and interaction norms. Discuss together how the team wishes to provide feedback and hold each other accountable, and how the team works best. Remote work does come with a degree of flexibility, but leaders should set clear expectations while still giving a degree of autonomy. Determine how conflicts will be resolved. Clashes in a virtual team setting are inescapable, as they are in a collective setting.

- **Rotational leadership.** Most members of high-performing teams are capable of leading themselves and the team, but unfortunately, they don't often get an opportunity. Rotational leadership allows each team member to lead the team; it could involve simple activities, like heading up the weekly phone call, formulating the agenda for the next meeting, or organizing a team-building activity.

- **Show Appreciation.** Make each individual feel they are valuable to the team. Although you may not be able to take everyone out to lunch, leaders can show appreciation and make employees understand how important they are to the overall success of the company. Whether it's sending gift cards and "Thank Yous" in emails, making simple phone calls, or doing a virtual happy hour event with your team once a month or so, you can make your employees feel valued. Employees who feel valued perform better. A team culture of recognition and reward will create a great environment for collaboration, as well as engagement.

- **Virtual team bonding.** Research shows that virtual teams who have participated in virtual team building exercises score significantly higher in leadership, decision making, and team performance than teams who haven't. Encourage members to engage in structured team-building activities such as online games to bring out their competitive spirit. Playing together will develop rapport. This could be useful to acclimate the team to company policies or just to have fun. The objective of virtual team-building activities and games is to help build trust among your team members, increase the level of cohesion and familiarity among your employees, and learn more about team members on a personal and professional level.

- **Measure the effectiveness of your team.** According to a survey conducted by FlexJobs and WorldatWork, over 80% of American organizations have implemented some type of flexible work arrangement. Surprisingly, though, only three percent of those same companies were measuring whether flextime actually makes people more productive and more likely to positively contribute to the bottom line. In an article for WorkFlexibility.org, Greg Kratz cited recent statistics compiled by Global Workplace Analytics that focus on large corporations. At JD Edwards, telecommuters were 20% more productive than in-office colleagues. And work-from-home American Express employees were 43% more productive than in-office ones. If you measure productivity, you can ascertain what areas you need to improve on to facilitate productive teamwork.

- **Get people together.** We are social beings; we were created for community, for friendship. People sharing common goals and a common purpose, and most of all, people who care about each other and who are dedicated to helping each other — that's what teamwork should be about. We have an innate ability to connect with others. As we grow and develop, we desire human interaction. Harmonious relationships do not happen by accident. We must be intentional about building relationships. Leaders need to constantly motivate remote team members to deliver their best. However, e-mails and conference calls may not be enough to keep up the momentum. In the absence of face-to-face interaction and body language, conflict often arises, and members begin to feel detached. So **it's important to meet up if logistically possible.** Get your people together to celebrate the achievement of short-term goals or to brainstorm difficult problems. Ritesh Idnani, founder and CEO of Seamless Health, a healthcare start-up that relies on dispersed teams of managers, is adamant about bringing everyone together in person at least quarterly.

PEOPLE HAVE BEEN PREDICTING A FOUR-DAY WORKWEEK FOR DECADES, BUT COULD THIS HAPPEN IN THE NEAR FUTURE?

Today, many employers are often unwilling to experiment with the four-day workweek due to a lack of faith in employees and little understanding of the benefits that a shortened week can offer. I believe business leaders could be convinced with more rigorous study. In most of the examples that are often highlighted, the standard is inconsistent. In some cases, one day of the week is simply removed, resulting in fewer hours worked. Some examples consist of cramming 40 hours of work into four 10-hour days. And some simply reduce the workweek to, say, 32 hours; sometimes the pay is cut. As a consequence, results have been mixed.

While shorter workweeks can improve productivity and bring clear benefits to employees' well-being, they also can be difficult to implement. The Wellcome Trust, a science research foundation in London, was considering giving workers Fridays off with no reduction in pay. But it abandoned its plans for a four-day workweek, saying it would be "too operationally complex to implement" for its staff of 800.

Microsoft Japan, on the other hand implemented, a four-day workweek in the summer of 2019, with employees working four days, having three off, and still collecting their full paycheck. As part of Microsoft Japan's trial, meetings were cut from one hour to 30 minutes and capped at five attendees. The company said employees reported being 40% more productive, and that the policy was particularly popular among younger workers. This announcement from one of the world's biggest tech companies breathed new life to the argument that a four-day work week is not only better for workers but better for the bottom line. **Several studies show various benefits such as reduced stress, increased productivity, and happier, more engaged employees.**

In 2018, New Zealand trust company Perpetual Guardian made its four-day working week permanent after a successful trial. The results: productivity increased by 20%, work-life balance increased from 54% to 78%, and stress levels dropped from 45% to 38%. "One of the overriding conditions of the four-day week at Perpetual Guardian was that customer service couldn't suffer," says Charlotte Lockhart, a former Perpetual Guardian executive. "So, all four workers decided they would buddy up digitally." This helped to strengthen their business model because staff were incentivized to find that solution for themselves.

Could employees really get all their work done in just 32 hours? According to a survey of UK office workers, **the average number of**

truly productive hours in an eight-hour day is two hours and 53 minutes. Wow. This is less than three hours of real work out of eight hours. We waste so much time on pointless meetings, unproductive emails and phone calls, etc. The four-day workweek encourages employees and managers to try to find smarter ways to get the job done. It takes re-examining work functions and structure to look for current time-wasting activities and see how they can be cut down or eliminated.

There's a widespread desire among employees to work shorter weeks. About two-thirds of workers favor a compressed workweek, according to recent surveys by the staffing firm Robert Half and the public radio program Marketplace. Work is changing, and there may still be hope for the four-day workweek. Millennials and the generation that follows, Generation Z, may drive this shift. Priorities are changing as these new generations enter the workplace. Motivating past generations was tied almost exclusively to pay and other extrinsic motivators. Millennials and Generation Z, on the other hand, seem to be focusing less on pay and more on growth and work-life balance. Working in an environment that offers them interesting challenges is rapidly becoming one of their most important motivators.

Should You Implement a Four-Day Workweek? It depends on the needs of your business and employees. Let's be realistic - in some cases it may not be feasible. But if you have an employee ask about working a four-day week, don't just dismiss the idea. It makes sense to look into it. See if it would work for this person in this position. Perhaps look at implementing a trial period. I think we've got a long way to go. However, I am bullish about the future of the four-day workweek. I have been speaking with companies in different industries from all over the world, and many are interested in learning more. We are in the age of big data. With so much information at our fingertips, we can now make data-based decisions. Leaders need to learn to give up control. Granting employees autonomy and empowering them to come up with better ways of working and self-scheduling can lead to greater efficiency, productivity, and profitability. It's time to stop measuring productivity by days and hours. We need to measure what matters - meaningful business results like productivity and customer service.

WORKSPACE OF THE FUTURE: ADAPTING TO CHANGING EMPLOYEE EXPECTATIONS.

The future workplace will be comprised of robots, VR tools, and AI hiring strategies. Let's be clear; the real the office will not go extinct. Why? There are some jobs that require us to be on location. What can an employer do to boost engagement in that case?

Workplace design has undergone a radical transformation. At the start of the 20th century, offices aimed to maximize efficiency by simulating the factory layout with rows of workers, as promoted by Frederick Taylor, the father of scientific management. The 1980s ushered in office cubicles. Today, corporate rooms filled with dreary rows of dim-lit desks in dreary uniformity are disappearing, replaced by sun-dappled open offices. We have seen the design of offices respond to the leading economic ideas and technologies of the time. The speed of that evolution is only intensifying. Today, the shift to more agile working is influencing the design of the future office. These new workplaces are furnished with everything from bold conference rooms to napping pods, plush office bean bag chairs to portable desks, idea incubators with circular couches to 3D holographic imaging projectors.

How we design workplaces must continue to evolve to reflect the changing world of work.

While the size of the human workforce may decrease, the value of employees and the highly skilled work they do, will only grow in importance. In an effort to support a healthier and more productive workforce, businesses are expected to increase their health and wellness benefits offerings. Some of the benefits companies are investing in include onsite gyms, standing desks, meditation rooms, workplace-funded childcare, etc.

The results of a recent Harvard study suggest that wellness programs, offered by 80% of large U.S. companies, yield unimpressive results. **It's time to stop spending money on futile office perks.**

Employees want the basics first: a high-quality workplace — air quality and good ventilation, access to natural light, comfortable temperatures, and the ability to personalize their workspace. These are often overlooked, yet they have the greatest influence on employee well-being, productivity, happiness, and the overall quality of the employee experience. Purposeful design — including inviting lighting, meeting spaces, and even how the office smells — influences how employees think, create, and collaborate. The design of a workplace should reduce stress but increase interactions among coworkers, fostering better collaboration and performance.

Research conducted by Gartner found that employees who are satisfied with their work environments are 16% more productive, 18% more likely to stay, and 30% more attracted to their company over competitors.

A good rule of thumb is to never assume that you know what your employees want. It's time to rethink your employee wellness strategy. **How about asking employees? "How can I make your job easier and your work experience better?"** According to a workplace wellness study by Future Workplace and View, which polled 1,601 professionals working in corporate offices, "more than two-thirds of employees said that a workplace that supported and enhanced their health and wellbeing would encourage them to accept a job offer (67%) — or to stay at their current job (69%)." A successful wellness program should be based on employees' goals and interests and provide opportunities for improvement. A workplace purposely designed around wellbeing must reach beyond the physical and environmental aspects of wellbeing to include social and emotional dimensions.

TAKE THE TIME TO ALIGN YOUR APPROACH TO EMPLOYEE WELLNESS SO THAT IT CONNECTS ALL OF THE IMPORTANT ARE AS, SUCH AS:

- **Physical wellness**: Employees spend over half of their lives at work. They want to be in a healthy and comfortable environment. Workplaces should be designed to bridge the gap between home and more traditional workspaces. Provide ergonomically designed workstations and healthy food and snack options. It shows a lack of concern or care for employees when the office vending machine is filled with junk food. Employees expect more. Show them you are genuinely interested in their health and wellness, and it's not just lip service. **Overall the workplace of the future doesn't feel like an office.**

- **Environmental wellness**: Some workplaces are just too cold for employees to effectively function in. The increasing prevalence of sensors in the workplace can help offices adapt to their users' needs. For example, sensors can learn and respond to people's individual preferences for temperature and lighting levels. Wearables will enable more personalization of space. Make sure your workspaces have good lighting and ventilation and proper acoustics. Those seem so basic, but just like Maslow's theory of needs, if they are not satisfied, everything else you do become pointless. As time goes on, employees' preferences in their workplace settings will become increasingly personalized and increasingly automated.

- **Emotional wellness**: Emotional wellness is sometimes a sensitive area to discuss in a workplace setting, but it's crucial. Ignoring emotional health — both on a personal level and on an organizational level — can lead to burnout, interpersonal conflicts, and decreased productivity. Without positive emotional well-being, employees aren't able to feel their best at work, and they're not likely to perform at their best either. Such employees can also spread their personal feelings of stress or unhappiness to other team members, thus affecting employee morale and the overall company culture. You can incorporate the emotional component of wellness into their employee wellness program through mental health days, stress management programs, and by providing emotional/mental health education and resources. Other initiatives or policies that can help companies improve their workforce's emotional health include flexible schedules, offering paid time off, allowing regular breaks, implementing a **"no eating lunch at your desk"** policy, or even a gratitude challenge that tasks employees to write down what they were thankful for every day for a month.

- **Social wellness**: This is another commonly overlooked aspect of employee wellness. Strong work relationships and emotional connections are essential for employee job satisfaction, happiness, and overall well-being. When employees feel disconnected in their work environments, this can lead to lower work performance. Employers can incorporate the social component of wellness into their employee wellness program through team activities, work celebrations, and creating social areas in the office.

According to "Absenteeism: The Bottom-Line Killer," by Circadian, unscheduled absenteeism costs roughly $3,600 per year for each hourly worker. Additionally, it also costs roughly $2,650 each year for salaried employees.

Take the necessary steps and show employees that you are committed to improving their work experiences. The most successful companies are those that embrace a more holistic view of workplace wellness. Your program needs to recognize all areas of your employees' health and well-being, including physical, environmental, emotional, and social wellness. From thermostats controlled by apps to integrated home entertainment controls, we're all getting used to personalizing our consumer lives. Employees are beginning to expect these same privileges in the workplace. This can have a major impact on your bottom line.

If these environmental improvements are not available to you now, you need to work with what you've got. Maximize your productivity at the office with the help of small, self-made perks, like a clean, organized desk, taking regular breaks, even if it's just to get up and walk for a bit, and keeping a firm handle on stress — and always look at the bright side of things to maintain a good mood and a positive mindset.

As the digital revolution in workplace continues, we need to look at work and its settings holistically. **It's a time of profound change in how design supports the work of building a collaborative, innovation-driven community.** Office spaces need to model this.

The workplace of the future calls for unprecedented changes. This means holistic design, a more virtual environment, and flexible work schedules. You manage processes and things, you lead people. This is done by respecting, empowering, and even challenging the people you lead to be better. Providing clear structure, continual feedback, and the autonomy to be creative builds loyalty.

Managers need to be open minded and flexible and get on board with the new work-life requirements or find themselves with a limited pool of talent to choose from. A large part of being successful in today's economy is the ability to adapt quickly. Being able to quickly innovate and adapt to changes in external influences are what makes or breaks a company.

CHAPTER FOURTEEN

THE IMPORTANCE OF ETHICAL LEADERSHIP

The technological advances of this decade have happened so quickly that it's difficult to comprehend. Speed of change during next decade? That... times ten. The first iPad came out just a decade ago. There were no food delivery meal kits. We weren't carrying on complex conversations with disembodied voices named Siri or Alexa. We stayed in hotels, not Airbnb's. When we needed a ride, we telephoned a cab company rather than pressing a button for an Uber. We didn't waste hours of our day on Instagram (though somehow, hours of our day still went missing).

A McKinsey report in 2017 predicted as many as 800 million jobs lost globally by 2030. It isn't just pizza delivery who will be replaced by artificial intelligence algorithms — the carnage will hit every career imaginable. But on a positive note: jobs that are now performed by hundreds of thousands of people didn't exist then either! Just think of all the new jobs that will be created in the next 10 years!

A lot of us are trying to see into the future of AI. We wonder what to expect from AI itself, of course, but we also wonder if the process of integrating AI into our lives will replicate the onslaught of the internet and the revolutionary effect of social media. For many of us, it's hard to imagine living without them now, but they've also resulted in negative effects, effects we often didn't see coming. We can expect that we will go through the same cycle with AI, and that after a while, we'll realize that we have exaggerated our positive expectations and start looking for solutions to AI's negative impact. Technology is a wonderful and marvelous tool that has changed the very fabric of our lives. However, we also need to be vigilant, and "just because we can doesn't always mean we should."

Fundamentally, AI is a tool, and like every tool, it can and will be used for good and bad.

I would like to start with the social context. That means people. And when AI touches the social context, ethical questions arise. Everything else derives from that. When training data doesn't mirror the population, for example, a constructed utility function will still give biased results. Everyone talks about bias which enters models through the selection of data and by the background of the developers, but that's just the start. Bottom line, the discriminatory effect of good intentions presents the obvious ethical issue: "I can build it, but should I?" Technologies are meant to serve humans, not the other way around.

Though artificial intelligence is capable of a speed and capacity of processing that's far beyond that of humans, it cannot always be trusted to be fair and neutral because its creators aren't always fair and neutral. Sophisticated algorithms can't overcome poor or insufficient data. AI is an innovative process where a machine is trained by feeding it large amounts of data. But if those datasets under- or over-represent certain groups, or use out-of-date or skewed historical records or societal norms, then any outcomes will necessarily be biased. Algorithms are unbiased, but if you feed these systems biased data, they will generate biased results. **When the data we feed the machines reflects the discrimination evident in our society, we are training them to be unfair.** But sadly, data can never become unbiased unless humans become that way. AI systems have the same flaws as their creators. If AI develops a certain bias towards or against a race, gender, religion, or ethnicity, then the fault will lie mostly in how it was taught and trained. The people who are developing the systems that currently drive much of this automation do not represent all of us and are not considering all of our needs equally.

There are some notable examples of AI bias. Male candidates have been preferred over female candidates in the recruiting process, and facial recognition systems have a hard time detecting darker skin tones. ProPublica published their investigation of a software application that was being used by a court to predict who was more likely to commit a crime for the second time. Appallingly, they discovered that the software rated blacks with higher probability than whites — 45% as compared to 23%. It was also found that a resume was more likely to be accepted if it was submitted by a European-American compared to one submitted by an African-American. I thought racism was slowly becoming a thing of the past. Seems not. Is history doomed to repeat itself? This is why we need to start having serious discussions on biases in AI, and ask ourselves if we are setting boundaries in the right places. And frankly, the sooner the better. It's likely to be easier if we shine a light on bias in AI now, before the damage becomes irreparable.

Given the scale of AI applications in fields like financial services, employment screening, and housing, the consequences of any single error are immense. Today, our sense of ethics provides a framework for making decisions. **But what if the developers of AI have a twisted ethical framework?** Or what if they answer to those who do? Like any other technology, AI knows no limits, and regulating the development and use of this technology will take an ever greater and more powerful global effort as AI becomes intertwined within society.

We must emphasize the importance of building trustworthy technology to prevent false profiling. With AI, using a facial recognition algorithm, your face and voice could be captured to create fake video and used to falsely convict you of a crime. How do we know what's real anymore? If we don't know how AIs make decisions, how can we trust what they decide? We need more transparency.

I don't know if you've ever seen the YouTube channel Ctrl Shift Face? They have short videos where they make one actor or talk show guest look like another actor. For instance, they have one where the little boy's face from the first Home Alone movie looks like Sylvester Stallone. The transitions are completely flawless. They use a program called DeepFake, and it's creeping out some of the commenters.

Deepfakes are synthetic media in which a person in an existing image or video is replaced with someone else's likeness. Deepfakes leverage powerful techniques from machine learning and artificial intelligence to manipulate or generate visual and audio content with a high potential to deceive. Deepfakes have garnered widespread attention for their uses in revenge porn, fake news, hoaxes, and financial fraud. Deepfakes have been used to misrepresent well-known politicians in videos. In one such video, the face of the Argentine President Mauricio Macri has been replaced by the face of Adolf Hitler. The Japanese AI company DataGrid created high-resolution whole-body images of non-existent people. We have fake news and now fake people. In June 2019, a downloadable application called DeepNude was released which used neural networks, specifically generative adversarial networks, to remove clothing from images of women. On June 27, the creators removed the application, but I am sure there are many more creators of this type of app. And if not, there soon will be. Many deepfakes on the internet feature pornography, often female celebrities whose likeness is typically used without their consent. This is all so eerie. The technology can make it seem like anyone is saying or doing anything at some point in time.

This has elicited responses from both industry and government to detect and limit their use. If this is public knowledge, could you imagine what superior technology the government or even competing nations have developed?

This technology is disturbing, even frightening. Soon we won't know if what we're watching is real or fake. Governments can use this technology to mislead the population. It's like the old curse — "May you live in interesting times." And it's getting more and more interesting.

Digital information technology's impact has been so pervasive that it's changing how we make choices and behave. The systems we require for sustaining our lives increasingly rely upon algorithms to function. Where energy grids, food distribution, supply chains, healthcare, fuel, and much more are becoming increasingly automated in ways that impact all of us, algorithmic models and techniques are now increasingly used as part of decision making in a variety of internet applications. Social inequalities illustrate the need not only for privacy rights, but also consideration for related dimensions such as fairness, accountability, and explainability of AI/ML systems.

LEADERS NEED TO GUARD AGAINST AI DATA MANIPULATION

While there is so much opportunity in this brave new world, we also need to be prudent. We must hold ourselves accountable and not be afraid to ask the big questions. What is our commitment to our employees, our customers and partners, our citizens? How we are dealing with their data? We don't have all the answers in all dimensions yet, but we need to be clear, honest, and transparent with our approach to using technology.

In the race to adopt rapidly developing technologies, organizations run the risk of overlooking potential ethical implications. And that could produce unwelcome results, especially in artificial intelligence (AI) systems that employ machine learning. Machines will reflect the values and principles of their creators. Therefore, we need morals and ethics in the development of AI.

Never has there been a time in history when so few people — the big tech companies — control the majority.

It scares me that there is so much discrimination that exists in our society, and it will continue to get worse. We need to fix these biases in AI because whether we like it or not, AI is silently reshaping our entire society. The damage caused can be irreversible when it comes to the algorithms that are used to decide more serious issues, like prison sentences, immigration, housing, or credit scores. It's all too easy to "weigh" algorithms to go in certain directions and still appear unbiased.

I have seen this happen personally, and I would like to share my experience with you.

THE DOWNSIDE OF DATA MANIPULATION: MY EXPERIENCE WITH LINKEDIN

In December 2019, LinkedIn Editors published the list of the Top Voices, and I was excluded as usual. LinkedIn tells the world these are the individuals driving engagement on the platform when it's not true. It's not a mistake. It's something that is very intentional. They have been consistently doing this for the past five years. Their post with this announcement couldn't even garner 3,000 likes because members on the platform don't even know the individuals on the lists. The worst was getting tons of email from members, asking "Brigette, how is it possible that you are not on the LinkedIn's Top Voices list?"

It's pretty simple. Manipulation of data.

So, what is their criteria for choosing the top voices?

"To find standout voices, we use a combination of data and editorial signals. We screen for engagement among professionals sharing in their area of expertise, looking at what kind of conversations — measured by engagement, including comments and re-shares — their original content is creating. We track relative follower growth, too: Are these professionals attracting dedicated fans in their particular sector? Finally, we emphasize quality and diversity; the list should reflect the world we work in." — LinkedIn Editors

But I continually surpass all the criteria. I have the top engagement on the platform, my following has grown substantially, and I am traveling and meeting my LinkedIn followers all over the world.

After purposely leaving me out for five years, this year they gave me the ammunition that I needed to prove it. **LinkedIn Marketing started publishing "The Water Cooler."** The Water Cooler is a monthly report released by the LinkedIn blog that highlights the top ten engaged with articles shared across the platform. The writing is now on the wall. Every single month my articles have been featured in these monthly lists, so much that **LinkedIn Marketing wrote an article on June 28th titled, "The Water Cooler: Why Jeff Bezos and Brigette Hyacinth Engage Readers on LinkedIn."**

The article stated, "If you want to engage the more than 630 million LinkedIn members on the platform, which is fast becoming the water cooler for global business professionals, here are two pieces of advice:

- Write about Amazon's Jeff Bezos.
- Have Brigette Hyacinth, the author of "The Future of Leadership: Rise of Automation, Robotics, and Artificial Intelligence," write your article.

Then on November 27th LinkedIn Marketing published another article, "The Water Cooler: What Does Brigette Hyacinth Know That You Don't?"

The first paragraph stated:

"What does Brigette Hyacinth know? Probably lots of things, but one thing the author of "The Future of Leadership: Rise of Automation, Robotics, and Artificial Intelligence" knows very well is how to get people to engage with her content on LinkedIn. In October, Hyacinth published four of the top 10 most engaging posts on LinkedIn. Actually, she held down all of the top four spots. Each of her posts on the list generated more than 8,500 comments, likes, and shares."

Apparently, the **LinkedIn Marketing team is using facts while LinkedIn Editors are ignoring and manipulating the data** to put whom they want on this list.

To make this deception more evident, I have the top five most-liked posts and articles for 2019. But LinkedIn will never make this public. I am including snapshots of my top posts just in case these posts mysteriously disappear from the platform.

1. My new employee asked to work from home. Then she started to tell me the reason.

Brigette Hyacinth
Author: The Future of Leadership: Rise...
5mo • Edited • ⊚ Anyone

My new employee asked to work from home. Then she started to tell me the reason. I told her "No need to apologize and I don't need to know the details."

I do not pay for seat warmers. Come to the office fine. 9 to 5? Fine. Work from home. Fine. Work from the garage while they fix your car? Fine. I don't need to know you will be late because of a doctor's appointment, or you are leaving early to attend a personal matter. Everybody works at a different pace. You choose how to get your work done. It's sad how we have infantilized the workplace so much, that employees feel the need to apologize for having personal lives. I am not a clock watcher. I trust you to get your job done. Keep clients happy. I am happy.

The future lies in flexible work patterns.

Agree?

👍👏❤️ 858,288   35,053 comments • 33,078,004 views

2. Never Punish Loyal Employees for being Honest

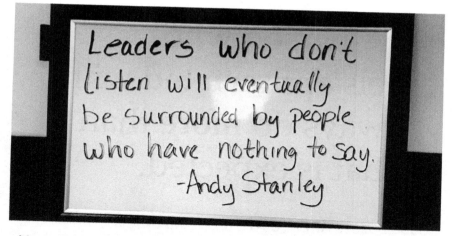

Leaders who don't listen will eventually be surrounded by people who have nothing to say.
-Andy Stanley

Never Punish Loyal Employees for being Honest

Brigette Hyacinth on LinkedIn

👍❤️👏 1,160,705   29,490 comments • 2,181,932 views

3. It's Nice To Be Important, But It's More Important To Be Nice!

I am not impressed by your money, position or title. I am impressed by how you treat others.

It's Nice To Be Important, But It's More Important To Be Nice!

Brigette Hyacinth on LinkedIn

👍❤️👏 857,849   13,299 comments

4. Good Bosses APPRECIATE Their Employees!

A person who feels **appreciated** will always do **more** than what is expected.

Good Bosses APPRECIATE their Employees!

Brigette Hyacinth on LinkedIn

820,745   12,572 comments

5. You Get the Talent that You Pay For!

If I do a job in 30 minutes, it's because I spent 10 years learning how to do that in 30 minutes. **You owe me for the years, not the minutes.**

You Get The Talent That You Pay for!

Brigette Hyacinth on LinkedIn

642,572   12,238 comments • 1,084,756 views

Moreover, thousands of posts have been shared on LinkedIn by the members about the positive impact I am making on the platform. The following post below was shared by a LinkedIn member on the 30th of December 2019 and I just think it captures the overall sentiments of most of my followers.

 Keynote Speaker & Leadership Advisor; Project Consultant & Preacher.
1w • Edited • ⊗

I want to wish all my connections and followers a wonderful 2020 ahead. Most importantly, I wish Brigette Hyacinth a year beyond her biggest expectations. I have had a LinkedIn account for years but only used it about once every three months. Then one day, a few months ago, I saw a post by Brigette whom I now call Miss LinkedIn and I found myself visiting LinkedIn almost daily just to see what this remarkable woman has to say. She is my Keynote Speaking mentor and the number 1 person I follow on this network and I recommend that you follow her if you aren't already.

She has completely changed my outlook on social media, networking, human resources and leadership and she is on a mission to put back the "Human" in Human Resources.

Thanks Brigette - you inspire so many...
SUEKS

I don't ask my LinkedIn connections to write posts about me like this, but many of them do and share it on the platform. Thankfully, I have been able to visit five continents in 2019, including North America, South America, Europe, Africa, and Asia and have met so many wonderful LinkedIn members in person. Some even take vacation and travel from different countries to meet me. I get so many emails daily in messages and in comments from individuals around the globe thanking me for inspiring them, and to let me know that after taking my advice, they have landed a job. The impact I have made is undeniable. Thus, I have been able to organically grow my following to 2.4M followers on the platform.

Why am I now coming out with this? I have never shared any of this on any social media platform. I have kept this to myself, but I think now is the time to tell the truth. I have nothing to gain from this but **sometimes you just have to stand up to Goliath even if all you have is a slingshot**. Imagine, I have had to fight for everything my whole life. And I still have to fight even when I work hard and rightly deserve something.

Just think about all the people and content they are deleting, hiding, and restricting for no apparent reason. Someone twiddling their thumbs behind the right computer has enormous power, the power to control, the power to judge — the power to impact lives. The world is becoming a very scary place. I am not afraid of AI. I am more concerned about unethical human beings.

We are becoming far too dependent on others thinking for us instead of us thinking for ourselves. When people stop thinking with their own minds, someone does the thinking and deciding in their place. The deceptively total knowledge and control of people's behavior through overestimated technological approaches (such as big data) is an obvious example of this strategy.

Take everything you see on social media with a grain of salt. Think for yourself. Ask questions. Don't digest everything they feed you. These companies want to control who we see, read, hear, and believe. They operate under the guise of fairness, but they are unethical to the core. Just ask LinkedIn to share the top posts and articles for 2017, 2018 and 2019? You can easily get information on the top tweets on Twitter or top Facebook posts but not for LinkedIn. Ask them to be transparent?

"I must stand with anybody that stands right and part from him when he goes wrong." — Abraham Lincoln

Let me be clear. I am not upset that I was not featured in the top voices list. What bothers me is how these companies can blatantly lie and the lengths they are willing to go to cover their tracks. When a member who does not fit the narrative or agenda, has more followers and gets more engagement that many of their official Influencers, it becomes a problem. **What has changed now is that as of November 2019, they have set the algorithms to block my followers from seeing my articles in their feed.** Many of my first-degree connections said they have suddenly stopped seeing any of my content in their feed. For example, my assistants do not see my posts in their home feed although they mainly follow and engage on my content alone. They have to go on my profile and check to see what I have posted. Hundreds of likes are disappearing from my posts. Many individuals said they also had to re-like the same posts. LinkedIn's machine-learning algorithm prioritizes content in your home feed based around your interests, groups, hashtags, and posts from members you have interacted with directly, through comments, shares, and reactions. Then what's the hitch in the algorithm? Why are the people who follow my hashtag and only engage on my posts not getting my content or activity in the home feed? The only explanation is — manual intervention.

There have been numerous times I had to call out LinkedIn on Twitter for shadow banning me and deleting my viral posts for absolutely no reason. Some of my posts will go viral and then go completely dead. A post doesn't gain 50K likes in one day and then all activity completely stops. When I complained, they would reinstate the posts with no explanation. But by then, engagement on the posts had gone completely dead. I would just have to repost those same articles. LinkedIn has been doing this all along. In 2016, they blocked me so much that I only published seven articles for the whole year. That was a tough time. I am thankful for my brother who encouraged me in that low period to keep posting articles and to not give up.

I would like you to read these excerpts from complains I made to LinkedIn:

In LinkedIn Case #:191110-001264 — **After I had the top four posts in October** 2019, **my articles started showing up blank in the feed.** This is what I wrote to LinkedIn customer support:

"There is either a glitch or restriction on my ability to post articles on LinkedIn. I have attached screenshots. I deleted and re-posted this article about three times and waited a week to see if it would rectify but it hasn't. The NAME of my article — Treat Employees like Assets — Not Liabilities! and the image DOES NOT APPEAR in the feed. It only shows HASHTAGS. My followers don't even know it's an article. Some were emailing me at times; they couldn't put comments or find the post. In five years of posting articles on LinkedIn, this has NEVER happened before. Something is CLEARLY WRONG. It's either a glitch or a restriction. Could you please resolve, so I could resume posting articles again?"

"There is something fishy going on here. **The person who copied my posts (I have reported him) has only 3700 followers. These copied posts garner over 270K and 60K likes...I have over 2.3M followers and SUDDENLY, none of my posts for November can even cross 35K likes**. This has NEVER happened before. You have manually restricted my account or are just blocking my followers from seeing my posts. After last month, achieving the four top posts on LinkedIn (with 800K, 800K, 600K, and 500K likes), someone has intervened to put a stop to me. My content is excellent. **It seems now, if I want to get back activity on my posts. I would have to change my name or give someone else my articles to post for me**."

In LinkedIn Case #: 191221-002411 Notice of Copyright Infringement, I reported a LinkedIn top voice who has been copying my posts.

This is what I wrote to LinkedIn customer support:

"And this is how you become a LinkedIn top voice — COPY Brigette Hyacinth's posts as your own. My work is not good enough to gain me recognition unless posted by someone else. Very sad and unfair."

Imagine this. The people who LinkedIn is naming as the top voices and who the editors feature as trending on LinkedIn are copying my posts. I have had to report so many of them. They are going viral with my content. It's beyond ridiculous. My content has been copied innumerable times on the platform - so much that it's humanly impossible to report all those who plagiarize my posts. **If you copy and paste one of my posts in the search tab on LinkedIn, you will see it comes up hundreds of time written by different people**. I report the top ones for plagiarism because I can't go through all of them. All my cases on LinkedIn are either about plagiarism or LinkedIn blocking my content. I don't post anything hateful or malicious. LinkedIn has never had any issues regarding this with me. All over the internet, I see my work being copied, and I don't get credit for it. It's not right.

I am so glad though that some people are finally seeing what is going on. Someone sent me this message even though I never mentioned anything to her.

"Brigette, you're one of the very few people on LinkedIn that are massively successful without LinkedIn using algorithms and tricks to support you at every stage. They don't give you LinkedIn Learning and live videos first, they don't promote you as a top voice, and they don't push you. They don't say you're an influencer. In fact, they've also held you back by not giving you opportunities you deserve!" — I. Mohan

After appearing on LinkedIn's Marketing Water Cooler Report consistently since it was started in 2019, I will no longer be on it because of manual intervention. At least I got the evidence to prove my case. There is so much politics happening behind closed doors. I **have been on LinkedIn since 2011**, and as an active user, I know everything that has been occurring on this platform. Many members who were active on the platform when I joined have become disillusioned and quit LinkedIn because of how they promote certain members and restrict others. I actually feel sorry for LinkedIn. I look at how hard they try to onboard celebrities from Gwen Stefani to Jennifer Lopez. These celebrities come on the platform once, LinkedIn heavily promotes them for members to follow, and then they disappear. Even many of the Influencers they try to push, only post content once in a blue moon. But as for the members who really drive daily engagement on the platform, LinkedIn keeps cutting our throats.

LinkedIn has a very narrow view of what an Influencer truly is. Their official influencers are mainly celebrities, athletes, and CEOs of

Fortune 500 companies from the USA. Just request that they give a geographical representation of where their Influencers are from, and you will notice the majority are all clustered in one region.

Imagine this: when LinkedIn rolled out their live videos, they forgot to include the region of Africa as a location. Additionally, when they released the Top Voices lists – there were no African Top voices. The total population of Africa is estimated at 1.2 billion, which represents almost 17% of the world's population. Yet Africa still seems to be the forgotten continent.

> *"Our lives begin to end the day we become*
> *silent about things that matter."*
> ~Martin Luther King Jr.

LinkedIn is supposed to be a global platform, but they have failed miserably at recognizing and including diversity. Then they go so far as to tell the world their "chosen few" are driving engagement on the platform – which could not be further from the truth. If you are dishonest about the little things, can I trust you with the big things?

I don't expect anything more from LinkedIn other than they will continue to delete my posts and all evidence of what I have verified. All I would like, though, is for an employee to come forward with the truth. **As my grandmother would always say, "What is hidden in the dark must always come to the light."**

A LinkedIn member shared a post in which he stated I had more engagement than Richard Branson and Bill Gates, and I believe this annoyed someone at the top. I have had more engagement than both of them with my published articles for the past two years, but this is not the case anymore. LinkedIn has put a stop to it.

It's very sad how unethical these companies can be. **The gap between the rich and the poor will continue to climb.** You are pushing Bill Gates' content; he is already the second richest man in the world. But when it comes to this hardworking woman from a third-world country, you are making sure to block all her efforts.

When LinkedIn blocks me, they block my visibility and reach. Not only do they prevent LinkedIn members who need, and who clearly choose, the encouragement from seeing my posts, but they block my reach to have a greater impact to help others. I spend a lot of time trying to assist my childhood community and help the less fortunate in the Caribbean. LinkedIn is supposed to be encouraging engagement, yet they are crippling it. Why? I simply can't understand it. I don't think those at the top know what's going on. I believe there are a few employees who are driving this unethical behavior.

As I write this, I just got a notification from someone that I have five of the top ten articles in the "LinkedIn Content Insights Quarterly Q3 2019," posted on December 30, 2019. **See list below:**

Top Articles on LinkedIn

1. Work for Someone Who Appreciates Your Ideas, Loyalty and Hard Work By **Brigette Hyacinth**
2. A Message to Business Owners Struggling With What to Charge By Scarlett Darbyshire
3. Positive Reinforcement By Ramesh Krishnaram
4. Don't Stay Where You're Tolerated, Go Where You're Celebrated By Raja Jamalamadaka
5. A Truly Great Boss is Hard to Find, Difficult to Leave and Impossible to Forget By **Brigette Hyacinth**
6. 5 Things to Stop Doing on LinkedIn Immediately By Robert Glazer
7. Good Leaders Don't Try to be the Smartest Person in the Room By **Brigette Hyacinth**
8. Empathy is the Most Important Leadership Skill Needed Today By **Brigette Hyacinth**
9. 5 Best Boss Behaviours I Want to Grow Into By Aanandita Bhatnagar
10. The Best Leaders Are Humble Leaders By **Brigette Hyacinth**

Furthermore, I just checked who viewed my profile, and LinkedIn is at the top again. Why do employees of LinkedIn keep viewing my profile for the past two consecutive weeks? I have no open cases and have not mentioned LinkedIn on any posts. **Every time LinkedIn views my profile, the engagement and views on my posts plummets.** It's as if they are up to something. It's a new year and they have already started. It's just sad. **See snapshots below:**

2382

number of times your profile appeared in search results between December 31 - January 7

Where your searchers work

LinkedIn
Internet

Global Goodwill Ambassadors (GGA)
Civic & Social Organization

University of South Florida
Higher Education

3106

number of times your profile appeared in search results between January 7 - January 14

Where your searchers work

LinkedIn
Internet

Global Goodwill Ambassadors (GGA)
Civic & Social Organization

Society of Petroleum Engineers International
Oil & Energy

When discussing ethics, we must understand passive ethics. It starts with a story that many of us learned at a very young age — the Parable of the Good Samaritan. The story is told by Jesus about a traveler who is stripped of clothing, beaten, and left for dead alongside the road. First a priest and then a Levite come by, but both cross the road to avoid the man. Finally, a Samaritan happens upon the traveler and helps the injured man. The Samaritan bandages his wounds, transports him to an inn on his donkey, and pays for the traveler's care and accommodations at the Inn. He also tells the innkeeper that if any addition costs are incurred, he would pay the balance when he returns.

The priest and the Levite operated under **passive ethics**. Technically, they did nothing wrong. But passive ethics is what is destroying our world.

> *"The world will not be destroyed by those who do evil, but by those who watch them without doing anything."*
> ~Albert Einstein

I was watching a video, a social experiment about a freezing homeless child on the sidewalk. He stood there shivering. But many people passed by and did nothing, except one homeless man who came forward and offered the child his jacket. It was heart wrenching to see this. How could society have become so callous? Never think someone else will do the right thing. It starts with each one of us. You might be the only one who takes positive action.

STEPPING FORWARD

Employees are usually the first to recognize wrongdoing in the workplace. A **whistle-blower protection system** needs to be established. Encouraging employees to report wrongdoing (to "blow the whistle") and protecting them when they do is essential to promote a culture of accountability and integrity. Empowering them to speak up without fear of reprisal can help organizations detect and deal with unethical behavior. Witnesses are usually scared to come forward because it could affect their job security. I have seen too often in the corporate world that once you become a whistle-blower, you enter a terrain loaded with land mines. We should create a safe space for employees to come forward. A whistle-blower protection system needs to be rigid, so that employees who have witnessed unethical behavior can feel secure when coming forward with information. Employees must be assured, when they report a matter and go through the required channels, it will be properly and objectively investigated. They should be able to come forward without the fear of being victimized. Their identity must always be protected.

USE AND PROCESSING OF DATA

We often read and hear that "Data is the new oil." Data is the fuel that feeds AI. The more data we produce, the more of it we can feed into AI systems. The more data you have, the more AI can learn and adapt. AI offers the best chance of quickly and accurately making sense of all that data and putting it to use to better serve customers and solve real-world problems.

But what happens if the data fed to the machine is flawed? Things could go very wrong remarkably quickly.

The processing of personal data in Europe falls under the General Data Protection Regulation (GDPR) guidelines for individual rights of consent, access, erasure, security, and accountability. Under the terms of GDPR, not only do organizations have to ensure that personal data is gathered legally and under strict conditions, but those who collect and manage it are obliged to protect it from misuse and exploitation, as well as to respect the rights of data owners — or face penalties for not doing so. Security of user data constitutes a large portion of GDPR and will lead to hefty fines in cases of data breaches. In 2019, the UK Information Commissioner's Office fined British Airways and Marriott for data breach-related violations totaling almost £300M. The penalties were the two largest issued under the European Union's (EU's) data protection regulation so far. Both incidents were the result of external hacking, whereby third parties managed to gain access to personal data through flaws in each company's online security.

More than a year after the EU enacted the General Data Protection Regulation (GDPR) (May 2018), half of the businesses in the United Kingdom are still not fully compliant. According to a survey conducted in July 2019 by the independent research organization OnePoll on behalf of Egress, only 48% of decision makers reported that their business was fully compliant. Implementing new processes around the handling of sensitive data has been the greatest area for compliance investment in the last 12 months, cited by 28% of those surveyed.

Under the GDPR, companies are required to have robust systems and processes to defend against both internal and external data breaches such as a hack. It is more important than ever that companies devote adequate resources to data privacy. Businesses should view GDPR as an opportunity to fortify their data safety measures as a way to protect themselves and their customers. Having well-trained, ethical employees and robust policies in place are vital to reduce the risk of data breaches. You can teach a skill, but you can't teach integrity. When you focus on intelligence and forgo this integrity, it can cost you heavily. The news headlines are littered with stories of employees and business owners who lacked integrity. Hunger without integrity is a disaster waiting to happen. An unethical employee can bring a company to its knees.

If a company's conduct in dealing with big data is perceived as less than ethical, this can negatively affect its revenues. When companies take personal information from a customer, the customer needs to know that their data will be kept safe and protected and will not be given to third parties without their consent.

Furthermore, do we conduct appropriate due diligence when sharing or acquiring data from third parties? Do the suppliers uphold similar ethical standards? A business decision should also be examined from legal, humanitarian, and ethical perspectives. The application of ethics and morality in decision making is beneficial for organizations both externally and internally.

THE IMPORTANCE OF ETHICAL LEADERSHIP

AI can be used for disturbing purposes such as social manipulation, social oppression, consumerism, and discrimination. What we are experiencing is just the tip of the iceberg.

For instance, in January 2019, I shared a post that I was going to Lagos, Nigeria. To my surprise, most of the comments were negative. Most people said, "Be careful," "Take your malaria pills"; others said they didn't have a good feeling about this. I got scared. When I reached Lagos and shared pictures of the area online, people were baffled. "Are you sure you are in Nigeria?" Lagos is like any other city. People are going to work. People are going to school. They are living normal lives. It's the media that only propagates negative stories about this country. I have traveled all over the world. There are good areas and bad areas in every country. As I look back, I was so surprised at how so many technologically connected professionals on LinkedIn, could be so misled into thinking I was going into a warzone. It shows that the degree of manipulation by these internet companies is astounding.

These social media and tech companies have too much power. They spread propaganda, fake news, and social discord. Elon Musk is calling for the regulation of AI. We need regulation of these internet/social media companies. They are getting away with too much. The sad thing for users is that when something happens, there is nobody you can report them to since they are privately held entities. You complain, they delete or block you, and there is nothing you can do.

TECHNOLOGY FORCES US TO FACE ETHICAL CHALLENGES OR DILEMMAS; SOME OF QUESTIONS THAT WE SHOULD ASK:

> Can we know if what we're seeing is the truth?

- ➢ Can we trust those who deliver it?
- ➢ Can we be sure that it is not prejudiced?
- ➢ Can we understand when it's taken too far?
- ➢ Can we tell if it's truly beneficial for all?
- ➢ Can we be sure that it is making the right decisions?

When will the sense of fairness prevail in our society, of just doing the right thing because it's the right thing to do? The almighty dollar has rendered some of these business leaders heartless. Our system has fallen into a self-reinforcing command loop construct as follows: increase shareholder value at all costs without regard for the human factor. Sadly, if you do not cure the cancer in the root of the tree, not only will the branches and leaves die, but so will the tree. The only thing that can cure the cancer and the root is having leaders with integrity.

A few years ago, I missed out on a huge promotion because I didn't comply with an action from a CEO of the establishment where I worked. He instructed me to hold back a delinquent customer's payment so their mortgage would be transferred to the non-accrual status. That would allow his colleague to submit an offer to purchase this prime property. Reality check: doing the right things may not bring on the welcoming committee; rather, you may be beaten for it. I faced the brunt of his wrath thereafter. I knew then I didn't have a future in that organization. I left with my integrity intact, which I value more than any job.

Every week in the newspaper, you are sure to find headlines about a leader or influential figure entangled in unethical behavior. Research on leadership has consistently rated integrity as one of the most important character traits of a respected leader. The seemingly trivial decisions and choices you make behind closed doors, when no one is looking, will ultimately carve your character. Eventually, the truth always comes to light.

Your ability to influence is not just based on skill or intelligence; it's based on trust and requires integrity, which is the foundation of

real and lasting influence.

Even if you possess emotional intelligence, creativity, vision, passion, in fact all the important leadership skills, but if you lack integrity, no one will believe or trust you. **Integrity is the foundation on which leadership is built.** If there is no integrity, your leadership influence will crumble. Lack of integrity renders all other leadership traits ineffective.

People want a leader who practices what he or she preaches and who follows through on promises. Many companies are struggling with low employee engagement. An employee's relationship with their manager sets the tone for their level of commitment to the organization's success. It's hard to feel passion for a job after you witness a lapse in integrity in your manager. Behaviors such as taking credit for someone's work, blaming, favoritism, treating others poorly, supporting unfair practices, and dishonesty are complete deal breakers.

A lot of business leaders don't even realize how closely they're being watched by their subordinates. Actions speak louder than words. People might tolerate a boring job or long commute, but they are more prone to leave if their boss lacks integrity. For loyalty, there has to be a relationship that develops between employee and employer. This relationship develops over time as trust grows. Even people without much else in common can build a solid and fruitful relationship based on integrity. Transparency, authenticity, and walking the talk are essential for building trust. You can't buy loyalty, but you can certainly foster and nurture it by being a person of integrity.

Society longs for leaders of integrity. Sadly, what we often see is greed, selfishness, and a lust for power. Integrity is something that is built over time, not overnight. It can take years to build and be destroyed in one moment. Once trust is lost, it is hard to regain.

Research from the Institute of Leadership and Management shows that while 83% of managers say their organizations have value

statements, only 38% consider they are closely aligned to those statements. That's a huge disconnect. Further, some 63% of people surveyed believe they have been asked to take action that goes against the values of their business. And the gulf between the values you hold and the values you live isn't just external. That gulf, that gap, becomes a part of you. That may be why so many people keep their values shallow - they may be afraid to go any deeper, afraid of what they'll find, or of what they'd have to change in their lives to fix what they find. Your vision and values should work in unison with each other, much like the nervous system and the muscular system. But for many people, that's not the case. *Often, their values are an afterthought.* Getting what we want, in and of itself, is not the problem. Our problem with integrity happens when we ask ourselves, "How can I get what I want?" Rather, the question should be "How can I honorably get what I want?"

INTEGRITY MEANS:

- Leading by example. It can be likened to a parent/child relationship. You cannot set policies that employees need to live by and not live by them yourself.
- Standing up for what is right.
- Keeping your word. Being reliable. Keeping promises, meeting important deadlines, and being there when people need you.
- Expressing concern for the common good.
- Being honest when no one is looking.
- Doing the honorable thing even when it's not popular.
- Loyalty under temptation or duress.
- Never compromising on a principle even when encouraged to.
- Making fair decisions.
- Communicating honestly.
- Giving credit where it's due.

- Displaying consistency in your words and actions.
- Treating everyone with respect.

Someone once asked a politician, "Have you kept all the promises that you made during the campaign?" He responded, "Yes . . . well, at least all the promises that I intended to keep."

Be Transparent — We know too well about office politics and favoritism. It's really sad when employees can tell who will be getting the next promotion based on a manager's relationship with some employees. Unfair practices relate to how vacancies are filled, disciplining inconsistently, and even in how a leader allows leeway in work schedules. This fosters low engagement. Give constructive feedback rather than criticism. Don't give preferential treatment to some employees and ignore others.

We have all come across leaders in the business that are great at displaying smoke and mirrors. Many times, the smoke and mirrors are simply a reflection of what management wants from them to grow the bottom-line. **Acting with integrity as a leader means that you won't always be the most liked because doing the right thing isn't always the popular thing.** Integrity is consistently behaving in a principled manner no matter who is watching. Consistency is an important concept in the framework of integrity. People need consistency. They need to know where they stand and what to expect. People want a leader who practices what he or she preaches and who follows through on promises. They must "walk the talk."

Building integrity starts with the smallest act and moves forward from there. snowballing into a reputation of trustworthiness and honesty.

Ethics is the way that we apply this understanding in our everyday life. Today, the most popular type of ethics is **situational ethics**, the premise of which is that there are no moral absolutes. It is often used to justify doing whatever is most beneficial for oneself in a particular situation. Not practicing integrity is similar to playing Russian roulette.

BE TRUTHFUL

In the words of Thomas Jefferson, a great thinker of his time, "Honesty is the first chapter of the book, Wisdom." Lying, in and of itself, is bad enough, but doing it in court and under oath is even worse. Perjury is a crime, and a serious one at that. The witness must therefore give a truthful testimony. Some people don't consider lying bad. In fact, it's not like you are killing anyone. Sadly though, if you are dishonest in small matters, you will be dishonest in large matters. It all starts as a small snowball and turns into an avalanche before you yourself have realized how far you have gone.

It is better to lose out, even in things that matter to us, if the alternative is having to lie or sacrifice our integrity. Integrity is a lot easier to talk about than to display. Even the best of us find ourselves easily compromised unless we are careful. Truly, in the littlest things, it is so easy to slip.

Unfortunately, early in our life, we learned that dishonesty could have great short-term benefits. It can get us out of trouble, and it can get us what we want. And all of us develop the habit (albeit, to varying degrees). Philosopher Sissela Bok has convincingly demonstrated how lying can be harmful for society. She writes: "A society then, whose members were unable to distinguish truthful messages from deceptive ones, would collapse." — *Lying: Moral Choice in Public and Private Life.*

If you lead long enough, you will face moral dilemmas, but integrity must always be in the front of your mind. Honesty builds confidence and strengthens your character. Dishonesty can be stressful, as it needs to be maintained. When you have nothing to hide, you are at peace because you don't have to maintain false stories or a double life. Remember, character is built over time and in the small moments. The seemingly trivial decisions you make when no one is watching will carve your character.

The leader is the one who upholds and enables the development of a moral system in an organization. Healthy organizations have a strong sense of moral order. It doesn't mean they are perfect, but they know who they are, and what they are about. There are certain lines they don't dare cross.

Integrity is essential; therefore, there must be accountability. Many people don't like to hear the truth. If it's negative, they see it as a personal attack on them. Is there someone in your life who can tell you when you are going down a wrong path and who will keep you in touch with reality? Society longs for leaders of integrity. To practice integrity means seeking out the best for your employees. This means that in your decisions, you set aside personal gain and put into consideration what would be beneficial to your people. Integrity entails that you become a "steward" of your people. You take care to the degree that you have an influence on their lives (and never underestimate that influence), and you take your share of responsibility for their well-being.

While most leaders don't engage in fraudulent behavior, many walk in the **"grey area."** In other words, while they aren't engaging in anything illegal, their behavior can be considered unethical. And it only takes one small step to cross the line. Leaders want their companies to be profitable, but this should be done only within the confines of sound legal and ethical precepts. Ethical leaders function within both the letter and the "spirit" of the law. They are sensitive to the fact that their everyday business decisions may have deleterious effects on others. The financial crisis of 2007-08 revealed that there is a higher need than we realized for ethical leaders and transparency in business processes. Success without integrity really isn't success at all. Integrity is the foundation of any good reputation. People will talk, and when they speak about you, it is best that you give them nothing unkind or unprincipled to discuss. Leaders with integrity are more concerned about their character than their reputation. Your reputation is merely who others think you are, but your character is who you really are.

When a company is struggling, it's logical that leaders take the short-term view, focusing on quick gains to cut costs and increase short-term revenue.

Don't cut corners or sacrifice quality. There are no shortcuts; they eventually lead to dead ends. Over the years, I've witnessed many brilliant leaders falling off the ladder because they were willing to cut corners by falsifying numbers on their results or embellishing their resume. I have also seen leaders crumble behind the facades they present. And then, when the pressure is on and the façade itself crumbles, the "real person" comes out. If you have integrity and are comfortable in your own skin, you won't need to deceive anyone.

I often say dishonesty is like digging a deep hole for yourself - you can't control the depth of the consequences.

Have a useful decision-making framework that works for you. Some useful ethical decision-making tests to consider:

> **The Golden Rule Test.** Servant leadership makes for ethical decision making. Do unto others as you would have them do unto you. Would you want others to treat you in this way?

> **The Sunlight Test.** When your decisions are brought into the full light of day, would you be comfortable if your actions were televised on the news tomorrow?

> **The Good Society Test.** It's about creating a better world. Will this decision result in making the world a better place?

> **The Authority Test.** It's including the views of an external authority you admire. What would this (named) authority think of your actions?

> **The Counseling Test.** Giving advice to others. What advice would you give to someone in your same situation?

> **The Legacy Test.** How will others remember you in future? Does this decision reflect how you want to be remembered?

Always wear your cloak of integrity and never leave home without your moral compass. An author once wrote a short story about two small-time crooks trying to pull off a robbery. In the plan, one of the crooks was to dress up in a policeman's uniform and stand in front of the place to be robbed. With him there, no one would be suspicious while his partner pulled off the heist itself. The story ended. however, with the partner dressed as a policeman apprehending and arresting the other one. Dressed as a cop, he started to act like one!

The further up the corporate ladder you go, the deeper your roots must be planted. Always be firmly grounded when it comes to integrity. The branches of growing trees not only reach higher, but their roots grow deeper. Strong, deep roots will anchor you firmly when the storms of an ethical dilemma begin to blow your way. I challenge leaders to live and lead with integrity. It will not only benefit the people you lead, but it will leave you free to enjoy more peace in your personal and professional life.

CHAPTER FIFTEEN

INSPIRATION LIES AT THE FOUNDATION OF SUCCESSFUL LEADERSHIP.

Think of a leader, future or current, who made an impact on your life. Can you name some of the qualities they possess?

I'll start first. My first boss was the best.

Once I had a family emergency, and before I could finish explaining the situation, he said, "And you are still standing here talking to me? Why aren't you out the door yet? I'll cover for you." I smiled, went to my desk, took my belongings, and left. Thereafter, he had my full commitment. He genuinely cared about people.

When I ask people this question, I get everything from "supported me," "stood up for me," to "cared," "humble," "empathetic," "patient," etc. Nobody lists intelligence or technical skills. Soft skills are what move people.

The managers we remember:

1. Cared about us.
2. Inspired us to be the best that we can be.
3. Defended us.
4. Provided a safe space to grow.
5. Created career opportunities for us.
6. Led us by personal example.
7. Appreciated us.
8. Were individuals of integrity.
9. Treated our mistakes as lessons.
10. Believed in us.

We need to think how to upskill ourselves with the skills leaders need to be successful in this new world. New technologies are coming out on an almost daily basis, which means we need to be more agile now than ever before. There is a growing risk that firms will become over-reliant on technology and ignore the value of people skills. Does all this suggest that leadership is radically different in the AI age? No, but there are two key distinctions. First, leaders' hard skills will continue to be surpassed by AI and smart technology, while their soft skills will become ever more important. It will be some time before AI can outperform humans in empathy, emotional intelligence, creativity, critical thinking, negotiation, problem solving, and collaboration.

Leaders need to balance the technological side as well as the human side. Big data will help leaders to make more informed decisions and serve customers better, but the focus must not be overly on numbers. When we only focus on the data points, we lose sight of a company's most important asset which is their people. To be successful in this AI economy, leaders need to stay engaged. Data processing will be relegated to computers, leaving interpersonal engagement to executives.What leaders can do better than any machine is form a connection with people. Individuals that motivate, inspire, and mentor will be sought after in years to come.

I had an employee who kept making mistakes and was coming into work late every day. He was put on PIP (Performance Improvement Plan) but with no improvement. His supervisor said she had tried everything.

Instead of firing him, I sat down with him to talk. It was obvious he was at a very low point. He had to move out of his home, he was going through a divorce complete with custody battle, and he was facing financial problems. He felt he was on the brink of a nervous breakdown. And asking for help wasn't one of his strong points.

I recommended him for counseling and sent him on leave so he could get it together. When he returned, he went from being one of the most difficult employees to one of the most positive influences in the workplace.

Managers, please use the HUMAN-to-HUMAN approach when dealing with employees. Take time to get to know your people, meet them where they are, and be flexible. It's a person you are dealing with and not just a statistic on a graph. A little empathy goes a long way.

My experience is that there are few bad employees but there are many "bad bosses" who lack people skills and are quick to cross people off.

Leadership is not about position or power. Too many managers get enthralled with the control and authority which comes with positional power. Being the leader means that you have been placed in a position to serve others. It is about how we treat people, how we make decisions, and the example we set. It's about looking for every opportunity to appreciate and inspire others. Your responsibility is to help your team achieve their goals, let them know that their work matters, and recognize and reward their efforts. Leadership is not a right but a privilege. You are privileged to be in a position where you can direct, shape, and positively influence the lives of others.

In these times of rapid change, what do employees need and want?

A gentleman from Iraq emailed me. He was the head of a medical transplant facility. He asked me how to lead under situations of duress. I told him the one thing you can give people is — HOPE.

Hope is the one thing that lifts the human spirit and keeps us going in spite of our difficulties. Hope looks beyond life's hardships to a better, brighter tomorrow. It keeps us believing and expecting that out of today's darkness, tomorrow's light will shine brightly. Hope is seeing the future, a future we can attain if we keep moving forward and, as needed, adjusting and adapting.

According to CNN/Opinion Research Corporation polling data taken in the United States in 1999, 85% of Americans surveyed were hopeful about the future. By December 2009, the number of those who were hopeful about their personal future had been reduced to 69%, and only 51% were hopeful about the world's future. By 2013, only 40% of those polled were hopeful about the world's future. I believe if the poll was taken today, the percentage of people who are hopeful would be far less. People are hope starved.

Murphy's Law is considered by some to be one of the central laws of nature - as universal as gravity and electromagnetism. It states in a nutshell: whatever can go wrong will go wrong. We all have moments and days that seem to follow Murphy's Law. Sometimes, our experiences can get us down. But we can always dig down inside ourselves to find some hope to hold onto, to fight off the inevitable moments of discouragement. A young woman who undertook counseling to recover from a predicament told her friends that one statement conveyed by the counselor was key to her successful recovery. "What helped me most," she said, "was the counselor insisting that my agonizing situation would come to an end. 'It looks gloomy and dark now,' the counselor used to say, 'but it will not last much longer.' This thought helped me gain resilience." In other words, the counselor kept the woman's hope alive.

I was in New Delhi, India, in August of 2019 speaking to attendees after I had finished my keynote speech. I noticed a gentleman standing in the corner of the room looking over at me. I knew he wanted to speak with me. I went over to him, and he said he was excited to meet me. He has been following me on social media for some time now, and this was on his bucket list to get a picture with me. He said he had flown from Bangalore to New Delhi for the first time ever and that he took his vacation from work just to be there. **He said I encouraged him at a difficult time and meeting me was on his bucket list.** It was such an honor to meet him. He even video called his wife to speak with me. It was an awesome moment. One that I will always cherish.

Then in September, I was walking through Amsterdam airport, and this woman stopped me and said, "You're Brigette Hyacinth, I follow you on LinkedIn. Can I take a picture with you?" She went on to say, "Just yesterday my friend and I were speaking about how inspiring you are. I speak about you so much that even my husband knows your name." I was blown over. She is from Turkey and invited me over; I should be there later this year. It made me realize people want to be inspired more than anything else. My platform on social media has primarily been about spreading hope and inspiring others. This is what I love to do.

Hope is essential in order to live our lives. A person who is in search of a job must hope that they'll find suitable employment, investors who have lost their money must believe that they will overcome this hurdle, or a lost traveler must hope to find his way back. Living with zero hope leads to depression, and eventually death. When Italian philosopher and poet Dante Alighieri (1265–1321) attempted to describe hell in his Divine Comedy, he proposed a big sign at the entrance, saying, "Abandon all hope, ye who enter here!" The worst punishment is to deprive someone of hope.

The world's greatest leaders all have one thing in common; they sparked hope in the face of despair. The Martin Luther King, Jr., "I Have a Dream" speech is stirring because it stirs hope for a more humane world. As he addressed the crowd, he acknowledged their plight. "I am not unmindful that some of you have come here out of great trials and tribulations." *He kept their eyes on the brighter road ahead.* "Let us not wallow in the valley of despair... This is our hope, and this is the faith that I go back to the South with. With this faith, we will be able to hew out of the mountain of despair a stone of hope."

Although he has passed on and most of us never had the opportunity to meet him, his words still continue to inspire millions around the world. And that is why we admire leaders like him. They give us something to hold on to; they make a personal connection with us by giving us hope.

"I have a dream that my four little children will one day live in a nation where they will not be judged by the color of their skin, but by the content of their character. I have a dream today!"
~Martin Luther King, Jr.

Challenging times, like these that we are facing, are the most difficult in which to lead, especially as the workplace changes, the economy struggles, and employees live in fear and uncertainty of their jobs. People are challenged to remain motivated. On top of that, leaders are asking for more and more, which does not directly correlate with an increase in remuneration. Leaders, therefore, need to make a positive impact in people's lives. Employees want to believe again in their leaders, but we are continually faced with inauthentic and selfish behavior. The need for inspirational leadership is at an all-time high. People are tired of false promises and rapid changes that leave them worse off. They want certainty during a time in history when the world is disillusioned by artificial relationships and the constant reminders that things aren't getting much better. In one word, they want hope.

It is even more critical that leaders inspire people to give their best. Inspiring a shared vision amid layoffs, downsizing, and radical changes in the way we do business is tough. Much like trust, inspiring hope in others takes time and patience. Emotions are contagious. Employees don't leave their emotions at the door when they report for work. If they are having personal problems, those emotions affect their work. Similarly, no one can sustain constant sacrifice. Almost every organization has been trying to do more with fewer resources lately, and it's taking a toll on employees. A leader's ability to tap into and know their workers' feelings, and to articulate a response to major events in ways that instill confidence and hope are key behaviors that enable leaders to resonate with their people. Leaders deal with people; people bring to the table skills, insight, and emotions. The first two of these may be constants in anyone's day, but it's our emotions that ebb and flow with our circumstances. Hope intersects the emotional needs that people have at any given moment; it's not a buzzword or a catchy slogan. Leaders must have a solid EQ (emotional intelligence quotient) to deal with people's emotions. There are many factors, both internal and external, to the organization and the individual that may make a person's belief in the mission waver.

One Monday morning, when I came out my office to greet staff, I noticed many employees were missing. I enquired with management on the floor, and it was determined many of them were facing personal problems, which included sickness, death of a family member, ill parents, children issues. The atmosphere in the office was dismal. Almost everybody was going through something. They were barely hanging on. I realized I had to do more because it was affecting their attendance and subsequent productivity. Our office had to be a place of hope. I wanted them to be inspired and not dread having to come to work in spite of all the troubles they were facing.

Hope is contagious. A wise leader will include hope in the vision and mission of their organization; they will work to make sure that everyone is focused on the task at hand. More importantly, they will make the vision bigger than the obstacles that threaten the mission itself. Giving hope to your team combines the alignment, engagement, and vision of the organization.

Studies show that hope is a critical factor in mental health. An attitude of hope found in hostages makes a difference in survival. Hope is a great motivator and a source of mental and physical endurance. Most depression treatments work well in patients convinced that their mood can improve significantly and that they can be helped. Indeed, depression and anxiety often afflict those whose outlook on life is pessimistic, catastrophic, and hopeless. A hopeful attitude can make a big difference in our entire mental outlook.

Hopelessness impairs cognitive functioning. Hopelessness is defined as having no expectation of goodness or success, and believing that cannot be changed, cannot to be helped or improved.

It is also the inability to learn, act, or perform. Synonyms for hopeless include words such as despairing, resigned, pointless, and impossible. When people feel uncertain, lost, and troubled in their careers and lives — sometimes all they want is a good dose of hope. Much like happiness, hope is an emotion that requires the individual to make good choices in order to sustain their positive impact. As such, the workplace culture can influence our degree of happiness and hope. **Hope promotes mindfulness.** Mindfulness is living in a state of full conscious awareness of one's whole self, other people, and the context in which we live and work. Mindfulness engages our passion and builds on positive emotional states. Many individuals just want a leader to tell them that everything is going to be okay. They want a sense of security, a feeling that their worries will soon be gone. People search for hope to recapture that moment in time when they had few and manageable problems and felt their best.

Inspirational leadership is about energizing and creating a sense of direction and purpose for followers, and the excitement and momentum to achieve goals. Inspirational leaders are capable of taking an organization and people to new heights. How you are able to inspire your team through your own actions and examples is an important component in achieving leadership success. In her Harvard Business Review blog titled, *Hope Is a Strategy (Well, Sort Of)*, Deborah Mills-Scofield clearly articulates, "Hope is a critical part of achieving a strategy when based on what is possible; perhaps not highly probable, but possible. Hope is the belief that something is possible and probable, and the recognition that the degree of each is not necessarily equal. When hope is based on real-world experience, knowledge, and tangible and intangible data, it results in trust, which is necessary for implementing any strategy."

Hope influences positive social engagement and mental/physical well-being. Hope gifts us with the belief that we can handle our problems, and opens our mind to finding the solutions we never thought existed. Research indicates that what really matters is that leaders are able to instill confidence, create enthusiasm, and be inspiring to the people they lead. **Hope is a motivational force that causes people to stay focused and hang on.** The fact is, no organization has ever become great without **Inspirational Leadership** as its cornerstone.

A leader's job is to spread hope, not despair. Without hope, we would all cease to live. The worst thing you can do is deny someone hope. Great leaders cast a vision of hope; they instill a positive outlook toward days to come, and they give people something to look forward to — a better tomorrow, a brighter future. Giving hope to your people combines the alignment, engagement, and vision of the organization. A leader's ability to do so will reap enormous benefits for your organization and your people. Hope is telling your team that getting this challenging proposal done on time will open up new doors of business. The walls of your difficulty might seem too high to scale, but don't look up and don't look down. Look straight ahead; find that first base and start to climb. Soon, that wall will become merely a steppingstone to the next phase of your life. Hope gives your people the drive to keep going in the face of impending failure. Hope is reassuring the employees that their efforts will pay off and tough times will get better.

Please don't misunderstand; hope is not a good way to manage a business. Budgets, strategic plans, targets, and forecasts are all tools that leaders use to manage a business on a day-to-day basis, but hope is needed to lead people. Hope is intangible, but it is a matter of human nature that we all seek.

HOPE THEORY

Recent organizational research includes hope as a factor in human and social capital management. This is referred to as positive psychological capital (Luthans & Youssef). Luthans and Avolio (2003) recognize, "the force multiplier throughout history has often been attributed to the leader's ability to generate hope." Hope theory (Snyder, Irving & Anderson, 1991), developed within the field of positive psychology, identifies hope as an activating force that enables people, even when faced with the most overwhelming obstacles, to envision a promising future and to set and pursue goals. It defines hope as a positive motivational state that is based on an interactively derived sense of successful (a) agencies (goal-directed energy), and (b) pathways (planning to meet goals), (Snyder, Irving & Anderson). **Hope is not just an emotion; it is a vibrant and potent force that contributes to leaders and followers expending the requisite energy necessary to pursue and attain organizational goals.**

Shorey and Snyder (2004) describe hope as a cognitive goal-directed process composed of well-defined goals, the perceived ability to develop routes to those goals, and possessing the requisite motivation. According to Snyder, Lopez, Shorey, Rand, and Feldman (2003), hope reflects individuals' perceptions regarding their capabilities to (a) clearly conceptualize goals, (b) develop the specific strategy to reach those goals (pathways thinking), and (c) initiate and sustain the motivation for using those strategies (agency thinking). Snyder (1994) pointed out that "high versus low-hope persons approach their life goals differently." Snyder stated people with high hope approach their goals with a focus on succeeding, have a positive emotional state, and have a perception of a high probability of goal attainment. By contrast, people with low hope approach the achievement of their goals with a focus on failing rather than succeeding, have a negative emotional state, and have a perception of low probability of goal attainment. Hope can be seen as a deeply creative process that allows the future to be shaped into possibility.

Shorey and Shorey (2004) argue that hope is a common process in leadership models and explain how leaders can instill hope in their followers by having high expectations, considering followers' needs and interests, and maintaining a positive, affirming attitude toward followers. These actions and attitudes of leaders have positive effects on followers, namely resulting in trust and self-efficacy. Effective leadership, it would seem, awakens hopeful thinking. Cerff (2006) supports the role of hope as a future orientation and notes the value of the inclusion of hope as an integral part of leadership development.

> *"A leader is a dealer in hope."*
> ~Napoleon Bonaparte

A couple of months back, I met one of my previous employees, Joanne, in the supermarket. She was accompanied by her mother. Her mother was so happy to meet me because she said her daughter spoke highly of me. We chatted for a moment, then, as I was about to leave, Joanne hustled across and said "Brigette, I can still hear your voice in my head telling me, "Don't give up." I never knew my words had such a lasting impact on her. And, if she had never gotten the opportunity to tell me, I would have never known.

Leadership is about making a difference in people's lives. It's about instilling and managing hope with real opportunities and goals that people believe they can achieve. A leader's hopeful outlook enables people to see beyond today's challenges to tomorrow's answers.

As we all know in life, you are either solving a problem, coming out of a problem, or heading into a new problem. More than ever in these uncertain times, leading requires inspiration. **People are looking for inspiration that speaks to their needs.** It's something they can take and use on their journeys in life. If I share a post about AI on social media, there is little engagement. But on the other hand, if I share something inspirational, it gets thousands of likes.

I was speaking to someone I met at a conference in Rwanda, and he said he was my biggest fan. He said his employee told him I encouraged her at her lowest moments before she even found that job. I have met so many people as I travel across the globe who say I encourage them. In December, I was speaking with an attendee at a conference in Morocco, and she said, "It's like you are always speaking to me. When I am depressed, I open LinkedIn to see what you posted, and it's always exactly what I need."

This weekend I had my four-year-old niece, Sarah with me. I've started back my exercise routine as one of my new year's resolution to exercise more, but I was really struggling with some of the moves. To my surprise, this little child came over and started clapping and saying, "You can do it Auntie." It made me laugh, but it also gave me the extra surge of energy to keep pushing. We all need a little encouragement along the way.

Without hope, society would collapse, as we would live our lives in despair. Hope enables us to believe that the future we envision is attainable, and that's crucial if we're going to move toward our visions and goals. And when we move forward in our lives, we can inspire others to do the same. Hope is an emotional magnet that keeps people going even in the midst of challenges.

Small trees, even though sheltered or hidden away, will always reach for the light. Leaders are like light. Let people feel that radiant energy when they are in your presence. Be a lighthouse to the ships lost at sea in these dark times. People are depending on you in difficult times to steer and anchor the ship in a safe harbor. Use your platform to encourage and uplift others. Never underestimate the depth of your influence. You may never know the impact you have made on others. One small word or kind gesture can change someone's day - or someone's life.

If you light one match in a dark room, it will illuminate the room. If, amidst a barrage of negatives, you have one positive thought and focus on it, you will magnify that one positive thought. Keep magnifying the positives. Keep spreading hope. Help people to keep their eyes on the light.

Our leadership ability won't be measured by our own advancement, but how well we advance the lives of others. "Let your light shine." Be a beacon of hope.

CHAPTER SIXTEEN

EMPATHY IN LEADERSHIP ISN'T A NICETY; IT'S A NECESSITY!

Employees don't leave organizations; they leave bad bosses. The worst place an employee can be, is stuck in an organization with a micromanager who doesn't care about his/her development and where there are no opportunities for growth and advancement.

We've all had a terrible boss at some point. Bad bosses can make you sick. Yes, a bad boss can take a negative toll on an employee's mental and physical health. Studies show having a bad boss raises a worker's chance of having a heart attack by as much as 60%. High levels of stress are directly linked with atherosclerosis, the disease of the arteries that in turn causes heart disease. What is it about a bad manager that increases the risk of heart disease? The stress and anxiety caused by unfeasible targets, lack of support, unfair practices, and threats of punishment.

There is an abundance of bad bosses in the workplace which accounts for employee engagement being at an all-time low. Self-serving leaders can be both destructive and ineffective. **Employees yearn for good bosses.** A recent study showed that 56% of employees would turn down a 10% raise to stay with a great boss. There is nothing like having a boss who genuinely cares about their team. They can make the working experience truly gratifying for their people. They support, empower and appreciate their employees. Employees who feel valued are willing to do more and give more.

Early in my career, I worked for a bad boss who put profit before people and sought to wring every ounce of productivity out of employees. We didn't even stop to celebrate the teams' successes. It was about speeding ahead to the next goal. There was no real leadership (vision and inspiration), only management (command and control). The culture was basically "do as you are told." Suggestions and recommendations by employees, and even the results of viewpoint surveys, were often ignored.

Employees became disengaged; salaries and weekends were the only high points, and very few of us went the extra step at work. Even with an overwhelming workload, employees poured out of the building at 4:00 pm sharp as if it was a fire drill - or a fire. Employee turnover was high, morale was low, and team spirit was nonexistent, unless you count the warm glow of griping in unison. Sadly, today the company is no longer in operation.

No matter how great a company's products and/or services may be, if management is dysfunctional, that company will have serious problems. Micromanaging is oppressive, fosters anxiety, and creates a high stress work environment. Eventually, employees will become disenchanted and leave.

In this digital age, there is a big disconnect between leaders and the people they lead. Many managers think they are doing a great job but when you ask the people they lead, it's quite the opposite. Many employees feel unappreciated and undervalued.

Employee engagement is at an all-time low. What seems to be missing link? **Empathy.**

Many organizations are focused on achieving goals no matter what the cost to employees. Treat your people right. Great leaders are concerned about getting the job done as well as the well-being of those under their care. **It doesn't mean being overly attentive or soft, but demonstrating that you value people**. Without empathy, you can't build a team, inspire followers, or elicit loyalty. Leaders that possess this trait always make time for people.

Creative Leadership surveyed more than 6,000 leaders and found that empathy is positively related to job performance. Managers that showed greater empathy toward their employees were viewed as better performers overall.

> *"To be kind is more important than to be right.*
> *Many times, what people need is not a brilliant mind*
> *that speaks but a special heart that listens."*
> ~F. Scott Fitzgerald

A couple of months back, I was speaking with Jill who had been on extended sick leave. She said, "Everything I did revolved around my job. However, when I was diagnosed with cancer in 2016, everything changed." She was hurt that not one of the managers called to see how she was doing. Her immediate supervisor would call but then quickly cut to the chase, asking her when she was coming back to work. The cancer is in remission now and she has returned to work, but Jill said, "I am not going the extra mile like before; they don't care about me and I don't care about them!"

The true test of mutual respect and value is when you need your manager to have your back and support you, or fight for you. When you go above and beyond and your manager responds with inflexibility and insensitivity, the relationship at that exact moment is lost.

I often find it's not all about what we say, but HOW we say it. Managers can sometimes demean employees by their tone and choice of words. Trust and empathy breeds loyalty. Just this week, I hung a new print on my office wall that reads, "In a world where you can be anything, BE KIND." You never know what people you come cross daily, are going through. So always be kind.

Too many managers have lost touch with the fact that it is people who make a company. They get tied up in policies and procedures. They are so focused on the business aspects of their company that they forget that their employees are the backbone of that company. The most successful leaders I have worked with cared about their people. The results were a loyal team driven to succeed. The motivation was fueled not only their need for success, but also to ensure their leadership longevity.

LEADING WITH THE HEART

There are three powerful words that you can say to someone to show you care about them and have their back - genuinely asking someone "Are you okay?" It is a simple phrase that someone may desperately need to hear. Choosing to ask if someone is okay will not always get you the most truthful answer but will authentically convey to someone that you care about them as a human being. Many simply ask "Are you okay?" to try and show concern, but in truth, they do not really want to know. Most people when asked will simply say "Yes, I'm good" or "Yeah, I'm okay," even if they are hurting inside. It's hard to be vulnerable without feeling like you'll be diminished in some way. If you ask someone if they're okay, and you are sincere in your question, then let your whole body say, "I'm sincerely interested." How? Be fully present. Stop and face the individual. Look them in the eye. Soften your voice. Show empathy by being attentive. If you sense that something is going on with the person and they say, "I'm okay," and your instincts tell you otherwise, then ask "Really? Are you sure there's not something you need to talk about? If you don't want to, that's okay. But if you do, I'm here." Then wait for a response. This way you let them know that you know they are not really okay and that's fine because you genuinely care. You want them to feel they are in a safe place.

These simple yet extremely powerful words exemplify true servant leadership. Far too many "so-called" leaders are hyper-focused on the metrics instead of how their employees are doing. Sincere leaders genuinely care about their people. I created an acronym to keep me centered and grounded for ensuring my intentions are honorable and true: S.A.G.E. SINCERE AUTHENTIC GENUINE ENGAGED.

THE HIGH CALLING OF LEADERSHIP

The road less traveled - imagine walking along a narrow path. Along the way, there are numerous paths leading in different directions. Some of these paths obviously go to places that we would not want to visit. Others look tempting; they appeal to our emotions, our feelings, and our desires. If we take any one of them, we get off the right path and go onto a road that might become exceedingly difficult to get off. Temptations can be very difficult because they appeal to things we really want, and they seem to come at our weakest moments. "Two roads diverged in a wood, and I took the one less traveled by, and that has made all the difference." So wrote Robert Frost in his poem "The Road Not Taken." The concept is of two roads or gates - one being broad and appealing (selfishness, pride, dishonesty), the other, narrow and foreboding (self-sacrifice, humility, love). Great leaders take the narrow road. The more we indulge in selfishness, pride, dishonesty, the more difficult it is to perceive the right decision in any given situation. On the contrary, the narrow road can be rewarding but it can be very rough. Yet it offers us genuine happiness that leaves us with a good taste in this life. We need to strive and press on, leading with purpose in spite of the many setbacks and obstacles faced.

TRUE LEADERSHIP STARTS WITH EMPATHY:

1. **Show That You Care** — Unfortunately, all too often leaders fail to recognize the importance of how they treat their employees. If we treat people only as the means to an end, we will never have their loyalty. Don't just consider them as a cog in the operational machinery. Treat your people right. It doesn't take much to show people that you care. If an employee is sick, don't force them to come to work. Tell them, "Stay at home until you feel better, rest up." If you have an employee on extended sick leave or who loses a family member, pick up the phone and call them. Be genuinely sympathetic. It will mean the world to them. Sending a card or flowers is good but take the time to call them. This is something they will never forget. You don't have to pry. Just a simple question,

such as, "How are you doing today?" will let them know that you care. Life happens to include sickness for employees, kids and parents, doctors' appointments, etc. A good employer will take care of their employees at their lowest, instead of kicking them when they are down.

2. **Show Respect** — Wanting employees to come in early and leave late on a daily basis shows a lack of respect for their personal lives. Additionally, contacting them after work hours or while they are on vacation should be avoided. Yes, there are situations where you will need to, but this should not be the norm. When employees realize that you don't care about their well-being, as demonstrated by infringing on their personal time too often, everything you do regarding relationship building activities will seem superficial.

3. **Connect with Your Team** — As a leader, you should be seen. Be visible. Make your presence felt. Don't just lock yourself in your office for the whole day and only communicate with staff when you want something done. How can you motivate the troops when you are out of sight? Come down from the mountaintop and mix and mingle with your subordinates. Sit at lunch with them. Get to know your employees. Find out about their interests. Empathy and listening go hand in hand. Listening forms the foundation of good relationships. Why? Because it shows you care.

4. **Advocate for Staff** — Exhibit loyalty to your employees. In some cases, if a complaint is made against an employee, the manager is quick to jump in, and suddenly all the good the employee has done is cast into the sea of forgetfulness. Don't be the judge, jury, and executioner. **Don't throw your people under the bus; let them know you have their back.** A good manager never leaves any of his team members to hang out to dry. It's never a good quality in a good manager even if it's not your fault. Own it. Taking ownership shows responsibility.

5. **Share and Give Credit**. — Don't brush over your team's successes with a bland acknowledgement while automatically working towards the next goal. Be generous with reward and recognition and say,

"Thank You" whenever you can. Recognize your team members publicly. Rather than just recognizing top performers, include those who are improving or doing their best. **Every team member is valuable, regardless of their job title or position and should be made to feel this way.** Furthermore, celebrate victories. Don't be a taskmaster! Yes, employees already know that they come to the office to do a job, but you should not stop them for having fun as well.

Leadership is about people - full stop! If you don't have a passion for people, you have no business leading them. In a perfect world, employees leave their problems at the door. In this not-so-perfect world, they bring them to work. We need leaders who will practice empathy. According to a number of studies, empathy is the single biggest leadership skill needed today.

Sometimes it's the little things we do that counts the most. It's the simple things people remember. The thoughtful gesture, the kind word, the much-needed support. It doesn't cost much to show employees you genuinely care, but it can make the biggest difference in keeping them loyal, happy, and engaged.

Lauralee emailed me this:

"I worked for a company in Brussels a few years ago when my brother (who was living in the USA) had cancer. In that year, I had 10 weeks leave visiting him & then, when he died, attending his funeral. When I asked my boss, Eric, how I repay the company for all these extra holidays, he simply replied 'They weren't holidays. Don't worry about it.' This attitude was not isolated & reflected the company culture . . . to this day, it was the best company I ever worked at & Eric was the best boss I ever had . . . I would walk over hot coals for him!"

You can manage budgets, processes, and schedules, but you have to lead people. They may never share your goals, but inspiring them to be the best they can be every day will bring the best results. Taking care of your employees as a leader means treating them with integrity, believing in their abilities, and showing them respect. This builds a strong relationship with all parties and encourages a successful business.

Leadership is about inspiring greatness in others. The true measure of a leader is revealed in how they treat others. It all starts from how one greets and treats all personnel. I am horrified to watch exec suite walking down the hall and not acknowledging their team, realizing they do not know their employees by name. One evening chatting with the security guard, he listed all the genuine managers in the office. And he pointed out all the execs passing by who had never once been courteous to him but were acknowledging him now because I was standing there."Empathy and respect should not be shown to a chosen few but to everyone.

TREAT EMPLOYEES RIGHT

In today's business environment, leaders see empathy as a show of weakness; being right is more important. What we fail to recognize is that people are human; they bring their full humanity to work with them every day. Being kind and being a good listener, listening with the heart - these are crucial to a leader's success (and more important to personal happiness) than an insensitive mind, no matter how brilliant.

Emotional intelligence is a foundational life skill, and yet some business owners underrate or even ignore it. I came out my office to speak to a supervisor. I noticed the employee next to her eyes were red. I was able to put two and two together and realized it was Mother's Day; she was crying because she just lost her mother two weeks ago. I called her in my office and told her how sorry I was about her loss and give her the rest of the day off. The saddest thing about this was the manager was right next to her but was so engrossed in the job, that she failed to notice what her employee was going through. Sadly, emotional intelligence is a valuable trait that not all leaders possess. Empathy displayed is directly proportionate to one's EQ.

Bill Gates and Jeff Bezos told stories about kindness versus brilliance from their personal experiences. The take home message from each was that kindness is a choice and the brilliant mind is an inherent gift. And given that it is a choice, it may be difficult to choose kindness over the ego satisfaction of being right, or the sense of control it confers. But what I found interesting is that they felt kindness, too, is a kind of power - the power to help us find a richer life.

Deep listening and compassionate communication come first in motivating and stimulating employee engagement. Being kind doesn't mean there is no accountability. Tough love is also necessary at times but should be wrapped in empathy. Leadership is being the captain of the team. Caring about your team in all aspects is extremely important; captains are chosen to lead teams to victory. When employees on this team are understood, are shown empathy, are connected with and listened to, they feel engaged. This engagement leads to knowing they have a voice, and what they say is important. If team members know and feel like they are truly a part of the team, and able to confidently do the job they were hired to do with the guidance of their captain, they're more mindful of the way they do their job. This is a win-win for all involved. Leaders take the time to truly learn about your people, to take care of and support those you lead and watch how smoothly and successfully your team evolves.

The link between employee loyalty and profitability is long established. Loyal employees = Loyal customers. Loyal employees are worth much more than their weight in gold. They uphold your brand and ensure the sustainability of your business. They make it possible for you to win.

When a loyal employee leaves, it costs the company. The impact on the organization's culture is also severe. Beyond the more tangible losses such as the cost of hiring and training and time with an unfilled role, it affects team morale and causes other employees to reconsider their loyalty towards the organization. Additionally, poor employee loyalty can damage a company's image. Sites like Glassdoor and Indeed offer employees a platform on which to air their true feelings about their employer. Fortune bases its "100 Best Companies to Work For" ranking on employee reviews of company culture.

Companies need to be more strategic about how they think about employee retention to remain competitive. It's important that managers focus on relationship building and encourage a family atmosphere at work. Get to know your employees, meet them where they are, and be flexible. Many organizations treat their employees as if they are a commodity. They use them until they can get no more out of them, and then cast them aside. This leads to poor morale, lower productivity, and higher turnover.

The following scenario happens quite often:

BOSS: You are late!

Employee: It is only 8:10 a.m.

BOSS: Work starts at 8:00 a.m. I will have to write you up for this.

Employee: But I am not usually late. I left late plus I was up late finishing a report. Could you just let me off this one time?

BOSS: We can't set the wrong precedent - that it's okay to be late.

Employee: Okay then, I am not taking any more work home from now on. I will arrive on time and leave on time.

This scenario happens too often. Many managers never complain when employees go the extra mile but are quick to point out employees' shortfalls. You can't buy loyalty, but you can certainly foster and nurture it.

Employees who have been pushed to the point where they no longer care, will not go the extra mile. They will not take the initiative to solve problems. They will end up treating customers the same way you treat them. **Instead of just focusing on the bottom-line; why not invest in the people responsible for the bottom-line?**

Leadership is about helping others become the best they can be. It is built on a foundation of servant hood and not selfishness. By providing employees with the opportunity to grow, we help them become more valuable members of the team at the same time that we're building the overall strength of the team. It's a total win-win situation. Your success is a result of your team. Build your employees up, and you build the company up. When you help others succeed, you will succeed! And you'll do it by having a positive impact and building a positive legacy.

I was supervising the morning shift one Friday when I noticed a cashier who seemed to be using the phone quite a bit. Another employee told me that her mother had just been rushed to the hospital, but she was afraid to ask for time off since she was on probation and might be fired. There were only four cashiers that day. I called her into my office and told her, "Next week, no one will remember what you did here today. But you will remember this time you spend with her for the rest of your life. Go." So, I was a cashier that day. I fumbled and made a few mistakes, but I realized the enormous pressure my team was under. Your job as a manager is to help everyone around you succeed. It's not about you. It's about them. And if extra work had to be done? Guess who always volunteered before being asked.

KINDNESS MATTERS

For far too long, being kind has been mistaken for being weak. In reality, kindness is a necessary quality of leadership for the world we're living in. It has become so rare that when someone does a kind act or goes out of their way to be nice to someone, it goes viral on social media. Being kind doesn't mean you can't make hard decisions or stand up to difficult people; it just means you are respectful, considerate, and show empathy to your employees.

The story is told of John, a young man, standing at the end of a bridge. He was waiting for the bus to take him to his home, nearly an hour's distance away. It was a warm summer day, and many children were swimming in the millpond below the bridge. As John watched them, he noticed one of the smaller boys began to drift farther and farther from the shore. Suddenly, the little boy threw up his hands and disappeared under the water. John's first impulse was to run down the bridge and try to help the little boy that was drowning. But as he looked up, his bus was fast approaching. He casually brushed it off and decided with so many good swimmers in the millpond, surely someone else would help him. So he boarded the bus and went home.

Upon arriving home, he found his mother lying unconscious on the floor. He hastened to bathe her face and rub her hands. As she regained consciousness, she cried out, "Oh John, your brother Willie has just drowned in the millpond." Then from John lips came the agonizing cry, **"If I had only known it was my brother William."**

As we help others, many times we are indirectly helping ourselves and our own families.

Just think about this for a moment. When you have to do a kind deed for someone, is it convenient? No, kindness is never convenient. It always requires sacrifice. Whether you have to go out of your way, or take time out of your schedule. But in the end, the satisfaction you receive is indescribable, plus it benefits the receiver. The seeds of kindness you sow will return to you, sometime down the road when you will need it. Kindness is the gift that keeps on giving. It creates a positive chain reaction which starts with you.

When kindness isn't modeled in the workplace, we find ourselves in an environment that is unhealthy and even toxic. Today **people are clamoring for a more human style of leadership.** In an age of automation and AI, leaders' hard skills are easily being replicated by smart technology. What will make the difference in effective leadership is soft skills.

Here are seven ways I've found being kind can bring you more success as a leader at work. You can start to encourage a culture of being nice to others by carrying out random acts of kindness during your day.

1. **Be considerate:** Hold the door open for the person behind you. If you are going to the water cooler, ask someone close to you if they would like water too.

2. **Smile at a colleague.** When you make eye contact and smile at someone, you are showing that they matter, which gives them a boost of happiness.

3. **Mind your manners.** Say "Good morning" or "Hello" to colleagues more often.

4. **Show appreciation**: Be more vocal in your praise. Acknowledge the contribution and efforts of others.

5. **Listen more.** Learn to listen with the intent to understand. Don't just dismiss or ridicule others' viewpoints. Listening shows that you care – even if you don't agree with them, it shows you care about them as people and as colleagues.

6. **Offer support** and help to team members who are struggling.

7. **Treat everyone** with the same level of respect, whether it be the janitor or the CEO.

"Everyone you meet is fighting a battle you know nothing about. Be kind always."

The way you treat others shows your values and reveals your true character. You can't influence others if you aren't authentic. Employees are looking at you as a leader to determine if they can trust you.

Over the years, I have learned it's all about teamwork. We win together, and we fail together.

In my experience, tough and kind don't have to be incompatible. Managers, please use the human-to-human approach when dealing with employees. It's people you are dealing with, not just a statistic on a graph. **Get to know your people, meet them where they are, and be flexible**.

Loyalty is a two-way street. It's just like any relationship. For a relationship to last, there must be mutual respect, love, trust, understanding, and appreciation. Without these, the foundation is shaky. Loyal employees show up, deliver results, and consistently go above and beyond to support the company. In the end, people make companies successful. Any strategy or business plan relies on motivated and engaged people to make it happen! This is why the most successful companies focus on people and relationships, making sure both are not just managed but valued and cared for. Want loyal employees? Treat your people well!

Leadership is not a competition. It's helping others to reach their full potential.

10 THINGS A BOSS SHOULD NEVER SAY TO AN EMPLOYEE

1. "This place falls apart without me."

Employees see this as implying they are not capable enough. It gives the impression that the organization revolves around you. A wise boss recognizes employees' contributions and is never condescending to them.

2. "I was here late last night, and I worked over the weekend."

Expressing indirect pressure that an employee should commit more time out of their personal lives is a sure path to dissatisfaction. Studies have shown that spending more time in the office doesn't make employees more productive - in fact, it has the opposite effect.

3. "I am not asking for suggestions."

Using this phrase will leave your employees demotivated and unwilling to participate in discussions. You are basically telling them your opinion alone counts. As a boss, you should actively seek feedback and input from employees. This promotes buy-in. If you discourage input from employees, you'll be breeding a culture of disengagement.

4. "We have to do more with less."

Here's what every employee hears: "You're going to have to work more hours without getting more pay." Business may be tough, but the solution isn't overworking employees or setting unrealistic expectations for them.

5. "Because I'm the boss, that's why!"

Employees already know you are the boss. You don't have to throw around your authority. "Unless you are the military, avoid pulling rank." An autocratic style does not inspire employees, it drives them away. Even if you do have the final say, most decisions should still be discussed.

6. "If you don't like it here, work somewhere else."

This is just rude. When employees have legitimate complaints, you need to address them rather than respond with scolding. You should show them you know that you are lucky to have them as part of the team.

7. "You can't go home." or "Don't come to me until this is finished."

Threats and power plays are not the way to inspire loyalty or great performance from the employees. Your employees are already stressed out, and this shows you don't care how an employee is coping with the workload or task.

8. "If you keep this up, you're not getting a raise."

Threatening employees with not getting a raise or bonus as a way to get them to do what you want is not sustainable. Sure, they will do what you demand, but eventually they will become unwilling to do more than the bare minimum to get by. And that's if they don't quit first.

9. "You need to think about where your priorities lie."

You should not make employees feel like they are doing something wrong and then not be specific about it. Don't beat around the bush leaving, them in limbo. Be specific about what you are insinuating.

10. "Personal issues cannot be brought to work."

We are human beings and yes, we bring our issues in the door with us. Try to be a little sensitive when an employee is dealing with a tough personal situation (divorce, bereavement, illness, etc.). You don't have to be so professional that you act oblivious to what an employee is experiencing. Show that you care.

True leadership relies on learning about the needs of people as well as their strengths, and then actively discovering what you can possibly do to help and encourage them. At the end of the day, looking out for people is the essence of leadership. It is not about your title but rather your commitment to care about others.

> *"You don't build a business. You build people*
> *and then people build the business."*
> ~Zig Ziglar

THERE IS NOTHING THAT CAN REPLACE THE "HUMAN TOUCH."

I received this disturbing message from Betty who was asking for my advice on what she should do in such a situation.

"I have not been able to communicate with my mom in Puerto Rico since Hurricane Maria hit the island. I had a surgery at the beginning of the year, so I ran out my paid time off. I requested next week time off to try to find my mom, HR says that my condition doesn't qualify as hardship. So, I went to the head of HR, she doesn't guarantee that I would not be written up for unapproved absenteeism. Let's see what happens. Either way I'm going to find my mom, and if they tarnish my record with a written warning, so be it. I'm so sad that sometimes I think this world should end, people has lost humanity and compassion. Maybe I will resign after coming back if I see that written warning."

My advice to this individual was: "Focus on your health and family (finding your mom). These cannot be replaced. You will get another job."

This company missed a great opportunity to gain an employee who would go above and beyond. Instead they broke her spirit. And even if she isn't dismissed, her engagement level will plummet. And remember, the way you treat employees who are having problems will be seen - and discussed - by the employees around them.

In contrast to this story, I heard of a manager that quietly hired a private investigator in Puerto Rico to locate the mother of one of his employees. He paid well over $1K out of his own pocket to bring peace to his distressed employee... and some help to the mother. He's rightfully earned loyalty, admiration, respect, and devotion. He's truly a great manager and a great role model!

Caring about employees means caring about what matters most to them. A good leader manages to balance a business mindset and being a human being, and knows how to emphasize one over the other. At some point being a decent human being has to outweigh just doing your job. We live in a time when empathy and intellect must meet.

I received this email from Steve:

"I got a call my wife who had been in a serious car accident. I told my boss I needed to leave immediately. He asked me to give him 10 more minutes. I was so disappointed because he could have covered for me. I come in early. I leave late. I hardly take any sick leave and that was the response I got. I looked at him and walked straight out the door. Next day I went back for my belongings and told him I quit."

Nobody cares anymore. Nor do they wish to care because they think caring is detrimental to the bottom line these days. This is because people have become as disposable and replaceable and upgradable as any other inanimate object, like cell phones or computers. Some managers would rather have someone they can plug in like a light bulb and then throw away once they have no more use for them.

I get so many messages from employees complaining about being treated badly by their employers. It seems that many companies have lost touch with the fact that it is people who make a company successful.

When your employees think about the company, does it leave a sweet taste in their mouths or make them sick to their stomachs? **Many organizations claim to put employees first, but often their practices run contrary to the sweet song.** When a company shows empathy to its employees, the employees become indebted to the company and go beyond the call of duty to defend and uphold the company's values. Lack of empathy breeds the lackadaisical attitude in employees which ultimately impacts the organization's performance.

> *"A drop of honey catches more flies than a gallon of gall.*
> *So with men. If you would win a man to your cause, first*
> *convince him that you are his sincere friend. Therein is a drop*
> *of honey which catches his heart, which, say what he will,*
> *is the highroad to his reason."*
> ~Abraham Lincoln

Julie sent me this:

"My company went out of their way to accommodate me while my husband was in hospice care, never asking about how much PTO time I had, never asking how many hours I put in. I give my all at every job I work at, but now I give 110% because of the respect and compassion that my employer gave to me. Then when he died, they even gave me three extra days. That was nine years ago and guess what, I still work there. This company has my loyalty till I retire."

If we want our employees to feel commitment to the organization, we need to show that we respect and value them, and that includes caring about what is of most value to them. Gaining loyalty through treating others this way should not be the goal either. This type of reaction should be simply natural.

Instead of giving employees vinegar, why not give them honey? I believe that weaving empathy into our business practices is not only an effective strategy but a powerful one.

Anyone can be a boss, but a good one will use leadership skills to inspire and motivate employees to deliver results. If you want to win the support and commitment of your team and improve engagement, you will have to use influence and inspiration rather than solely relying on designated power. Listen, encourage, recognize, and show that you appreciate your employees, you value their contributions, and you genuinely care about them.

Leadership is a give-and-take relationship. If you fight for your employees, they will fight for you. If you have their back, they will have yours. Many of the other managers would ask me how I always got all my team to come out at events. Whenever we had some event and I needed the commitment of my team, they always showed up and, in some cases, they would solicit the help of their families. From visiting homes for the aged or orphanages, to beach clean ups. It's not rocket science, and it does not take a big budget. I just simply showed that I cared for them, and I looked out for them. It came back tenfold to me.

Over the years I have learned to get the best from employees. Just treat people well. It is so basic, and it is sad and difficult to understand — why is it that so many managers don't get this? If you want employees to go the extra mile, you have to go the extra mile too. Show people that you are interested in their welfare. Your success is a result of your team. Take care of your team.

In October 2019, I had the honor of speaking at a Cable and Wireless conference in Miami. The night before the event as we were going through the rehearsals. I was brought to tears as they showed video clips of their relief efforts in Abaco Islands, Bahamas, in the aftermath of Hurricane Humber to. Imagine this - when the hurricane hit the Bahamas, they evacuated their employees and put them up in a hotel, and they did not charge customers for calls or using their data service. Now that is having a heart for people! An employer that puts people first. Who wouldn't want to work for such an organization?

If we can put people before profits, technology, and processes, we would create a positive and lasting impact. Employees are the most valuable asset of any company. We need leaders with human qualities who will put people first. A little respect and empathy go a long way in building relationships and commitment. It may seem simple, but it works wonders.

In whatever we do, let's consider humanity first. The unrestrained effects of capitalism in our culture are more destructive than we would like to believe. The question is, how do we turn this around? We live in a world where numbers, budgets and year-over-year profit increases, etc., *are* all that seem to matter. Many employers view employees as human capital — employee units — and not people. I hold onto the hope that the time is coming when humanity will take first priority, ahead of the bottom line.

When companies put profits before people, it's a slow-rolling disaster. In March 2019, the Boeing 737 MAX passenger airliner was grounded after two new airplanes crashed within five months, killing all 346 people aboard. Three hundred and forty-six people lost their lives because of greed and callousness. This could have been easily avoided. Boeing has admitted that it knew about a problem with its 737 Max jets a year before the aircraft was involved in these two fatal accidents, but they took no action. As someone who flies frequently, this breaks my heart. The world moves on to the next hottest story, but I will never again have the trust I had in one of humanity's greatest achievements.

On my way back from Singapore, the airplane experienced turbulence like I have never felt before. It was very scary. The plane shook like paper and plunged twice. All the passengers screamed out. Even a flight attendant got injured. The woman next to me began to cry uncontrollably, and I tried to comfort her. I then took out my little Bible from my handbag and started to pray. I wondered if I would ever get home. I looked around at all the passengers; many were so young. I just prayed to God that this wouldn't be our last day. I thought that if this plane were to crash in the ocean, they wouldn't even find a trace of us.

My mind then ran to those people who had lost their lives in the Boeing crashes (Ethiopian Airlines Flight 302 and Lion Air Flight 610). I can't imagine the horror they must have been going through as those planes plunged to Earth at incomprehensible speeds. I thought of their families at the airport eagerly waiting for them, only to receive the devastating news.

No financial settlement can compensate for the loss of life. I wish the leaders of Boeing would realize (and had realized before they let problematic airliners carry passengers) how valuable and precious human life is. Boeing has expressed hope the plane will be cleared for flight in mid-2020. I hope not – not ever. A company that has so little regard for human life cannot be trusted. Boeing has put the total cost of the two deadly crashes of its 737 Max airliners at nearly $19bn as it slumped to its first annual loss in more than two decades. Not putting people first is a *lose-lose situation. Nobody wins.*

In the end, people are what truly matters. It's not buildings, systems or procedures. If we can put people first, everything else will fall into place. I urge leaders to develop a heart for people.

Conclusion

Imagine a world where everyone can come to work and feel fulfilled, supported, valued, appreciated and cared for. This is something we all want, and although it seems unrealistic, the vision is possible.

Research continues to emerge showing that human-centered companies significantly outperform those operating from a "mechanistic" approach. By building a sense of hope, well-being, and purpose in each employee, you'll create a deep connection and vested interest in your organization and its goals. And that's the key to business success.

I really hope that a seed has been planted, whereby you will apply the various strategies shared in this book to make a positive impact. It's all about having a heart for people.

References

Harvard Business Review. May–June 2018 issue (pp.122–129)

Matthias Klumpp, Marc Hesenius, Ole Meyer, Caroline Ruiner, Volker Gruhn. Production logistics and human-computer interaction—state-of-the-art, challenges and requirements for the future. *The International Journal of Advanced Manufacturing Technology*, 2019

https: //en. wikipedia.org/wiki/Deepfake

https:// www2.deloitte.com/global/en/pages/human-capital/articles/gx-human-capital-trends-library-collection.html

https:// www.gallup.com/workplace/231668/dismal-employee-engagement-sign-global-mismanagement.aspx

https:// www.gallup.com/workplace/231587/millennials-job-hopping-generation.aspx

https:// www.mercer.com/our-thinking/career/global-talent-hr-trends.html

https:// www.mckinsey.com/featured-insights/gender-equality/women-in-the-workplace-2019

https:// www.payscale.com/data/economic-trends-2019-2020

https:// www.thepeoplespace.com/practice/articles/were-more-machine-now-man-hr-and-digital-journey

Epilogue

We have come to the end of this book. Thank you for staying with it. I hope you have known at all times that the author has your best interests in mind. Leading the Workforce of the Future: Inspiring a mindset of Passion, Innovation and Growth is geared to helping you become **the leader you were destined to be**. It combines wisdom from the ages with the author's insights; thus, giving a winning formula for success.

If you have enjoyed this book, please consider writing a review on Amazon. It really does make a difference.

Thank You and I wish you the very best in life!

Sincerely,

Brigette

BRIGETTE HYACINTH
BRIDGING THE GAP
KEYNOTE SPEAKER & AUTHOR

Made in the USA
Middletown, DE
16 January 2022